HUMAN TORCH

BURN

WRITER:
KARL KESEL

PENCILS:
SKOTTIE YOUNG

INKS:
JOE SEUNG
WITH PIERRE-ANDRE DERY

COLORS:
STUDIO F

LETTERS:
VIRTUAL CALLIGRAPHY'S
CORY PETIT

ASSISTANT EDITORS:
MARC SUMERAK
& ANDY SCHMIDT

EDITOR:
TOM BREVOORT

COLLECTION EDITOR:
JENNIFER GRÜNWALD

SENIOR EDITOR, SPECIAL PROJECTS:
JEFF YOUNGQUIST

DIRECTOR OF SLAES:
DAVID GABRIEL

PRODUCTION:
JERRY KALINOWSKI

BOOK DESIGNER:
PATRICK McGRATH

EDITOR IN CHIEF:
JOE QUESADA

PRESIDENT:
DAN BUCKLEY

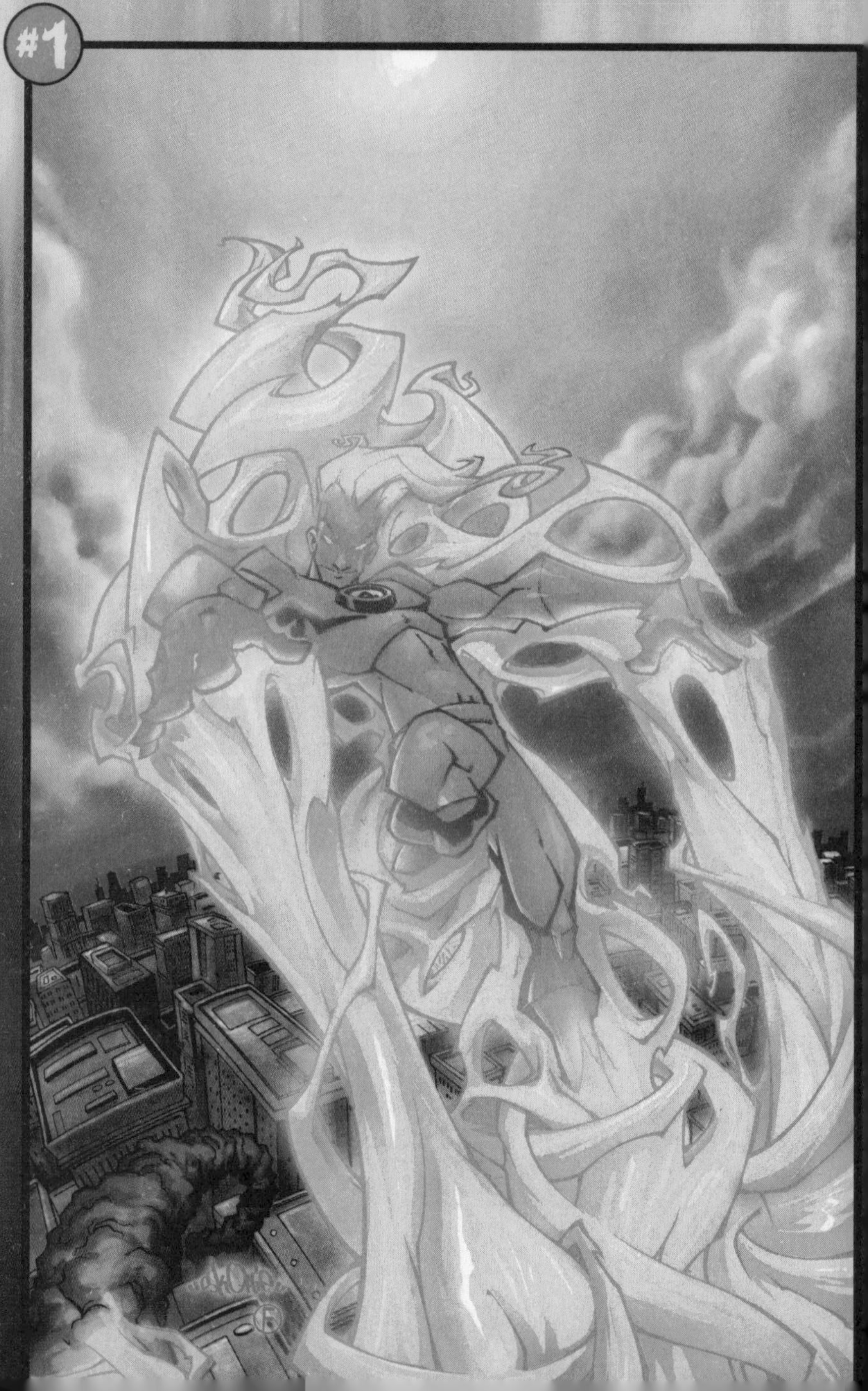
#1

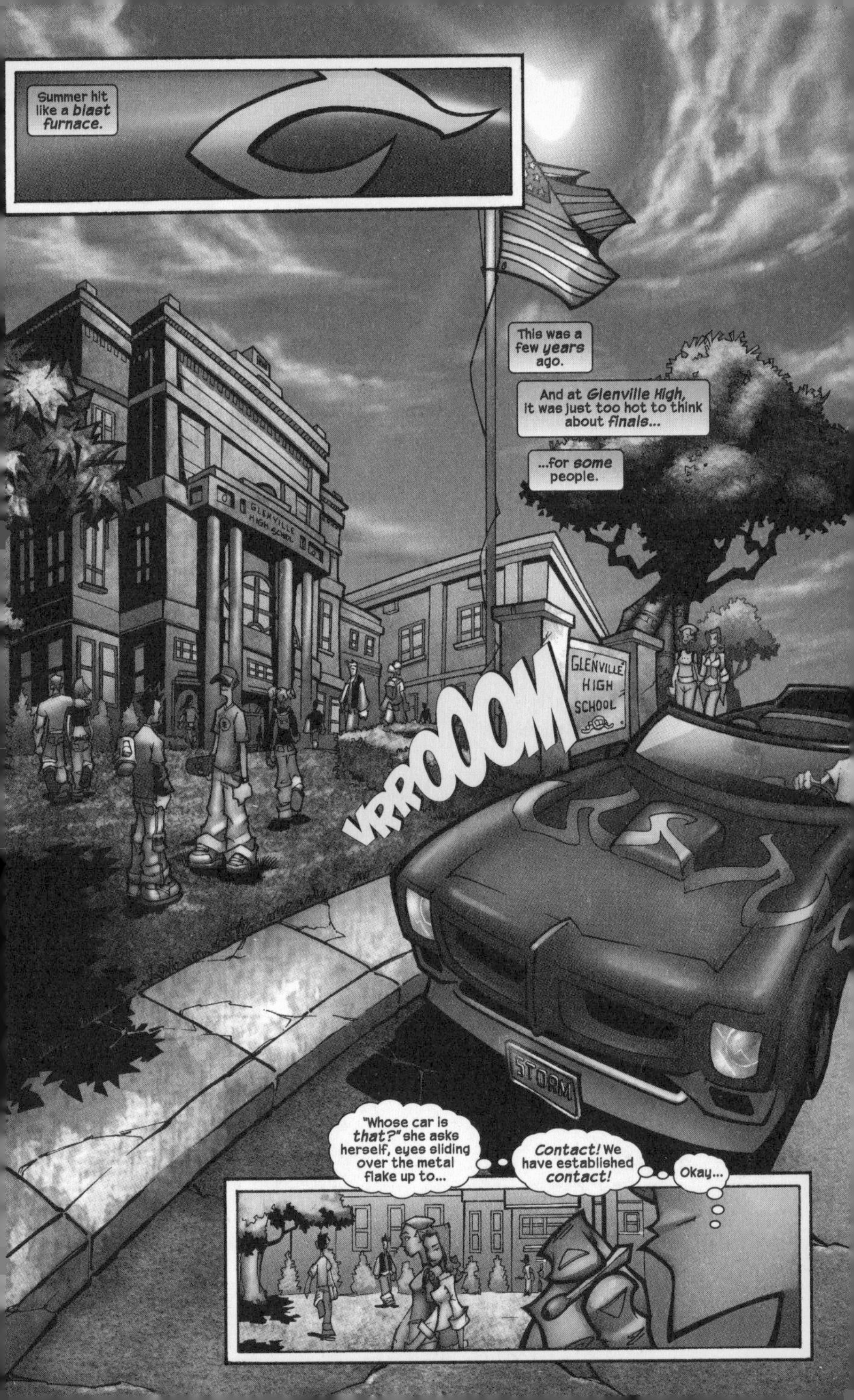
Summer hit like a *blast furnace*.
This was a few *years* ago.
And at *Glenville High*, it was just too hot to think about *finals*...
...for *some* people.
GLENVILLE HIGH SCHOOL
GLENVILLE HIGH SCHOOL
VRROOOOM
STORM
"Whose car is *that?*" she asks herself, eyes sliding over the metal flake up to...
Contact! We have established *contact!*
Okay...

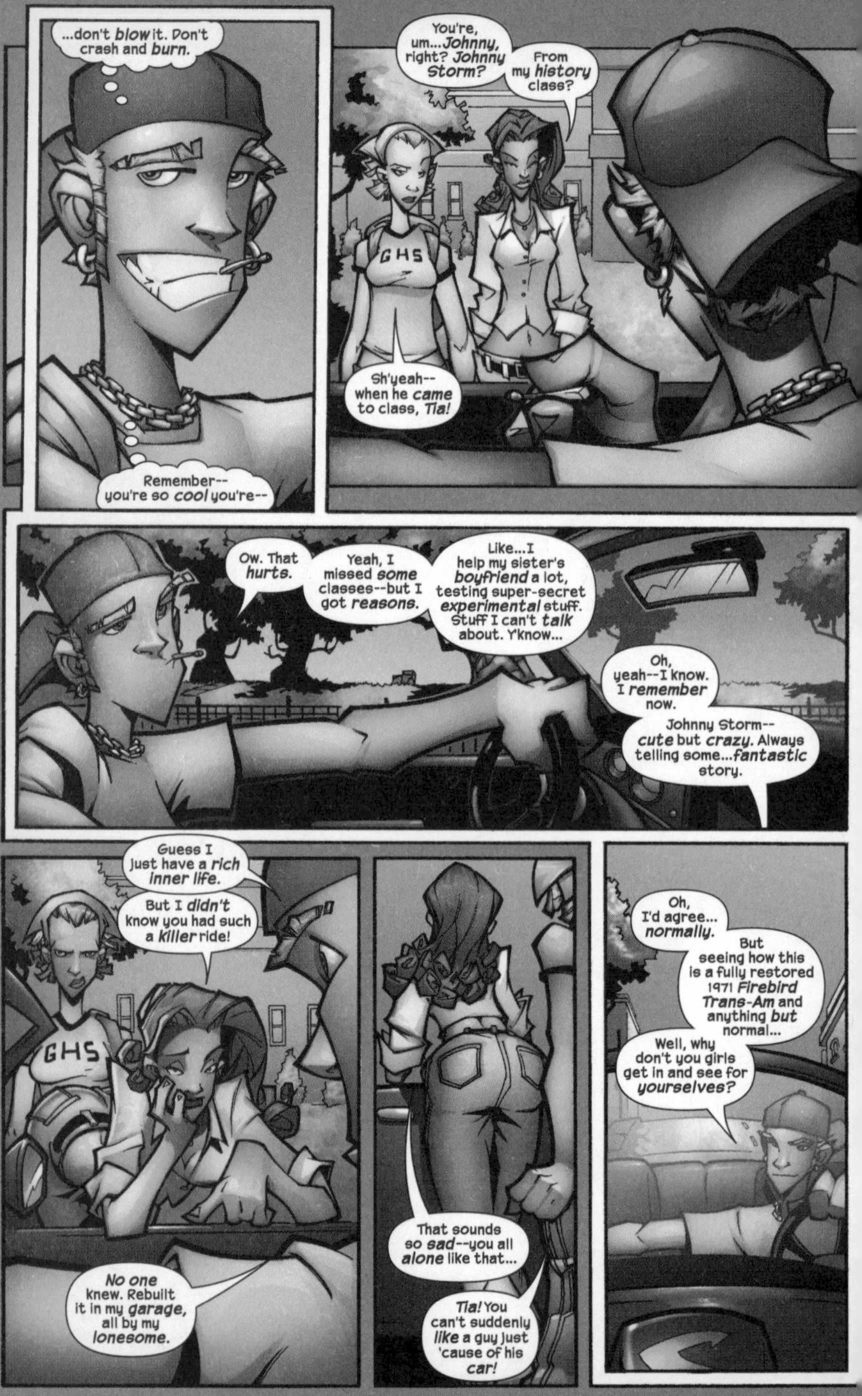

...don't blow it. Don't crash and burn.
Remember-- you're so cool you're--
You're, um...Johnny, right? Johnny Storm?
From my history class?
Sh'yeah-- when he came to class, Tia!
Ow. That hurts.
Yeah, I missed some classes--but I got reasons.
Like...I help my sister's boyfriend a lot, testing super-secret experimental stuff. Stuff I can't talk about. Y'know...
Oh, yeah--I know. I remember now.
Johnny Storm-- cute but crazy. Always telling some...fantastic story.
Guess I just have a rich inner life.
But I didn't know you had such a killer ride!
No one knew. Rebuilt it in my garage, all by my lonesome.
That sounds so sad--you all alone like that...
Tia! You can't suddenly like a guy just 'cause of his car!
Oh, I'd agree... normally.
But seeing how this is a fully restored 1971 Firebird Trans-Am and anything but normal...
Well, why don't you girls get in and see for yourselves?

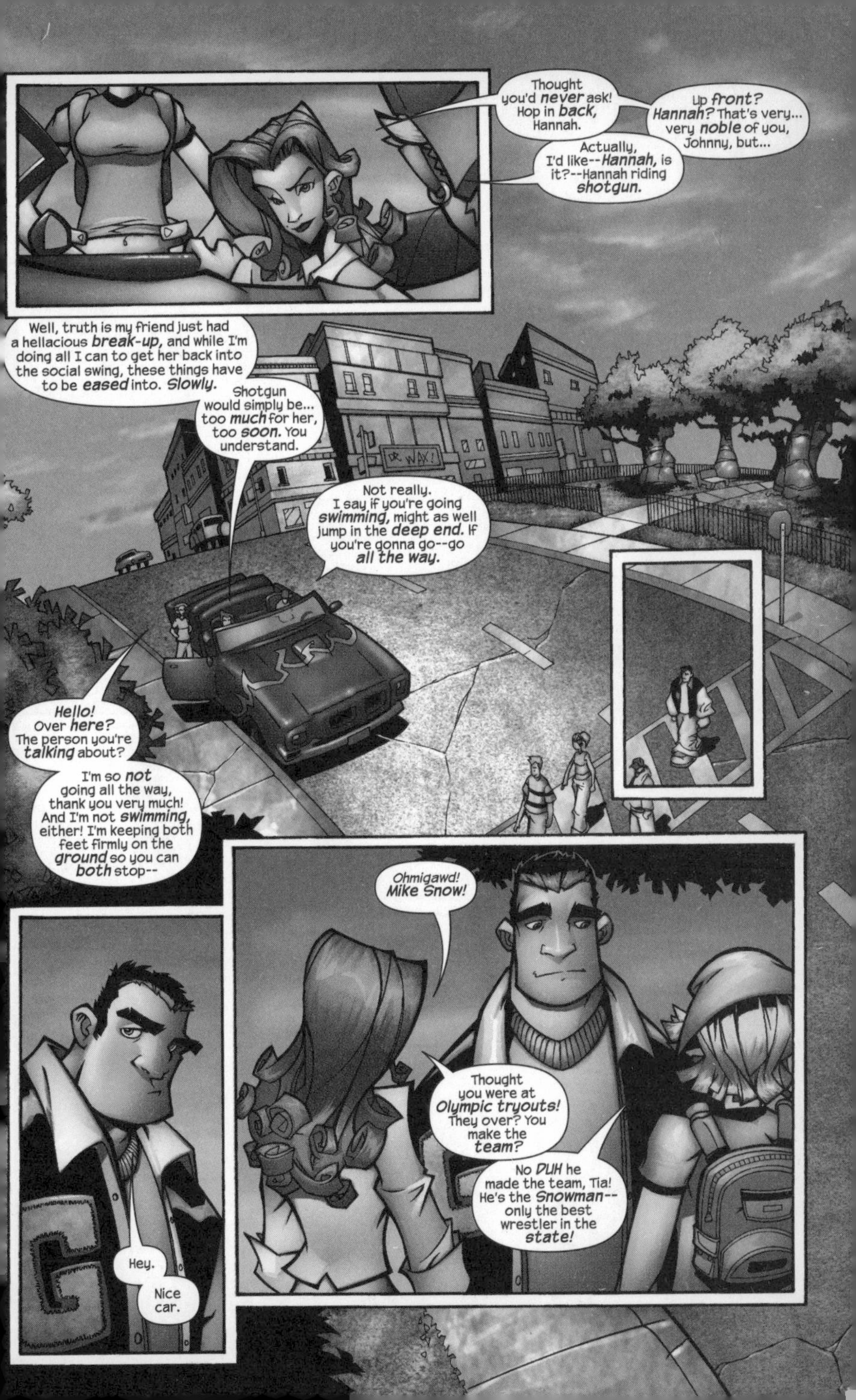

Thought you'd never ask! Hop in back, Hannah.
Up front? Hannah? That's very... very noble of you, Johnny, but...
Actually, I'd like--Hannah, is it?--Hannah riding shotgun.
Well, truth is my friend just had a hellacious break-up, and while I'm doing all I can to get her back into the social swing, these things have to be eased into. Slowly.
Shotgun would simply be... too much for her, too soon. You understand.
DR. WAX!
Not really. I say if you're going swimming, might as well jump in the deep end. If you're gonna go--go all the way.
Hello! Over here? The person you're talking about?
I'm so not going all the way, thank you very much! And I'm not swimming, either! I'm keeping both feet firmly on the ground so you can both stop--
Ohmigawd! Mike Snow!
Thought you were at Olympic tryouts! They over? You make the team?
No DUH he made the team, Tia! He's the Snowman-- only the best wrestler in the state!
Hey.
Nice car.

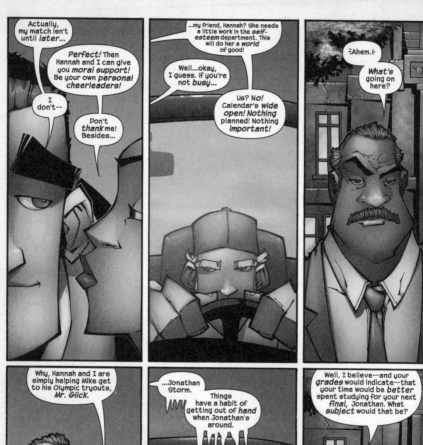

Actually, my match isn't until *later*...

Perfect! Then Hannah and I can give you *moral support!* Be your own *personal cheerleaders!*

I don't--

Don't *thank* me! Besides...

...my friend, Hannah? She needs a little work in the *self-esteem* department. This will do her a *world* of good!

Well...okay, I guess. If you're not *busy*...

Us? NO! Calendar's *wide open!* Nothing planned! Nothing *important!*

¿Ahem.¿

What's going on here?

Why, Hannah and I are simply helping Mike get to his Olympic tryouts, *Mr. Glick.*

Oh. Oh! Can't miss *that,* can we?

My mistake. I had the impression this little gathering was masterminded by...

...Jonathan Storm.

Things have a habit of getting out of *hand* when Jonathan's around.

Was just showing them my *car,* Mr. Glick.

Sir.

Well, I believe--and your *grades* would indicate--that your time would be *better* spent studying for your next *final,* Jonathan. What *subject* would that be?

Science.

Or English. Always get those two *mixed* up.

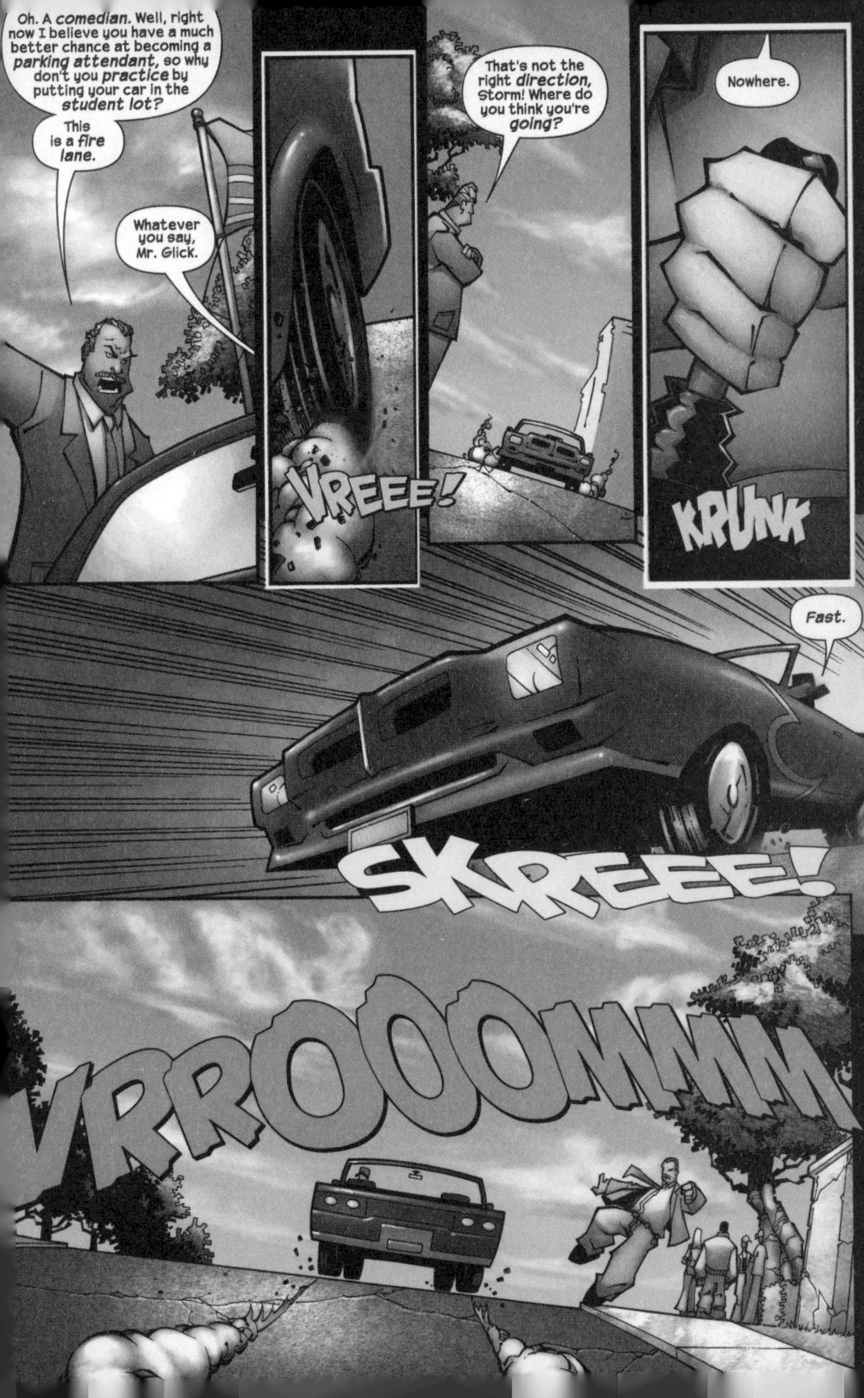
Oh. A comedian. Well, right now I believe you have a much better chance at becoming a parking attendant, so why don't you practice by putting your car in the student lot?
This is a fire lane.
Whatever you say, Mr. Glick.
VREEE!
That's not the right direction, Storm! Where do you think you're going?
Nowhere.
KRUNK
Fast.
SKREEE!
VRROOOMMM

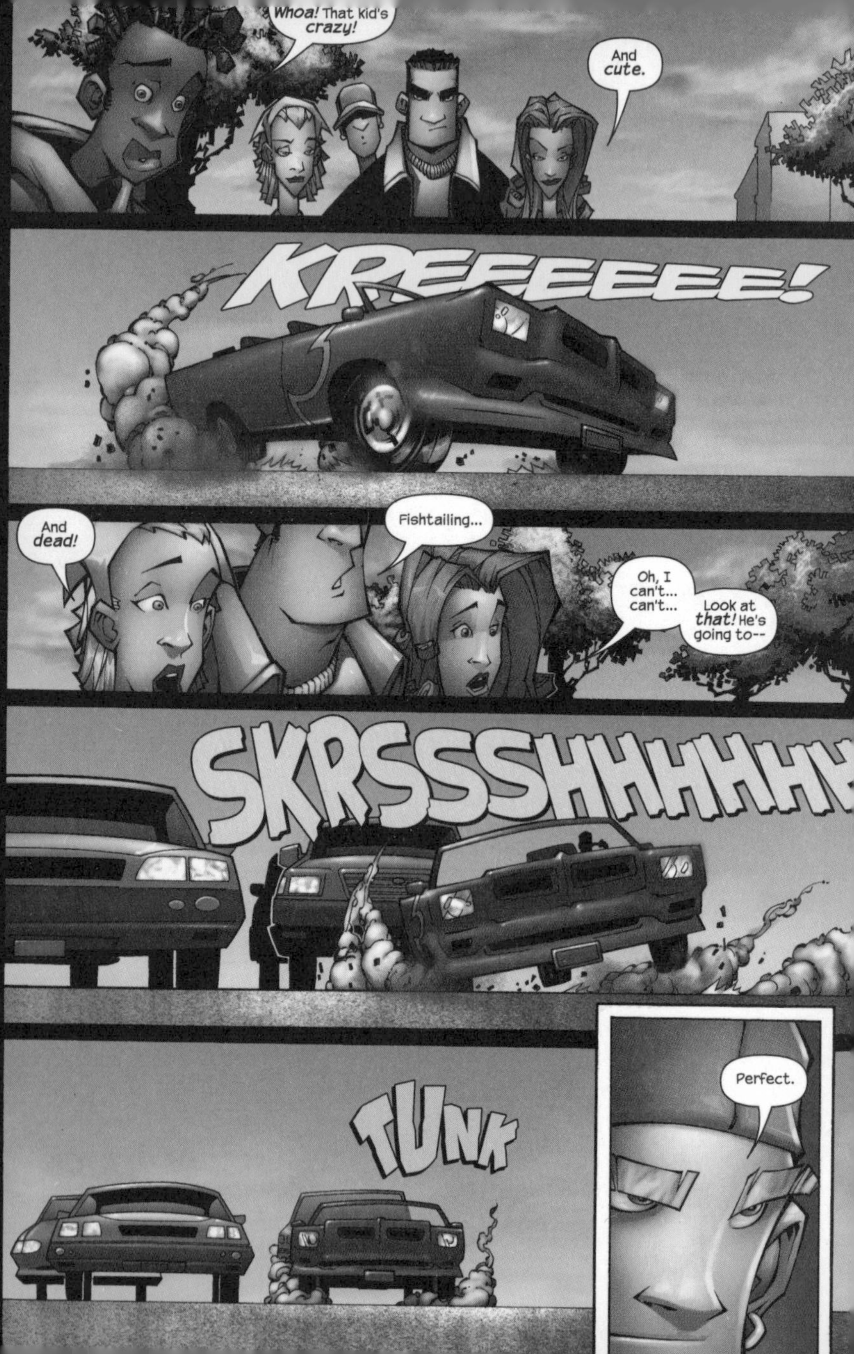
Whoa! That kid's crazy!
And cute.
KREEEEEEE!
And dead!
Fishtailing...
Oh, I can't... can't...
Look at that! He's going to--
SKRSSSHHHHH
TUNK
Perfect.

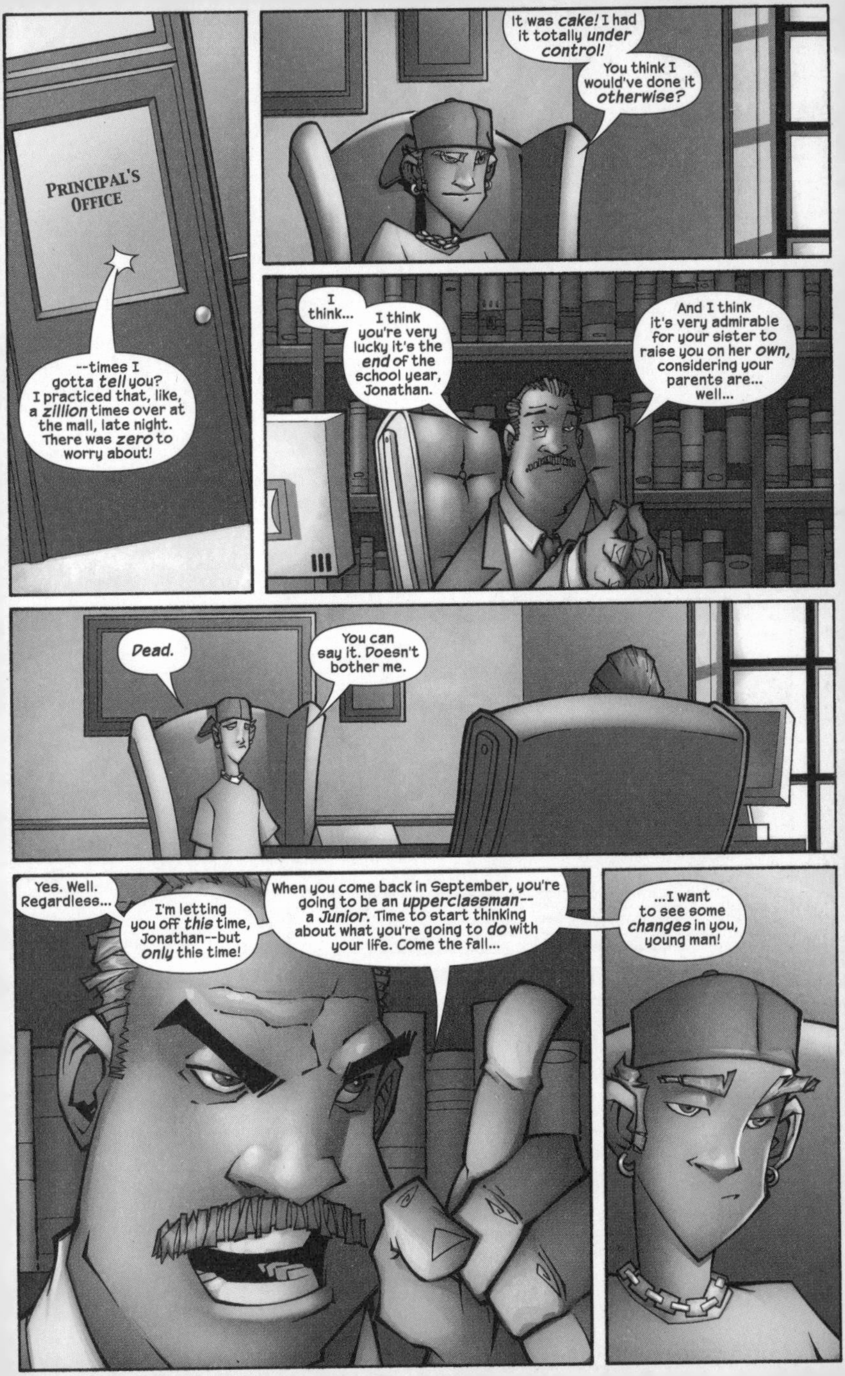
PRINCIPAL'S OFFICE
--times I gotta tell you? I practiced that, like, a zillion times over at the mall, late night. There was zero to worry about!
It was cake! I had it totally under control!
You think I would've done it otherwise?
I think...
I think you're very lucky it's the end of the school year, Jonathan.
And I think it's very admirable for your sister to raise you on her own, considering your parents are... well...
Dead.
You can say it. Doesn't bother me.
Yes. Well. Regardless...
I'm letting you off this time, Jonathan--but only this time!
When you come back in September, you're going to be an upperclassman-- a Junior. Time to start thinking about what you're going to do with your life. Come the fall...
...I want to see some changes in you, young man!

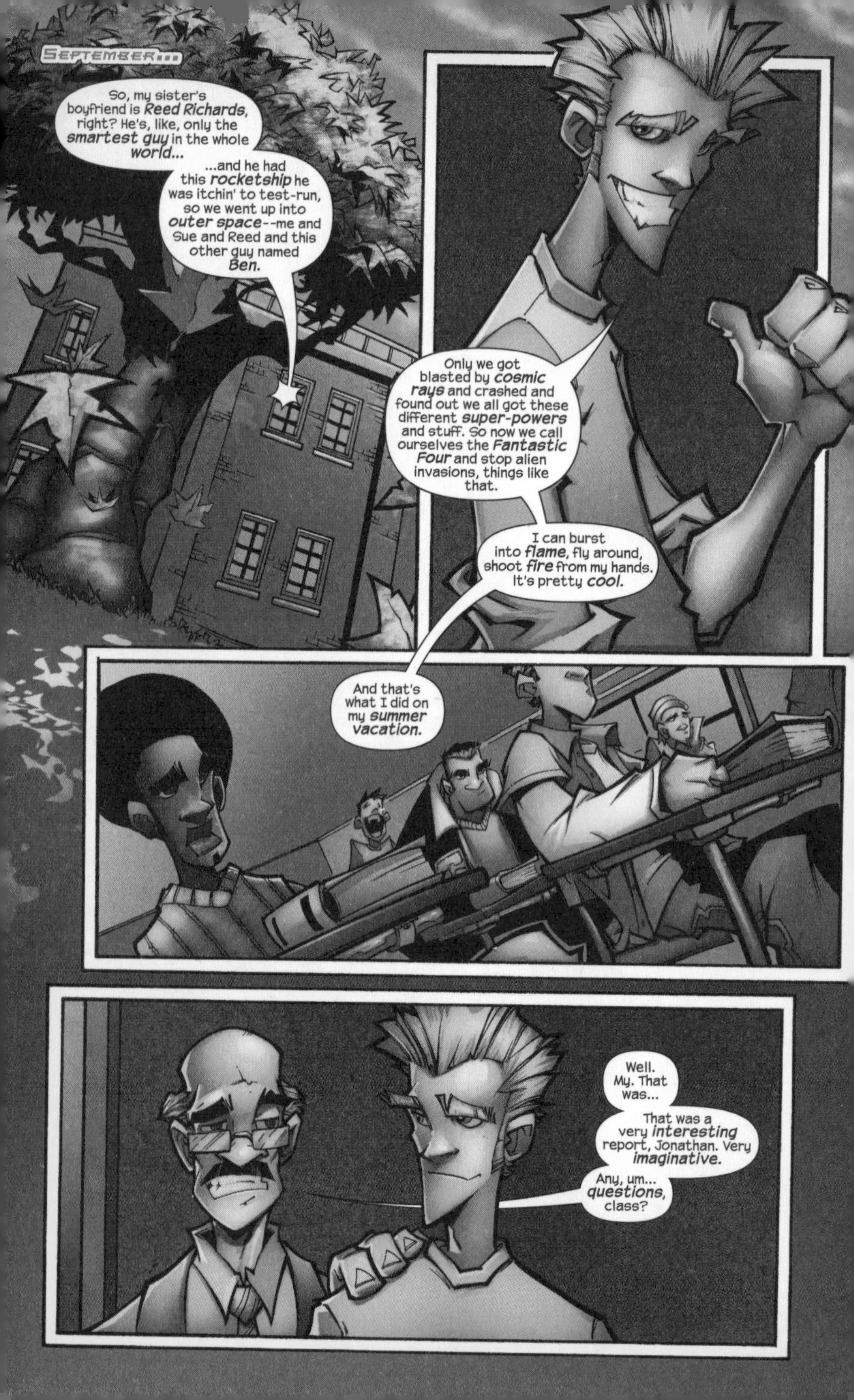
September...
So, my sister's boyfriend is Reed Richards, right? He's, like, only the smartest guy in the whole world...
...and he had this rocketship he was itchin' to test-run, so we went up into outer space--me and Sue and Reed and this other guy named Ben.
Only we got blasted by cosmic rays and crashed and found out we all got these different super-powers and stuff. So now we call ourselves the Fantastic Four and stop alien invasions, things like that.
I can burst into flame, fly around, shoot fire from my hands. It's pretty cool.
And that's what I did on my summer vacation.
Well. My. That was...
That was a very interesting report, Jonathan. Very imaginative.
Any, um... questions, class?

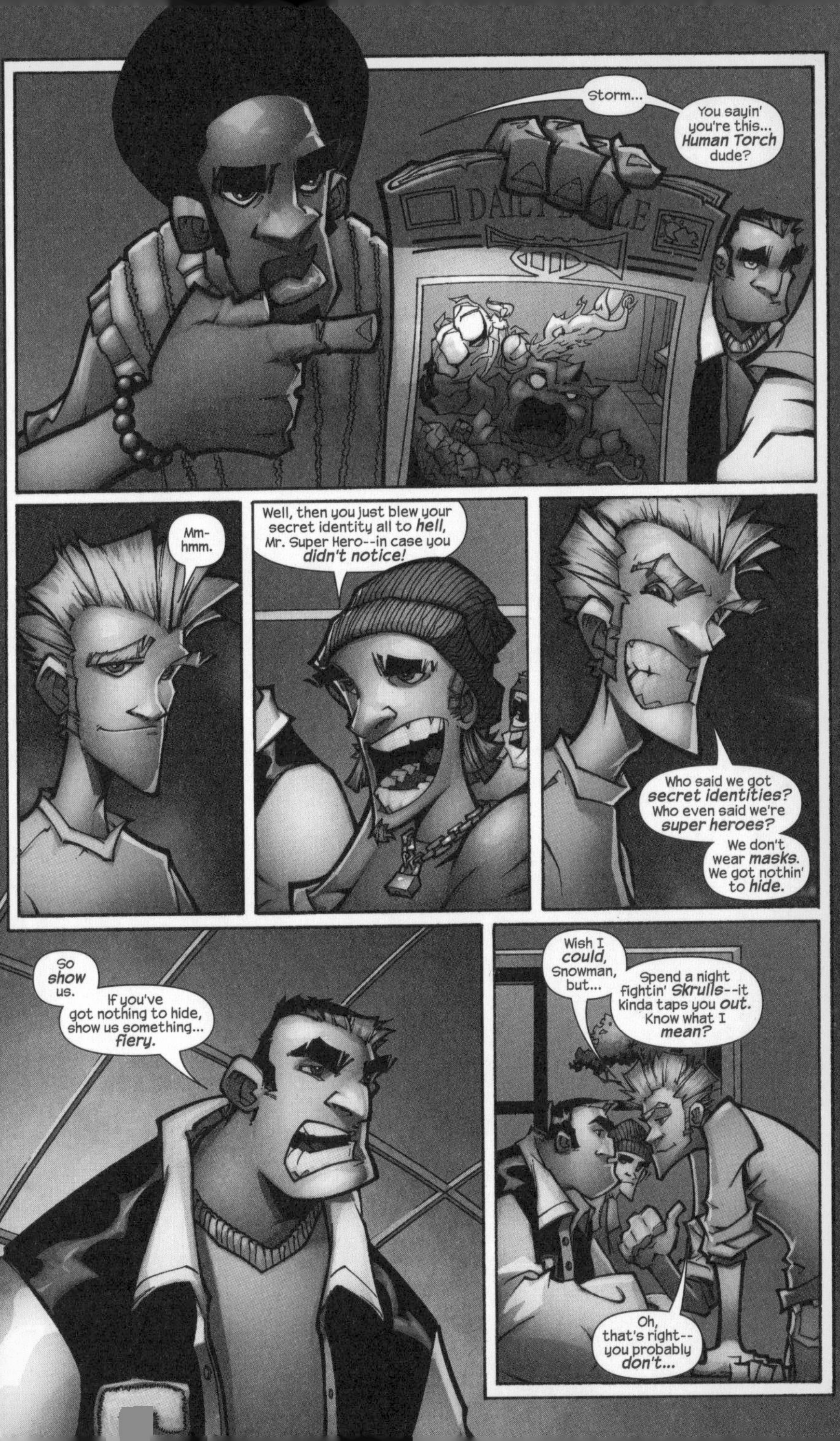
Storm...
You sayin' you're this... Human Torch dude?
Mm-hmm.
Well, then you just blew your secret identity all to hell, Mr. Super Hero--in case you didn't notice!
Who said we got secret identities? Who even said we're super heroes?
We don't wear masks. We got nothin' to hide.
So show us.
If you've got nothing to hide, show us something... fiery.
Wish I could, Snowman, but...
Spend a night fightin' Skrulls--it kinda taps you out. Know what I mean?
Oh, that's right--you probably don't...

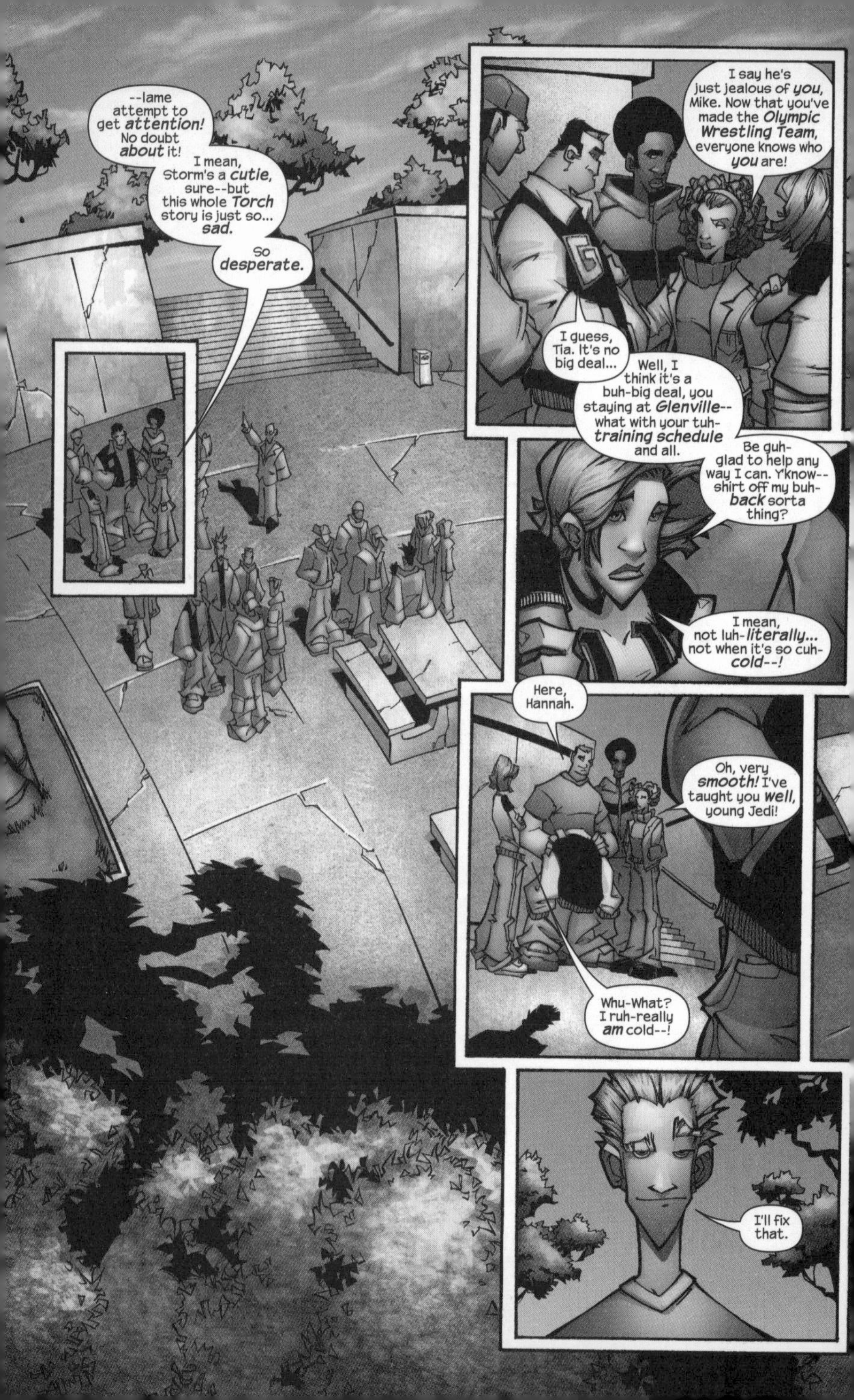
--lame attempt to get attention! No doubt about it!
I mean, Storm's a cutie, sure--but this whole Torch story is just so... sad.
So desperate.
I say he's just jealous of you, Mike. Now that you've made the Olympic Wrestling Team, everyone knows who you are!
I guess, Tia. It's no big deal...
Well, I think it's a buh-big deal, you staying at Glenville--what with your tuh-training schedule and all.
Be guh-glad to help any way I can. Y'know--shirt off my buh-back sorta thing?
I mean, not luh-literally... not when it's so cuh-cold--!
Here, Hannah.
Oh, very smooth! I've taught you well, young Jedi!
Whu-What? I ruh-really am cold--!
I'll fix that.

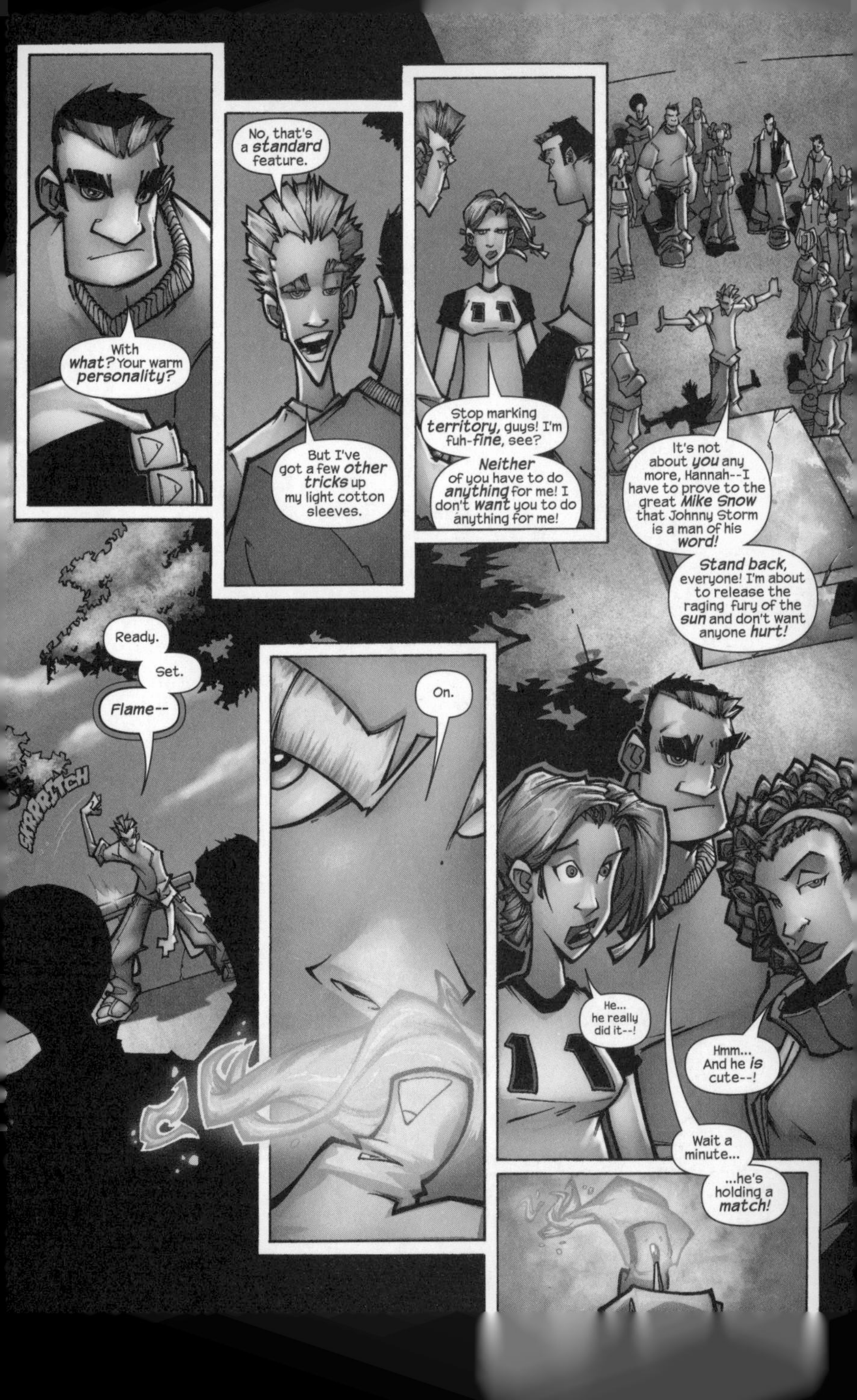
With what? Your warm personality?
No, that's a standard feature.
But I've got a few other tricks up my light cotton sleeves.
Stop marking territory, guys! I'm fuh-fine, see?
Neither of you have to do anything for me! I don't want you to do anything for me!
It's not about you any more, Hannah--I have to prove to the great Mike Snow that Johnny Storm is a man of his word!
Stand back, everyone! I'm about to release the raging fury of the sun and don't want anyone hurt!
Ready.
Set.
Flame--
SKRRITCH
On.
He... he really did it--!
Hmm... And he is cute--!
Wait a minute...
...he's holding a match!

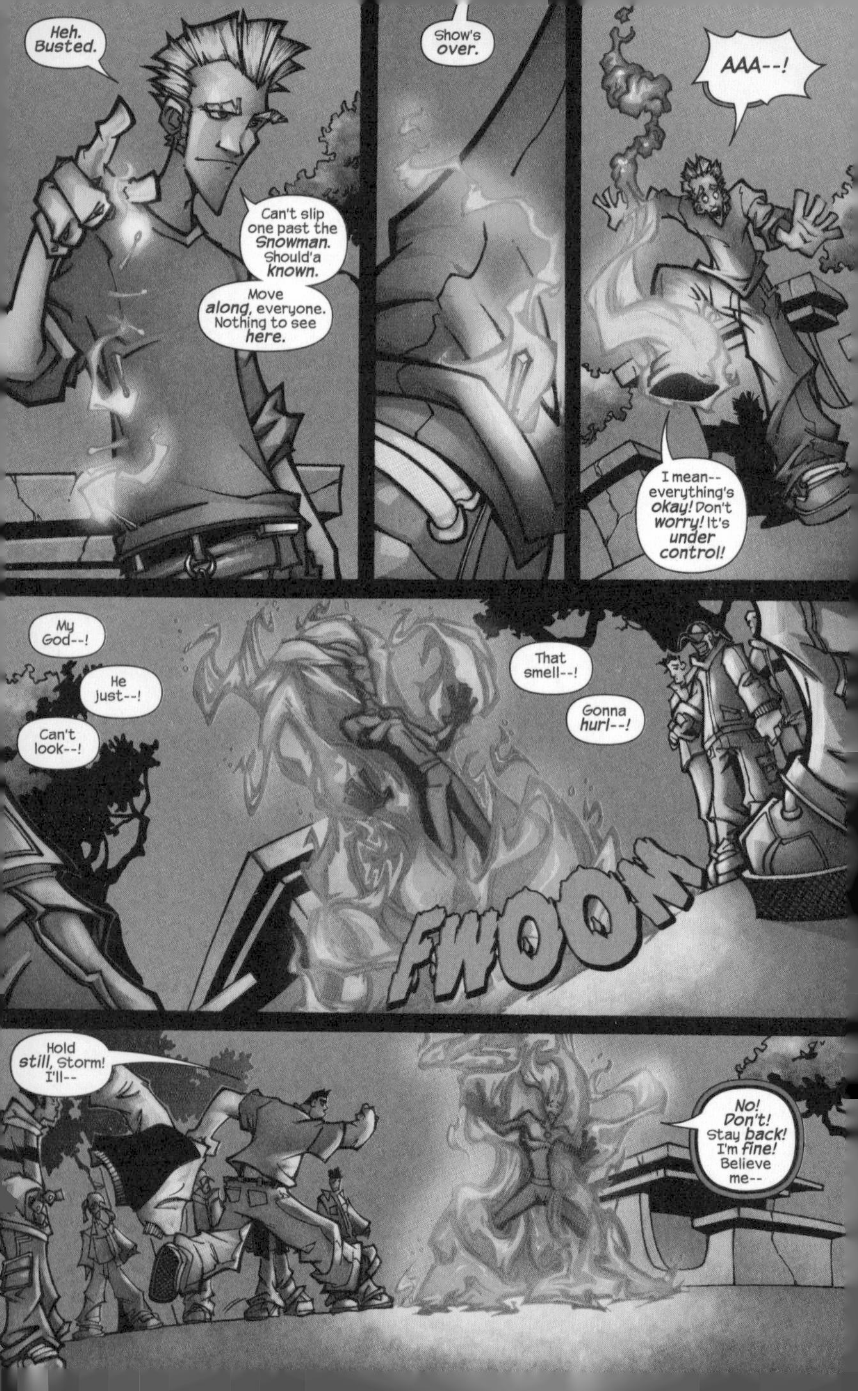
Heh. Busted.
Can't slip one past the Snowman. Should'a known.
Move along, everyone. Nothing to see here.
Show's over.
AAA--!
I mean-- everything's okay! Don't worry! It's under control!
My God--!
He just--!
Can't look--!
That smell--!
Gonna hurl--!
FWOOM
Hold still, Storm! I'll--
No! Don't! Stay back! I'm fine! Believe me--

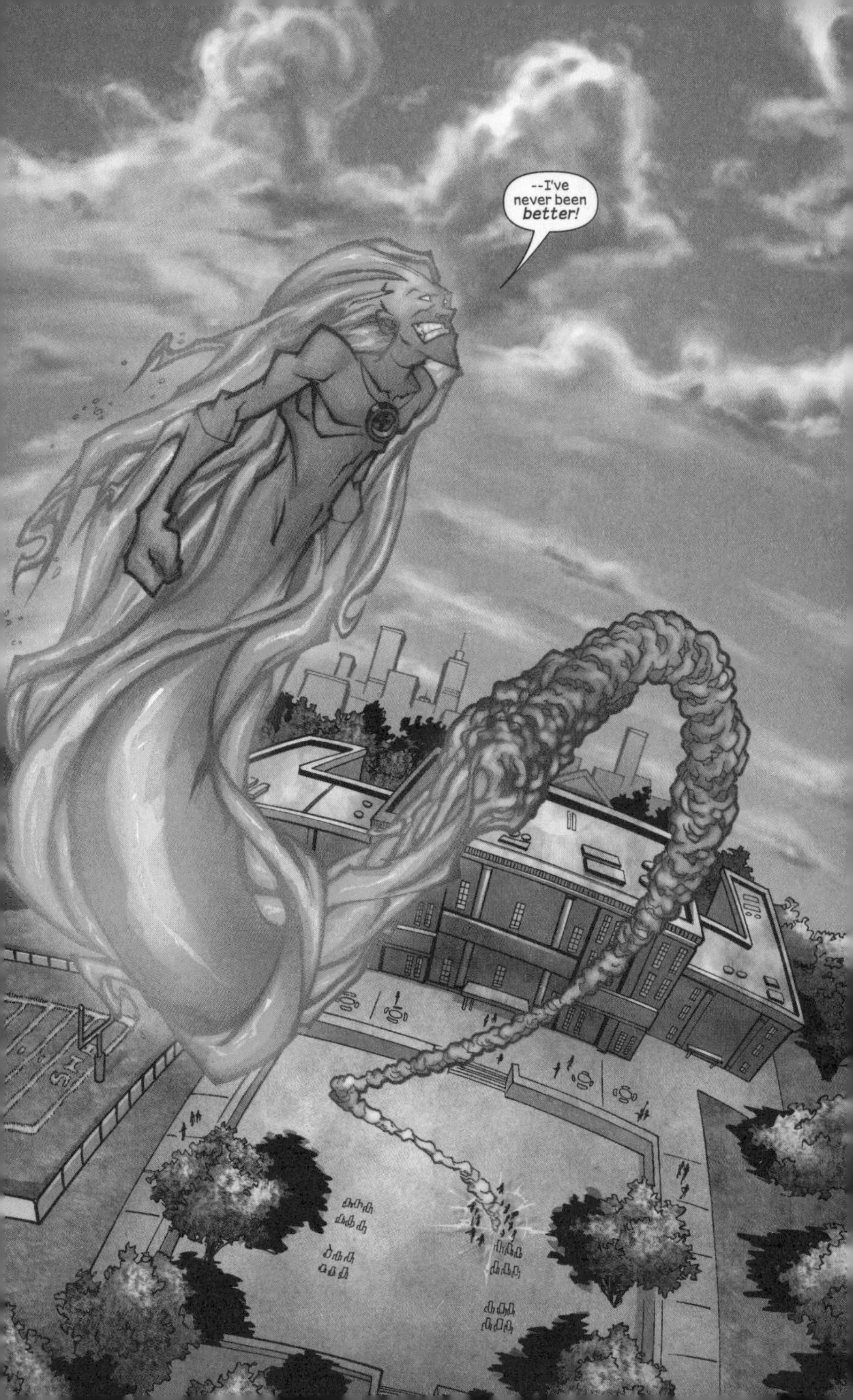
--I've never been *better!*

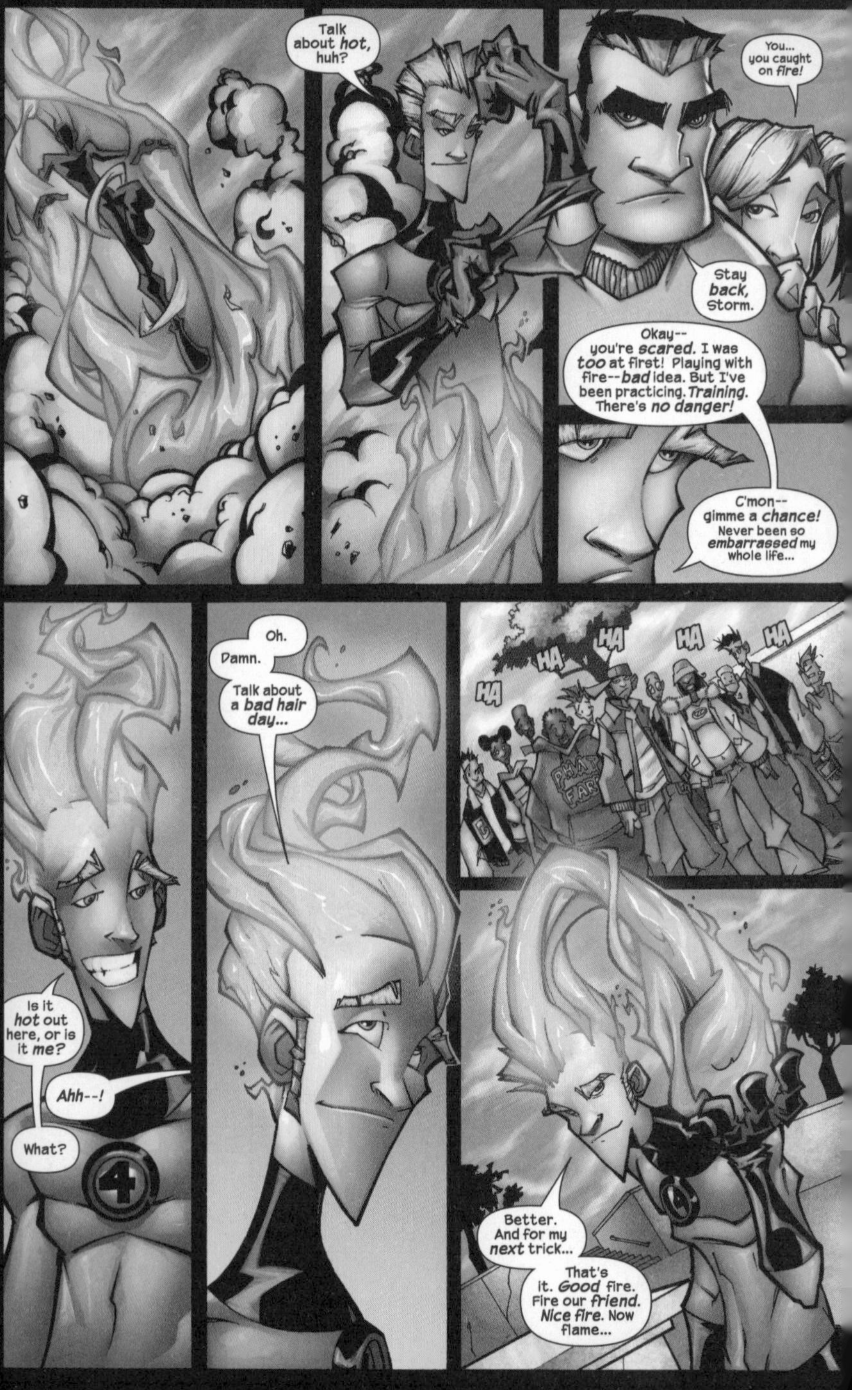
Talk about hot, huh?
You... you caught on fire!
Stay back, Storm.
Okay-- you're scared. I was too at first! Playing with fire--bad idea. But I've been practicing. Training. There's no danger!
C'mon-- gimme a chance! Never been so embarrassed my whole life...
Is it hot out here, or is it me?
Ahh--!
What?
Oh.
Damn.
Talk about a bad hair day...
HA
HA
HA
HA
HA
Better. And for my next trick...
That's it. Good fire. Fire our friend. Nice fire. Now flame...

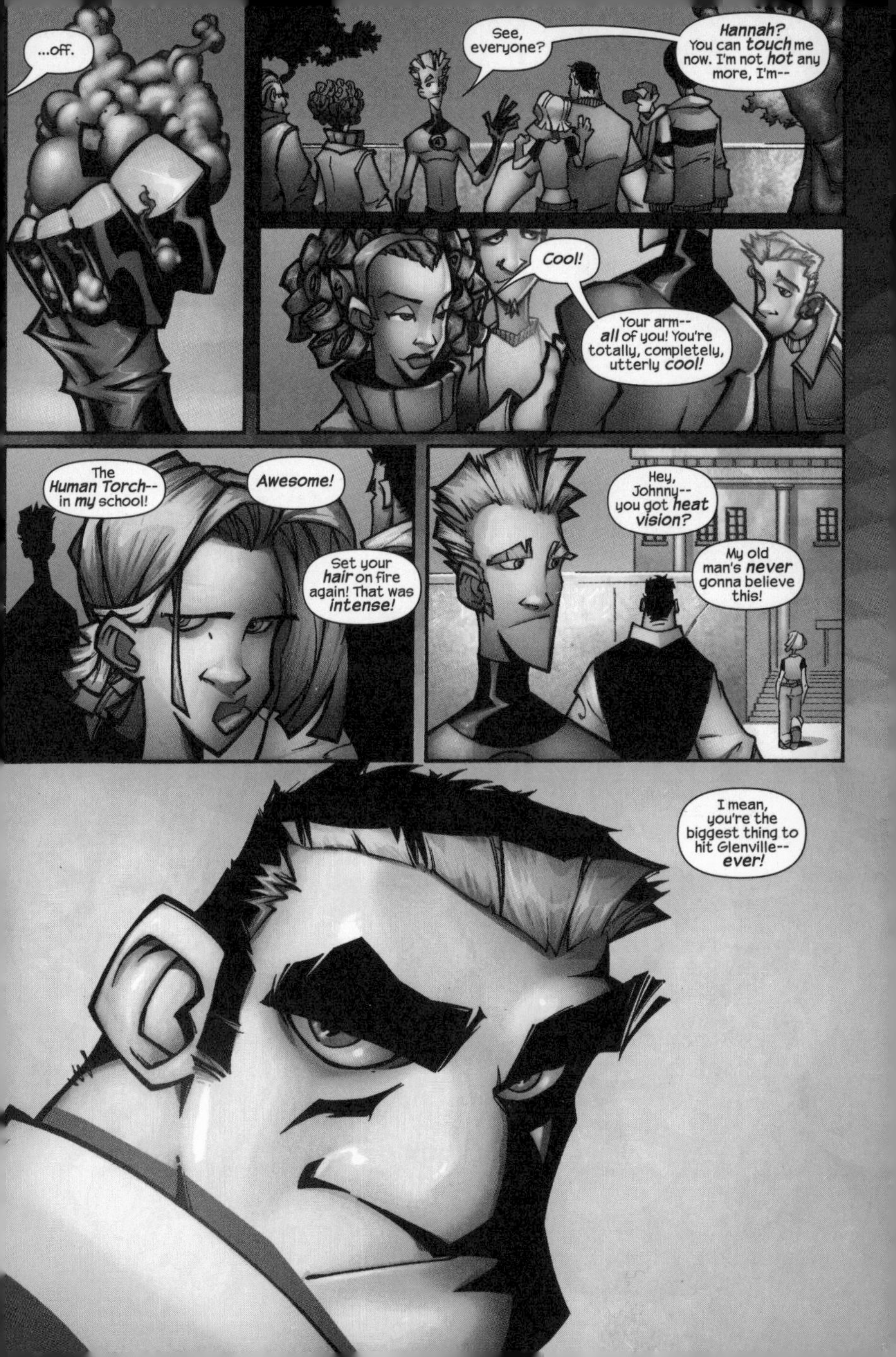
...off.
See, everyone?
Hannah? You can touch me now. I'm not hot any more, I'm--
Cool!
Your arm-- all of you! You're totally, completely, utterly cool!
The Human Torch-- in my school!
Awesome!
Set your hair on fire again! That was intense!
Hey, Johnny-- you got heat vision?
My old man's never gonna believe this!
I mean, you're the biggest thing to hit Glenville-- ever!

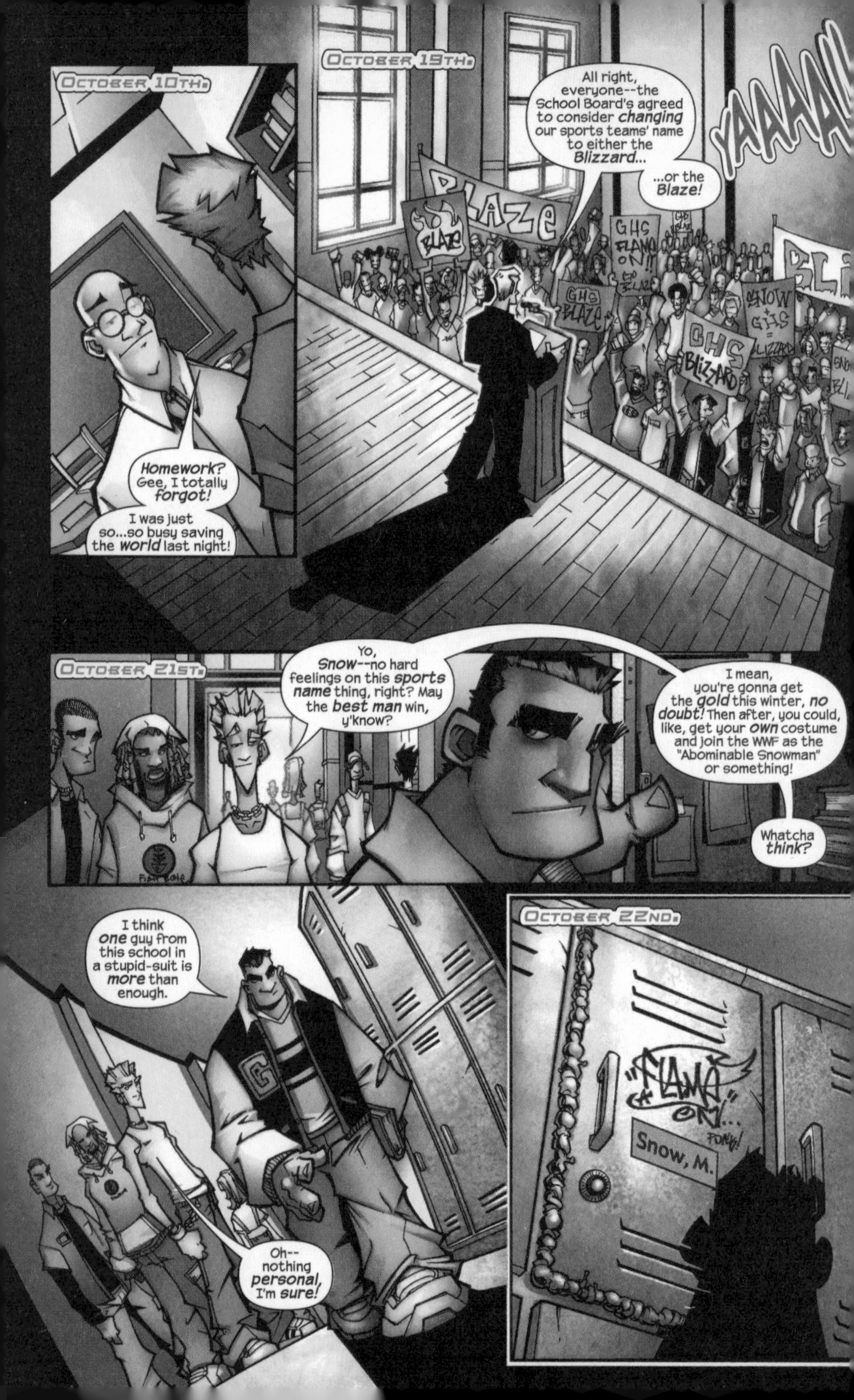
October 10th.
Homework? Gee, I totally forgot!
I was just so...so busy saving the world last night!
October 19th.
All right, everyone--the School Board's agreed to consider changing our sports teams' name to either the Blizzard...
...or the Blaze!
YAAAA
BLAZE
BLAZE
GHS FLAME ON!!
GHS BLAZE
GHS BLIZZARD
SNOW + GHS = BLIZZARD
October 21st.
Yo, Snow--no hard feelings on this sports name thing, right? May the best man win, y'know?
I mean, you're gonna get the gold this winter, no doubt! Then after, you could, like, get your own costume and join the WWF as the "Abominable Snowman" or something!
Whatcha think?
I think one guy from this school in a stupid-suit is more than enough.
Oh--nothing personal, I'm sure!
October 22nd.
"Flame on"...
Snow, M.

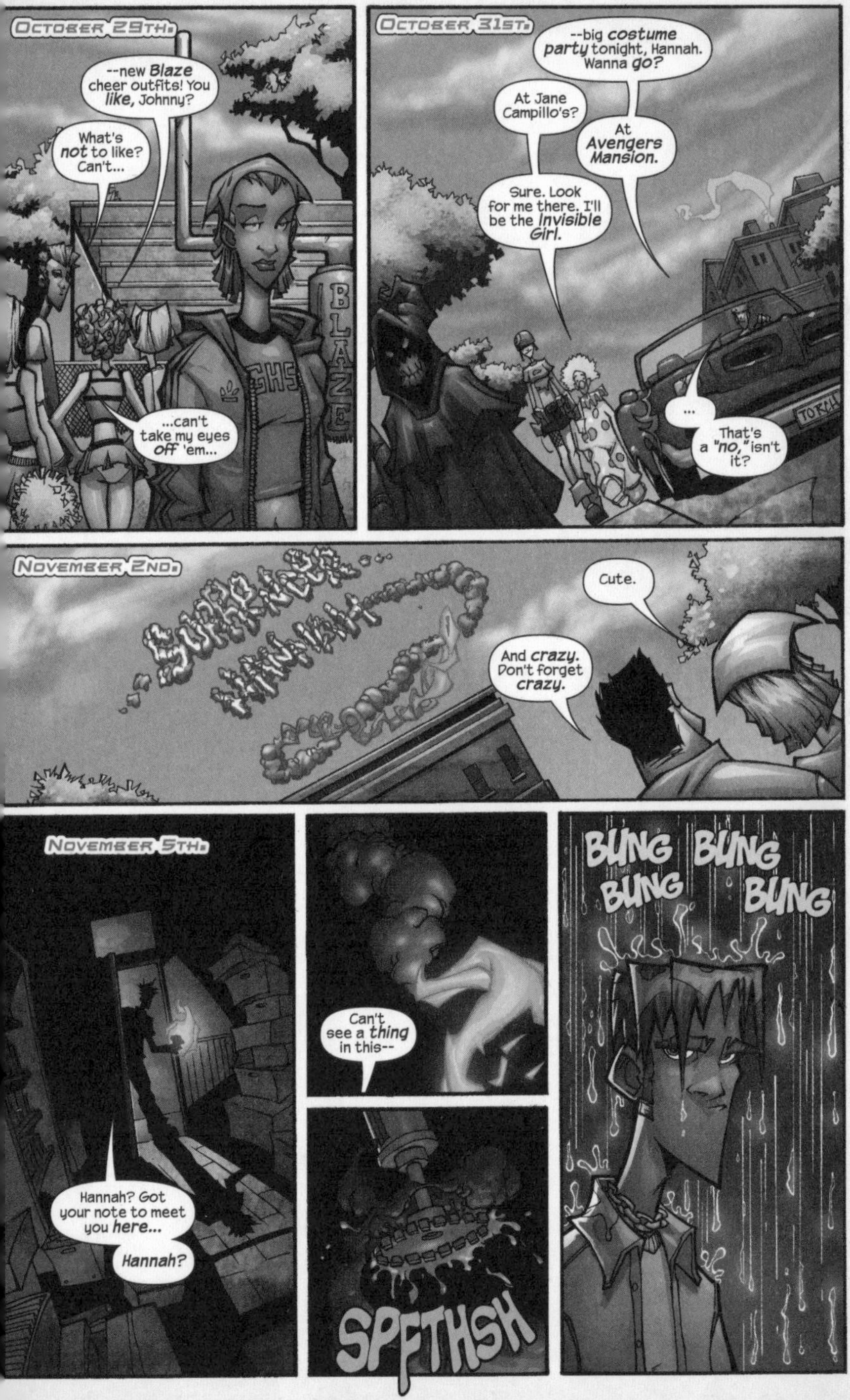
October 29th.
--new Blaze cheer outfits! You like, Johnny?
What's not to like? Can't...
...can't take my eyes off 'em...
BLAZE
GHS
October 31st.
--big costume party tonight, Hannah. Wanna go?
At Jane Campillo's?
At Avengers Mansion.
Sure. Look for me there. I'll be the Invisible Girl.
...
That's a "no," isn't it?
November 2nd.
Cute.
And crazy. Don't forget crazy.
November 5th.
Hannah? Got your note to meet you here...
Hannah?
Can't see a thing in this--
SPFTHSH
BUNG BUNG
BUNG BUNG

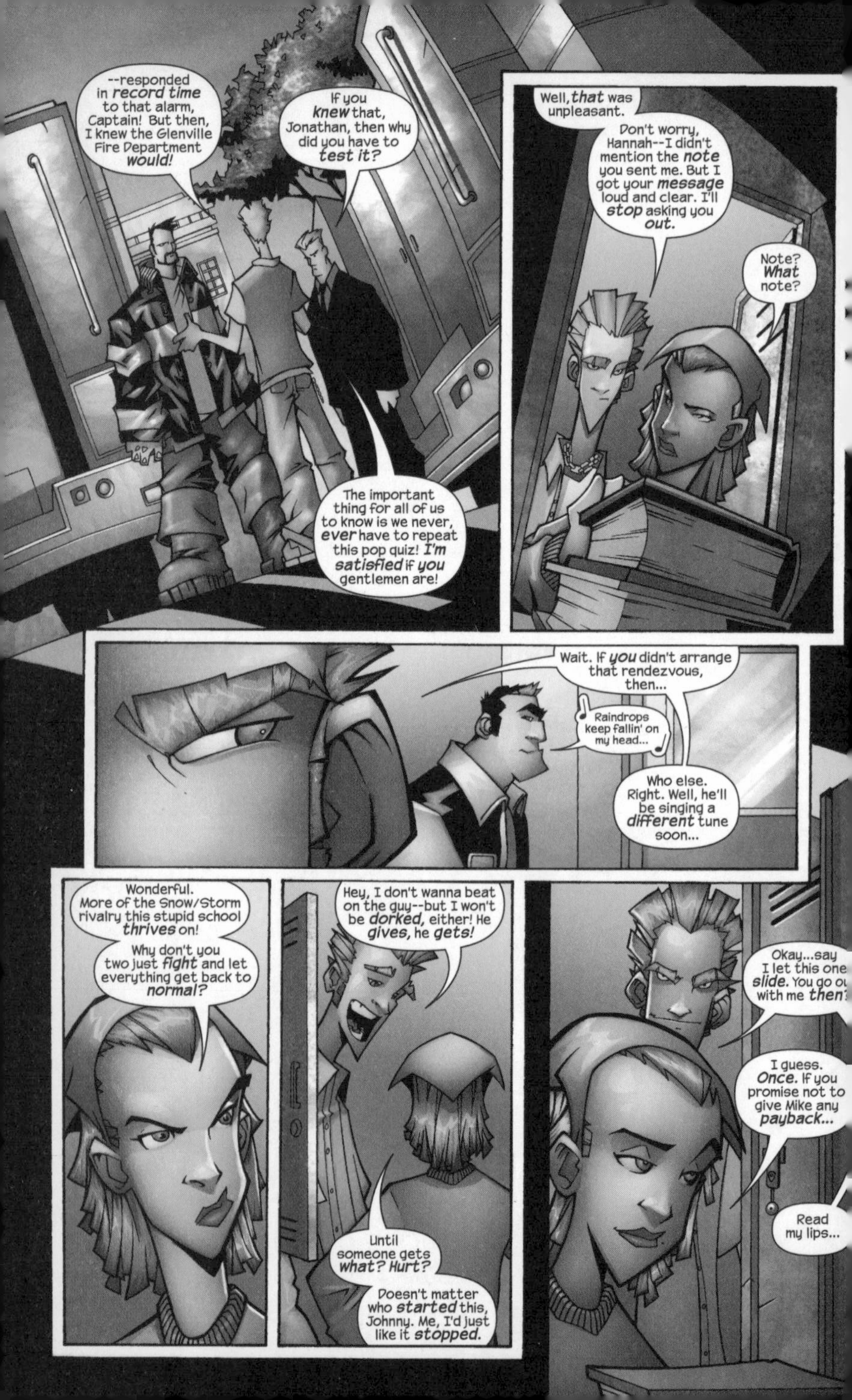
--responded in record time to that alarm, Captain! But then, I knew the Glenville Fire Department would!
If you knew that, Jonathan, then why did you have to test it?
The important thing for all of us to know is we never, ever have to repeat this pop quiz! I'm satisfied if you gentlemen are!
Well, that was unpleasant.
Don't worry, Hannah--I didn't mention the note you sent me. But I got your message loud and clear. I'll stop asking you out.
Note? What note?
Wait. If you didn't arrange that rendezvous, then...
Raindrops keep fallin' on my head...
Who else. Right. Well, he'll be singing a different tune soon...
Wonderful. More of the Snow/Storm rivalry this stupid school thrives on!
Why don't you two just fight and let everything get back to normal?
Hey, I don't wanna beat on the guy--but I won't be dorked, either! He gives, he gets!
Until someone gets what? Hurt?
Doesn't matter who started this, Johnny. Me, I'd just like it stopped.
I guess. Once. If you promise not to give Mike any payback...
Read my lips...

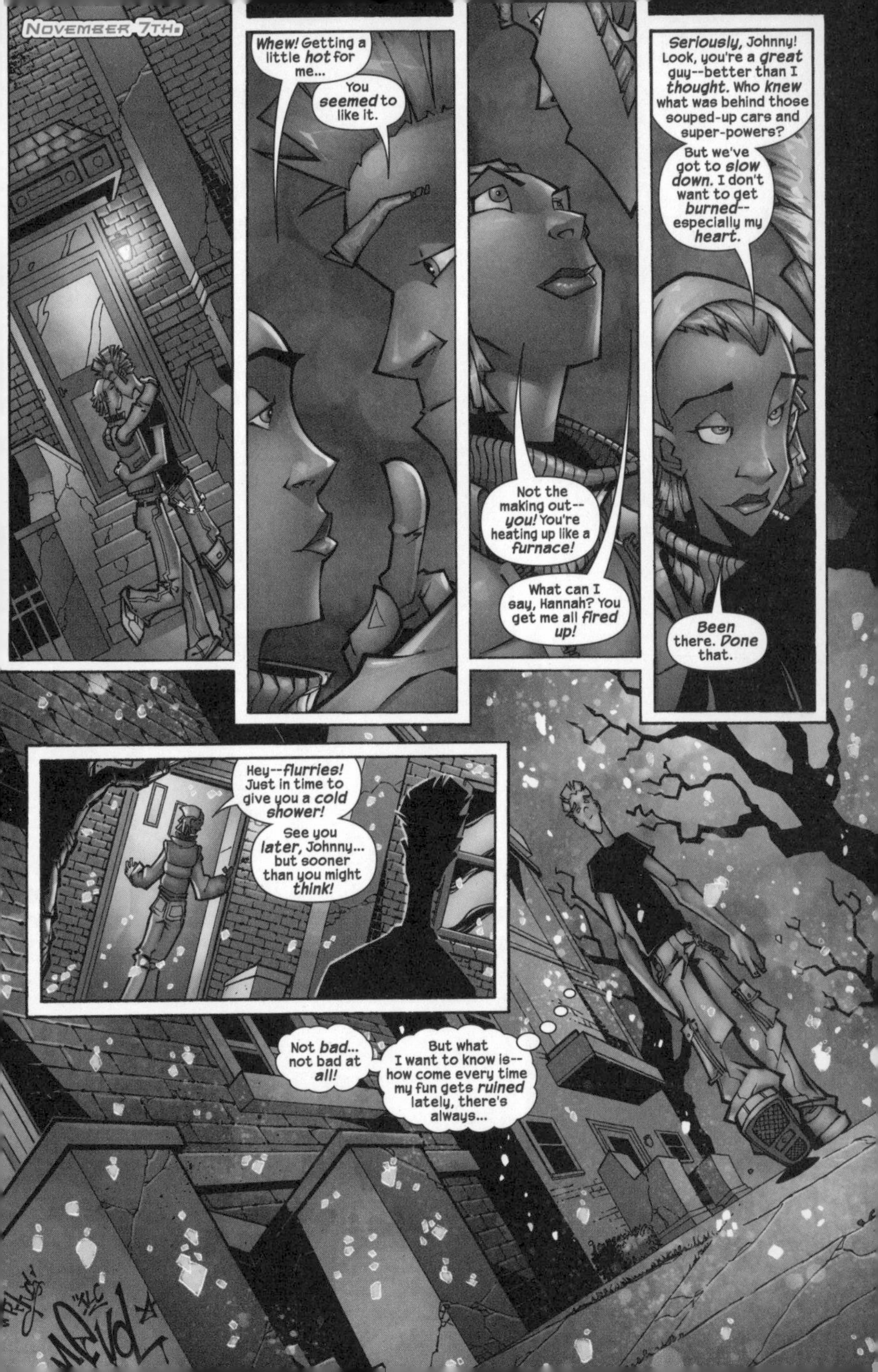
NOVEMBER 7TH.
Whew! Getting a little hot for me...
You seemed to like it.
Not the making out-- you! You're heating up like a furnace!
What can I say, Hannah? You get me all fired up!
Seriously, Johnny! Look, you're a great guy--better than I thought. Who knew what was behind those souped-up cars and super-powers?
But we've got to slow down. I don't want to get burned-- especially my heart.
Been there. Done that.
Hey--flurries! Just in time to give you a cold shower!
See you later, Johnny... but sooner than you might think!
Not bad... not bad at all!
But what I want to know is-- how come every time my fun gets ruined lately, there's always...

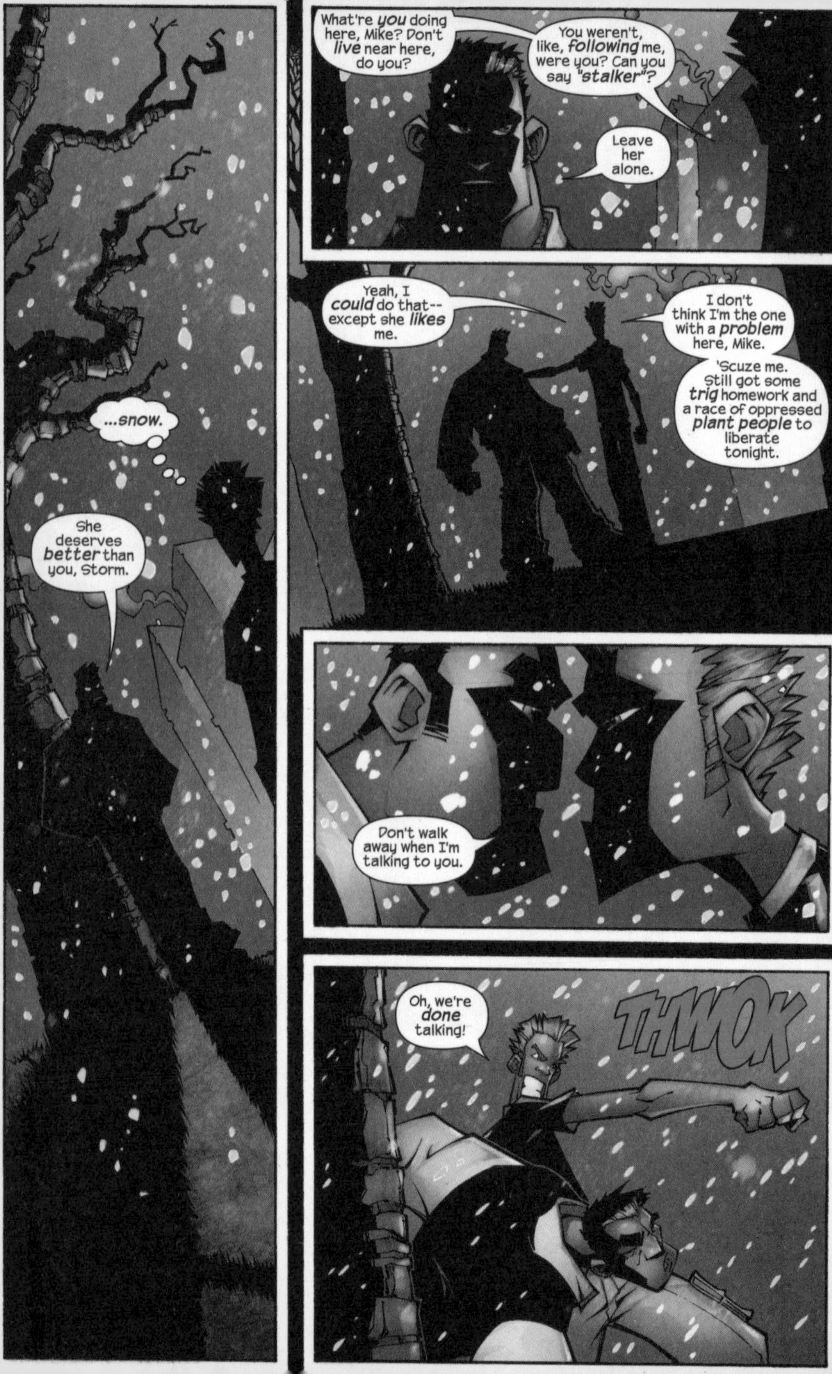
...snow.
She deserves better than you, Storm.
What're you doing here, Mike? Don't live near here, do you?
You weren't, like, following me, were you? Can you say "stalker"?
Leave her alone.
Yeah, I could do that--except she likes me.
I don't think I'm the one with a problem here, Mike.
'Scuze me. Still got some trig homework and a race of oppressed plant people to liberate tonight.
Don't walk away when I'm talking to you.
Oh, we're done talking!
THWOK

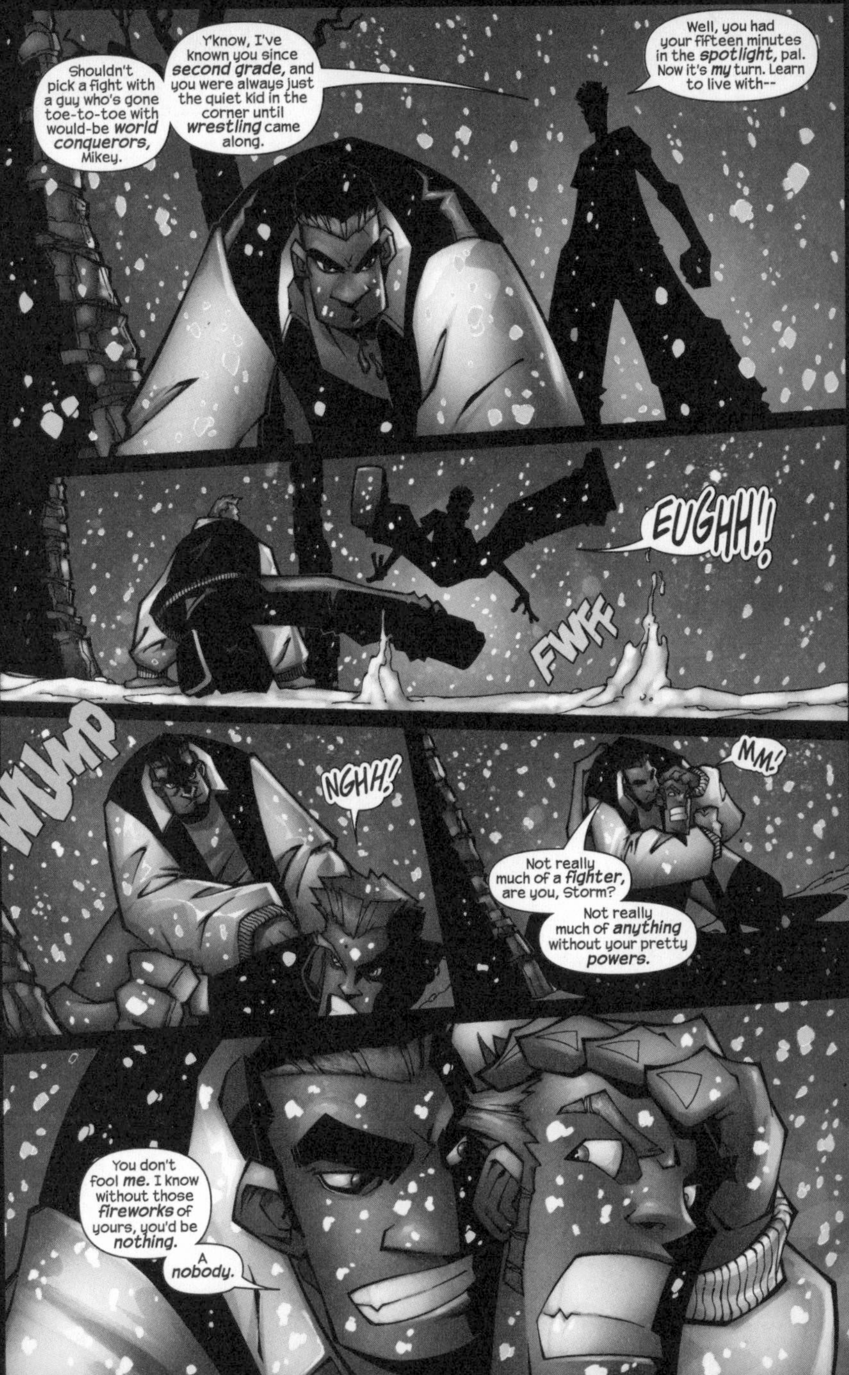
Y'know, I've known you since second grade, and you were always just the quiet kid in the corner until wrestling came along.
Shouldn't pick a fight with a guy who's gone toe-to-toe with would-be world conquerors, Mikey.
Well, you had your fifteen minutes in the spotlight, pal. Now it's my turn. Learn to live with--
EUGHH!!
FWFF
WUMP
NGHH!
MM!
Not really much of a fighter, are you, Storm?
Not really much of anything without your pretty powers.
You don't fool me. I know without those fireworks of yours, you'd be nothing.
A nobody.

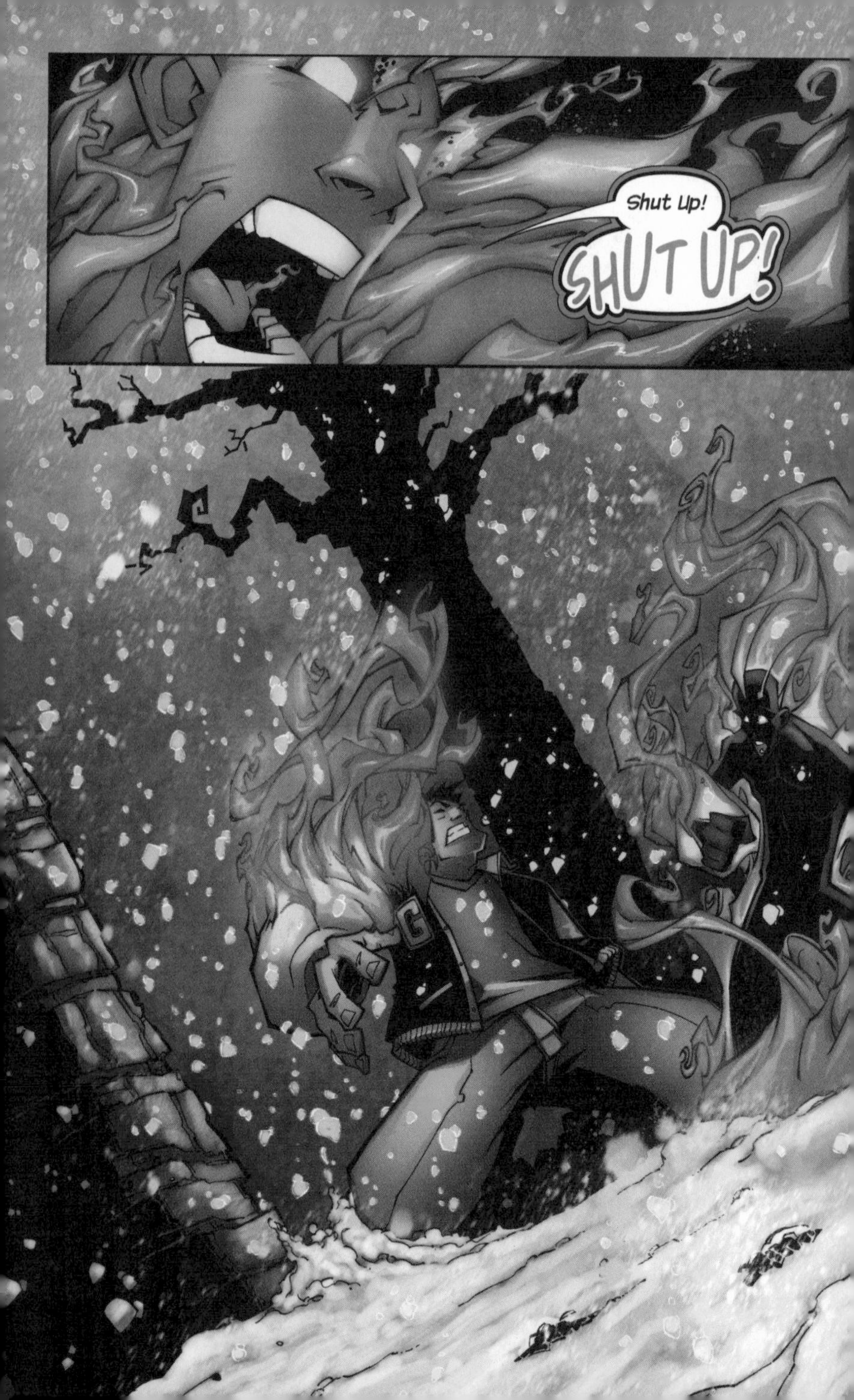
Shut Up!
SHUT UP!

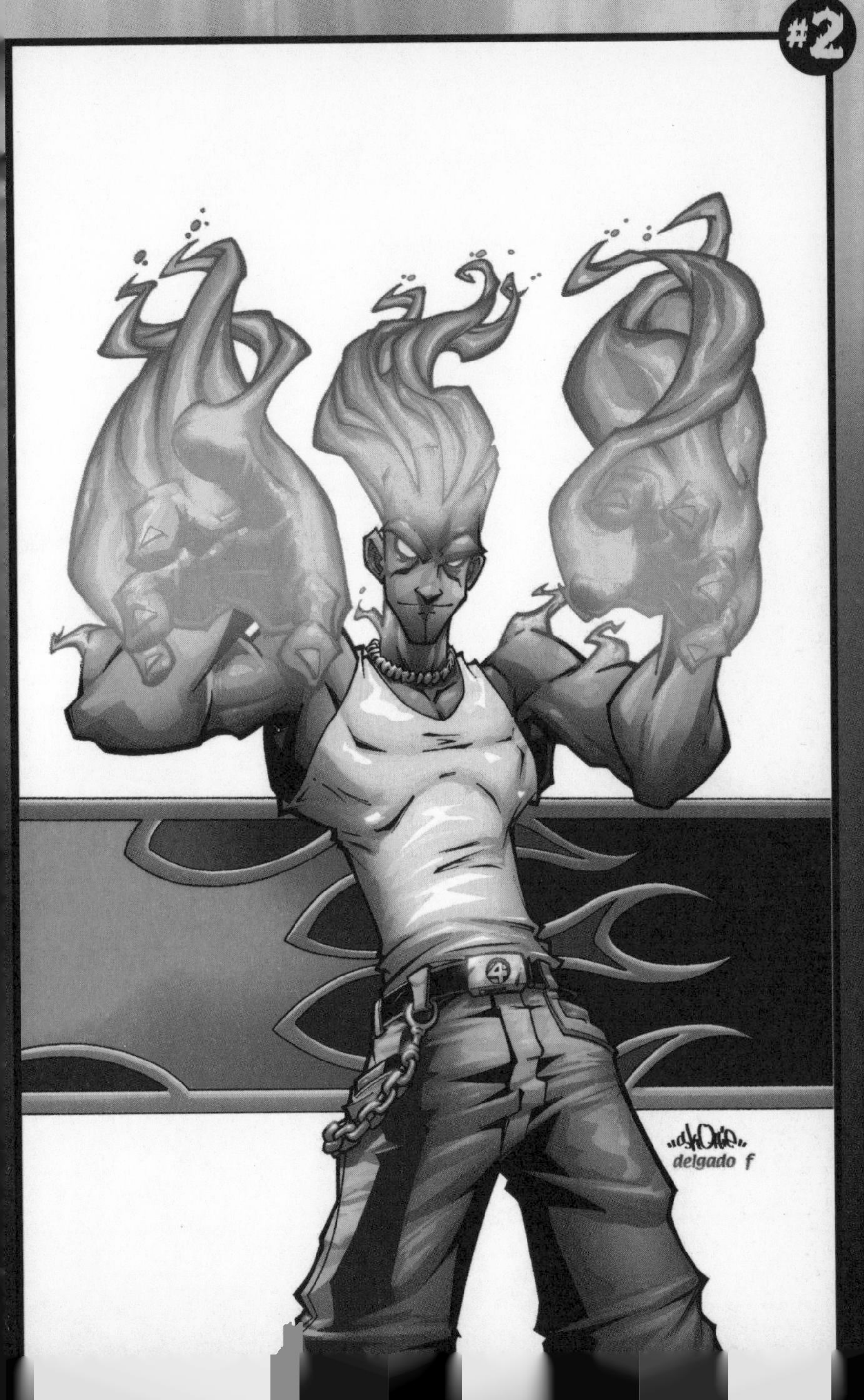
#2
delgado f

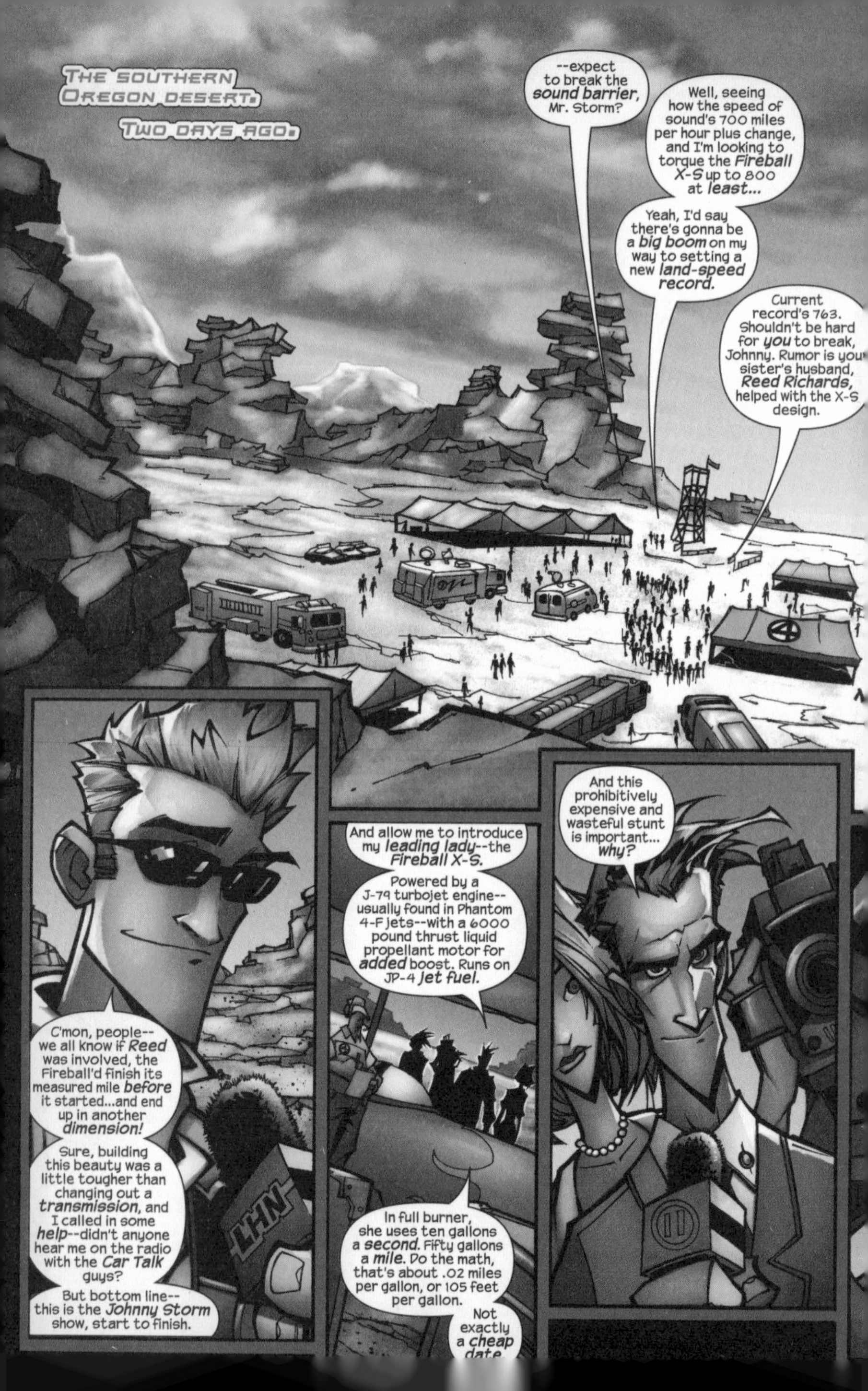
THE SOUTHERN OREGON DESERT.
TWO DAYS AGO.
--expect to break the sound barrier, Mr. Storm?
Well, seeing how the speed of sound's 700 miles per hour plus change, and I'm looking to torque the Fireball X-S up to 800 at least...
Yeah, I'd say there's gonna be a big boom on my way to setting a new land-speed record.
Current record's 763. Shouldn't be hard for you to break, Johnny. Rumor is your sister's husband, Reed Richards, helped with the X-S design.
C'mon, people-- we all know if Reed was involved, the Fireball'd finish its measured mile before it started...and end up in another dimension!
Sure, building this beauty was a little tougher than changing out a transmission, and I called in some help--didn't anyone hear me on the radio with the Car Talk guys?
But bottom line-- this is the Johnny Storm show, start to finish.
LHN
And allow me to introduce my leading lady--the Fireball X-S.
Powered by a J-79 turbojet engine-- usually found in Phantom 4-F jets--with a 6000 pound thrust liquid propellant motor for added boost. Runs on JP-4 jet fuel.
In full burner, she uses ten gallons a second. Fifty gallons a mile. Do the math, that's about .02 miles per gallon, or 105 feet per gallon.
Not exactly a cheap date.
And this prohibitively expensive and wasteful stunt is important... why?

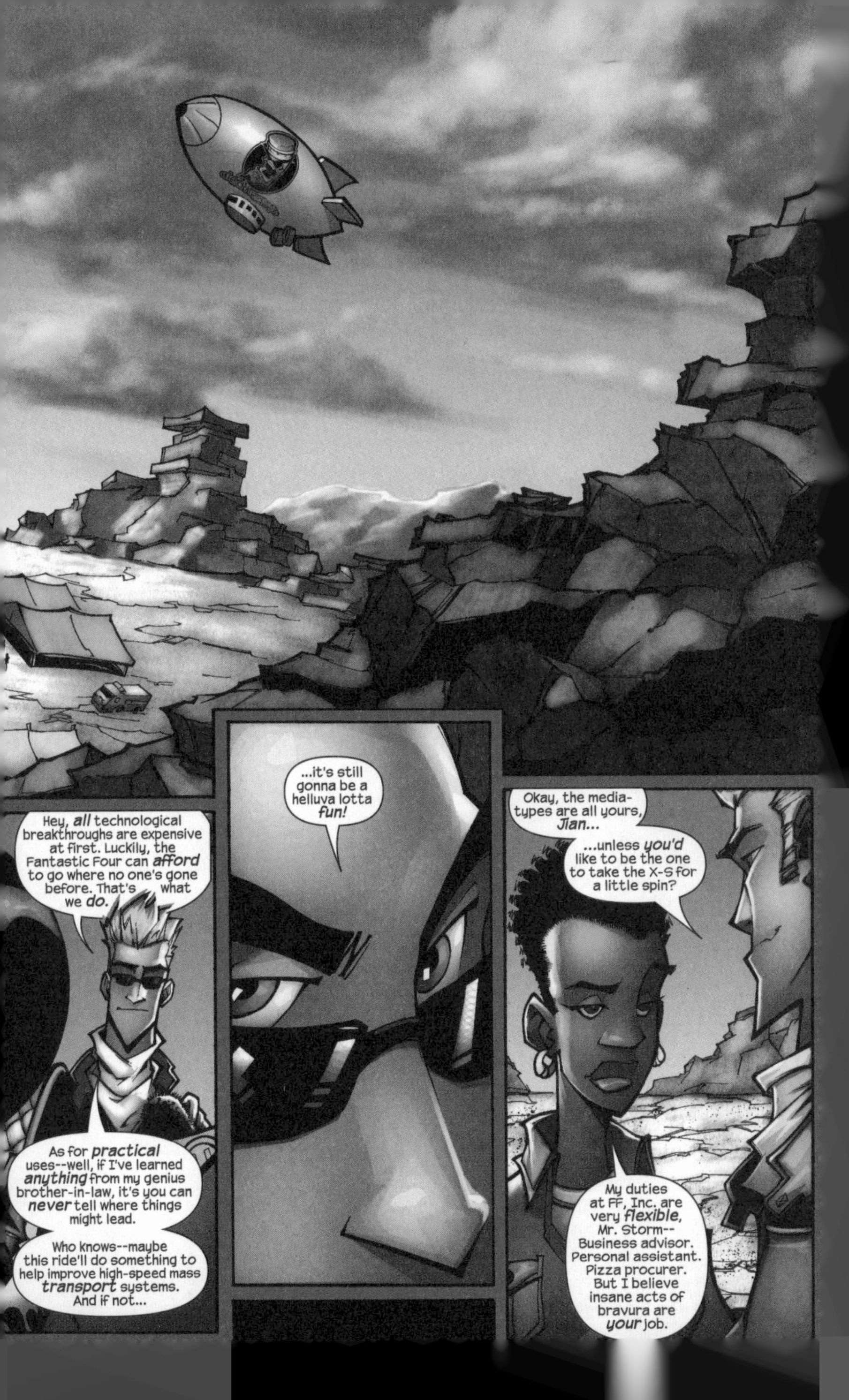
Hey, all technological breakthroughs are expensive at first. Luckily, the Fantastic Four can afford to go where no one's gone before. That's what we do.
As for practical uses--well, if I've learned anything from my genius brother-in-law, it's you can never tell where things might lead.
Who knows--maybe this ride'll do something to help improve high-speed mass transport systems. And if not...
...it's still gonna be a helluva lotta fun!
Okay, the media-types are all yours, Jian...
...unless you'd like to be the one to take the X-S for a little spin?
My duties at FF, Inc. are very flexible, Mr. Storm-- Business advisor. Personal assistant. Pizza procurer. But I believe insane acts of bravura are your job.

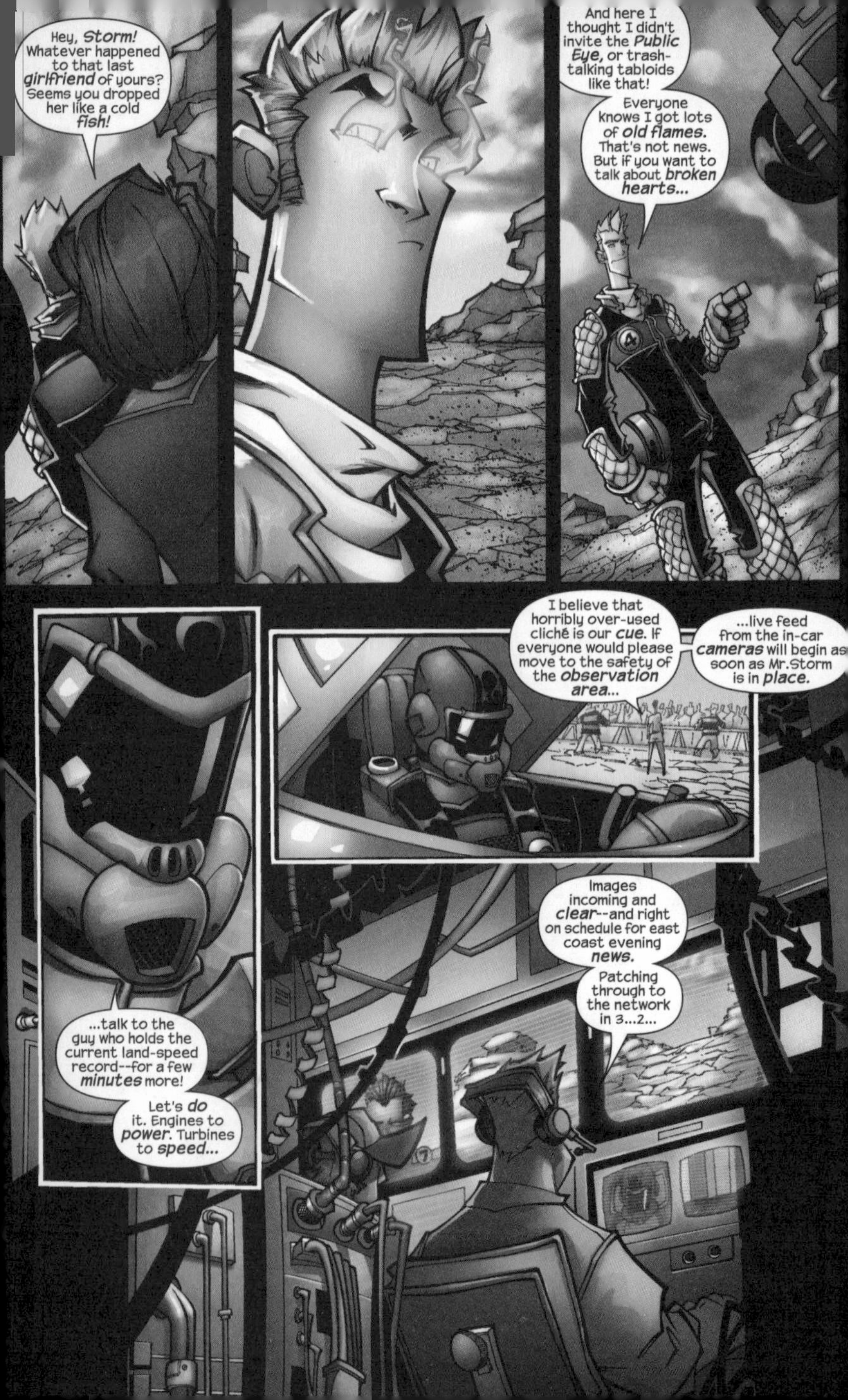
Hey, Storm! Whatever happened to that last girlfriend of yours? Seems you dropped her like a cold fish!
And here I thought I didn't invite the Public Eye, or trash-talking tabloids like that!
Everyone knows I got lots of old flames. That's not news. But if you want to talk about broken hearts...
...talk to the guy who holds the current land-speed record--for a few minutes more!
Let's do it. Engines to power. Turbines to speed...
I believe that horribly over-used cliché is our cue. If everyone would please move to the safety of the observation area...
...live feed from the in-car cameras will begin as soon as Mr.Storm is in place.
Images incoming and clear--and right on schedule for east coast evening news.
Patching through to the network in 3...2...

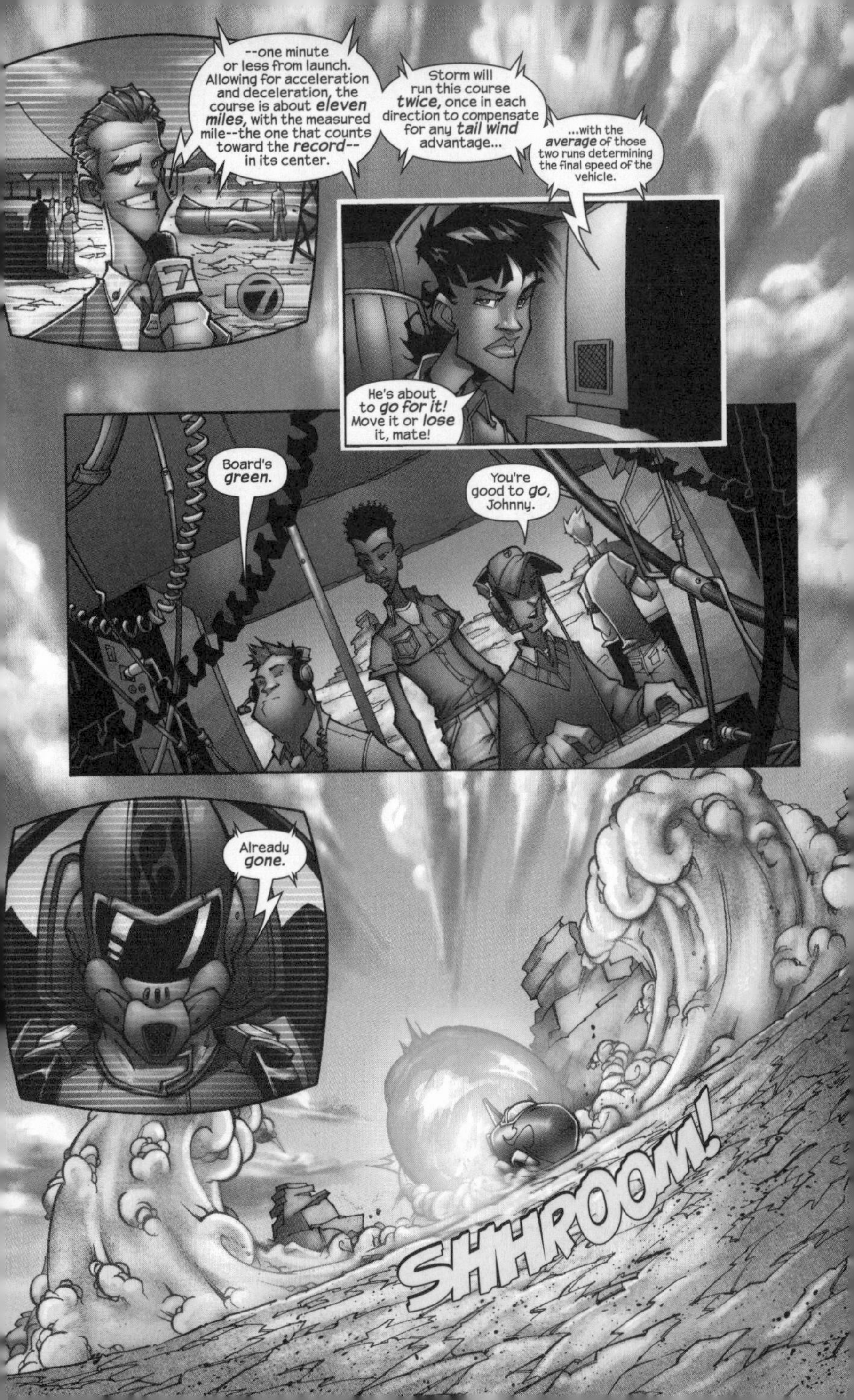
--one minute or less from launch. Allowing for acceleration and deceleration, the course is about eleven miles, with the measured mile--the one that counts toward the record--in its center.
Storm will run this course twice, once in each direction to compensate for any tail wind advantage...
...with the average of those two runs determining the final speed of the vehicle.
He's about to go for it! Move it or lose it, mate!
Board's green.
You're good to go, Johnny.
Already gone.
SHHROOM!

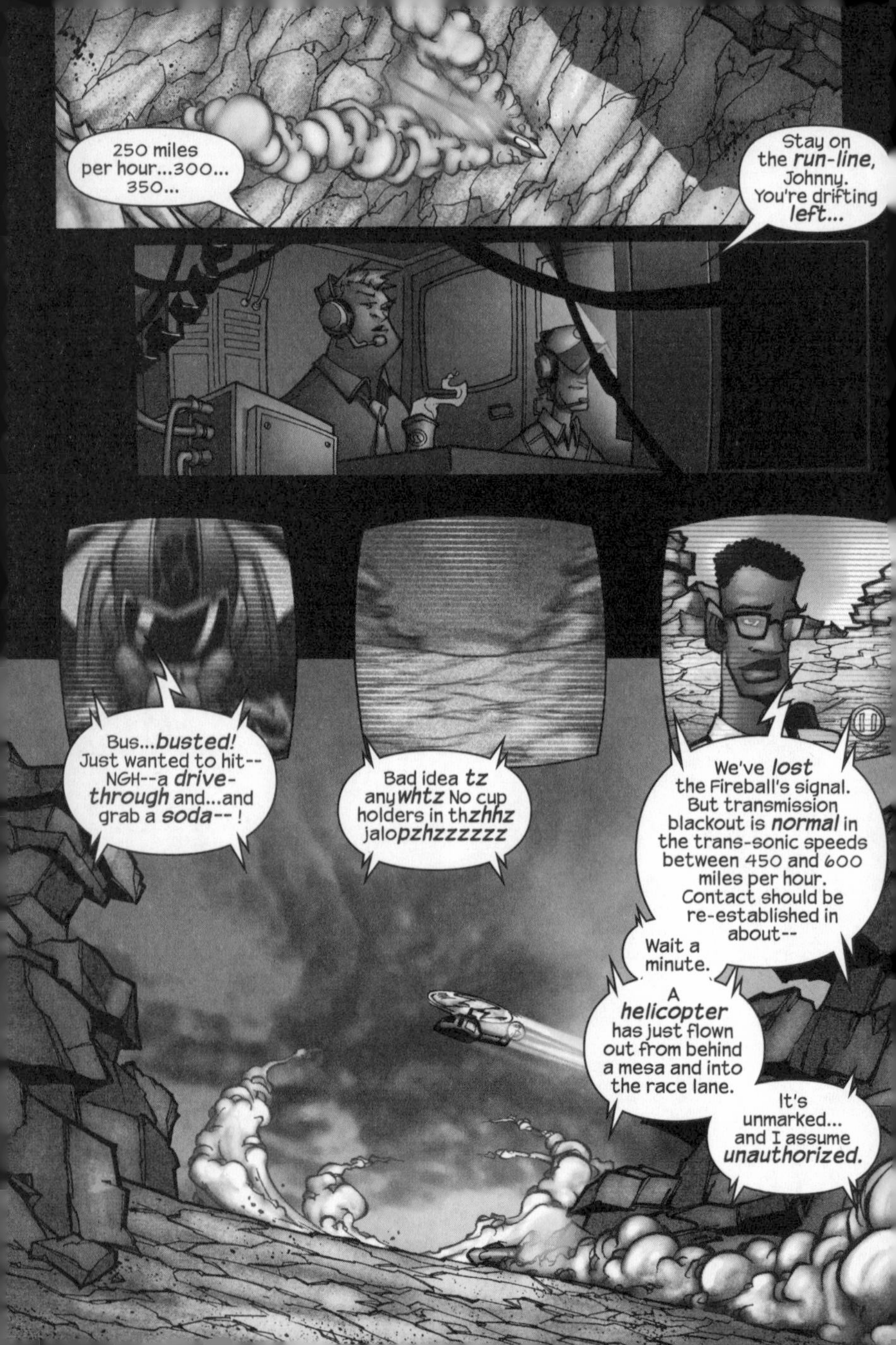

250 miles per hour...300... 350...
Stay on the *run-line,* Johnny. You're drifting *left...*
Bus...*busted!* Just wanted to hit-- NGH--a *drive-through* and...and grab a *soda*-- !
Bad idea *tz* any *whtz* No cup holders in th*zhhz* jalo*pzhzzzzzz*
We've *lost* the Fireball's signal. But transmission blackout is *normal* in the trans-sonic speeds between 450 and 600 miles per hour. Contact should be re-established in about--
Wait a minute.
A *helicopter* has just flown out from behind a mesa and into the race lane.
It's unmarked... and I assume *unauthorized.*

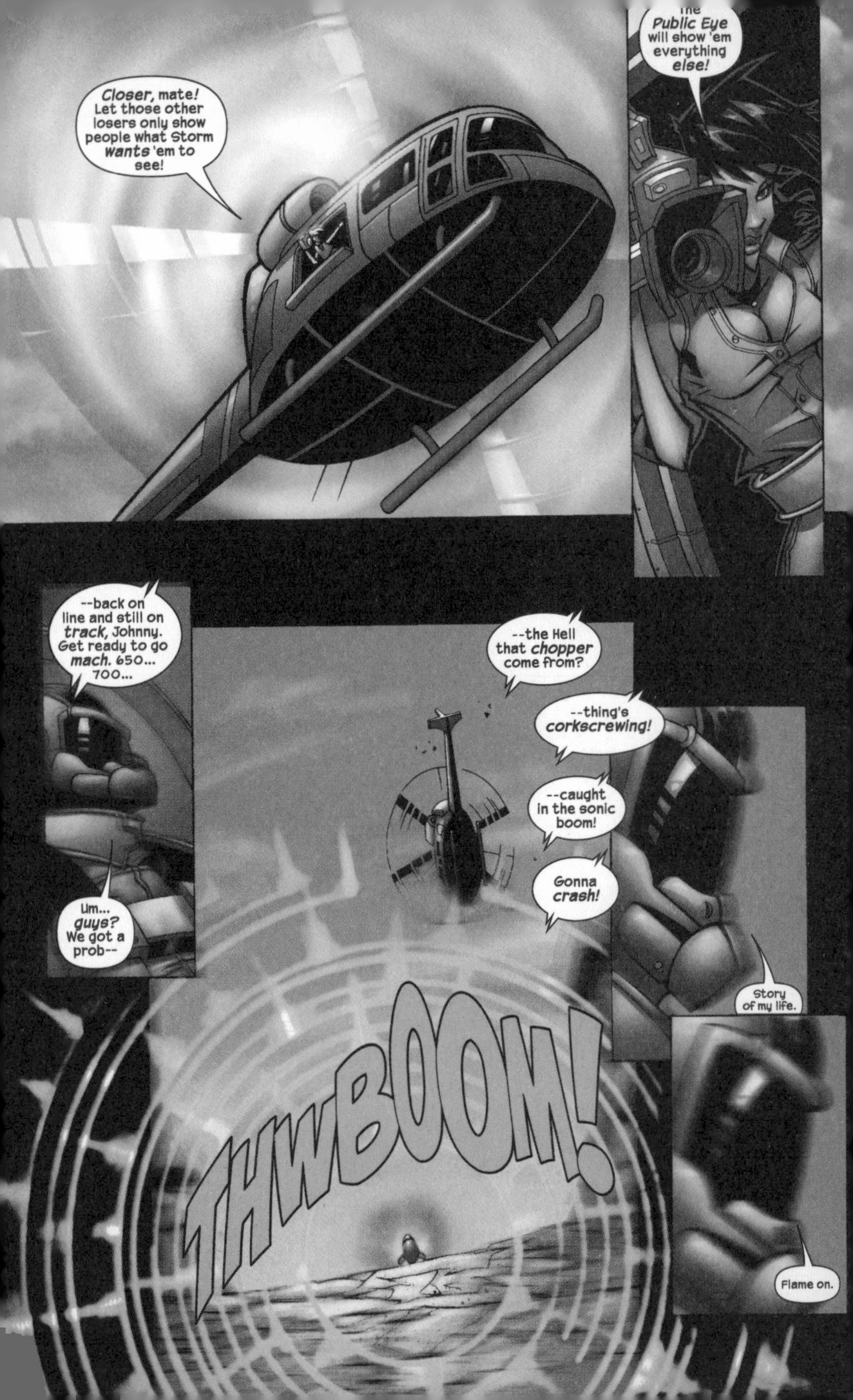

Closer, mate! Let those other losers only show people what Storm wants 'em to see!
The Public Eye will show 'em everything else!
--back on line and still on track, Johnny. Get ready to go mach. 650... 700...
--the Hell that chopper come from?
--thing's corkscrewing!
--caught in the sonic boom!
Gonna crash!
Um... guys? We got a prob--
Story of my life.
THWBOOM!
Flame on.

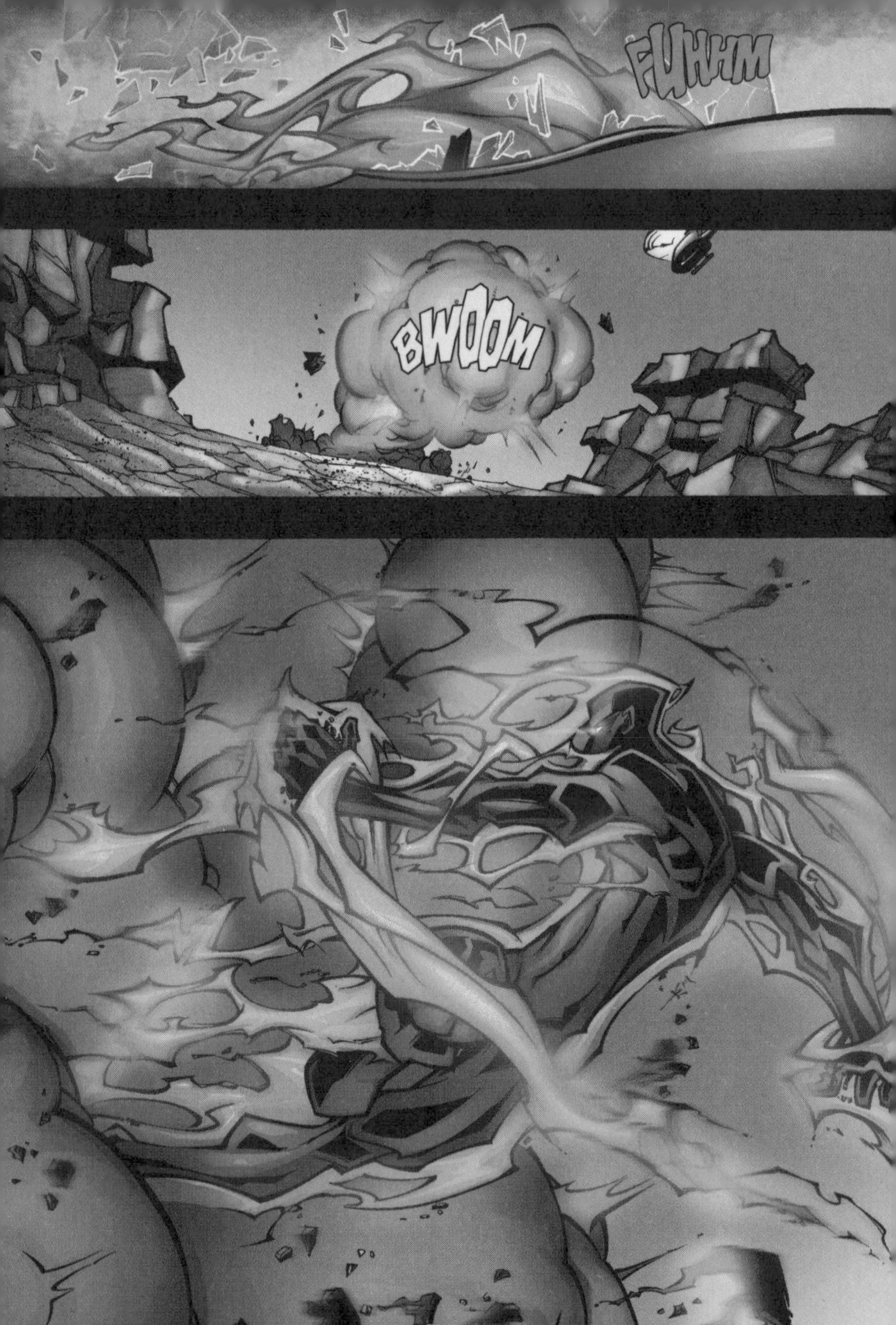
FUHHM
BWOOM

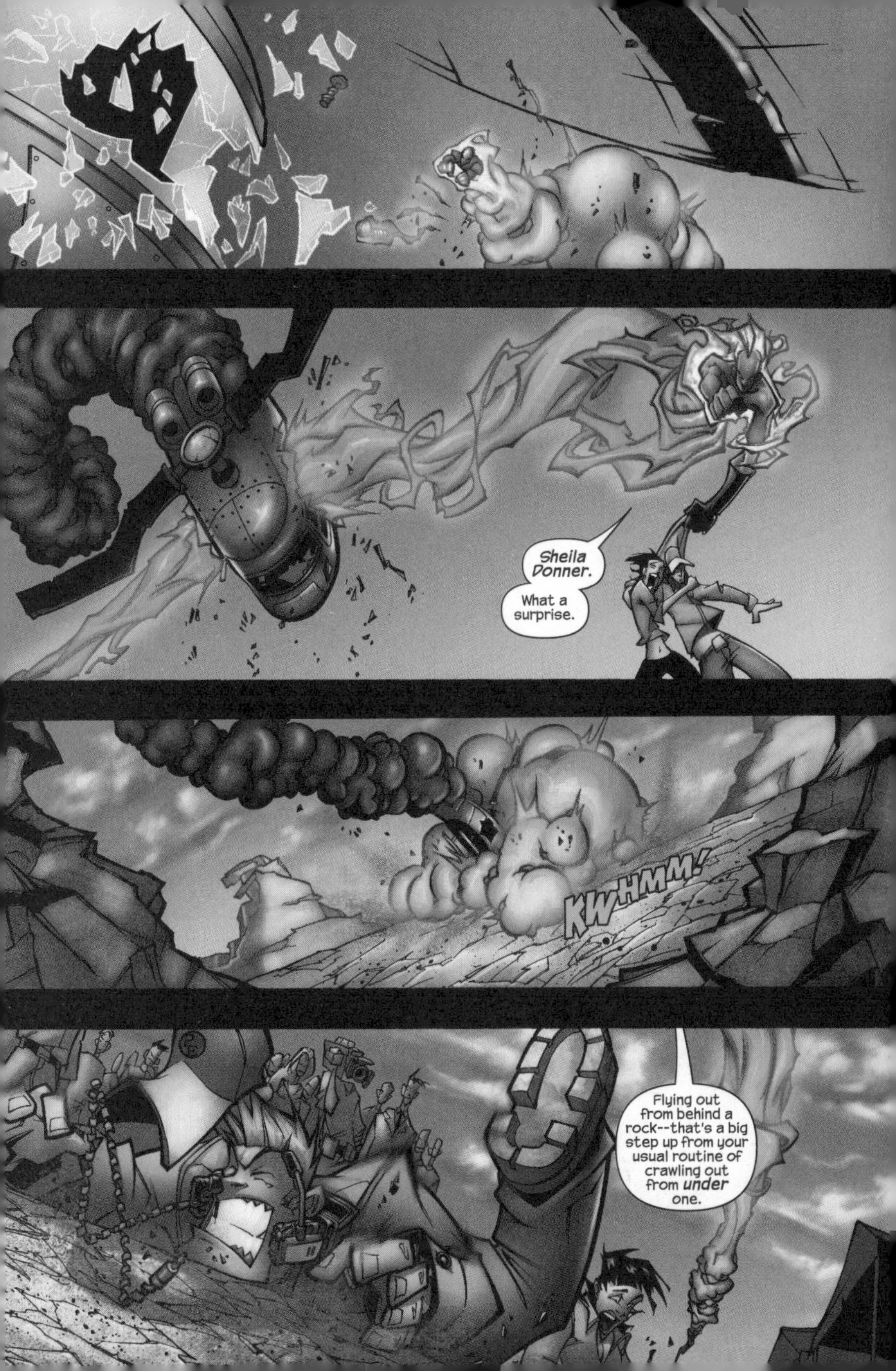

Sheila Donner.
What a surprise.
KWHMM!
Flying out from behind a rock--that's a big step up from your usual routine of crawling out from *under* one.

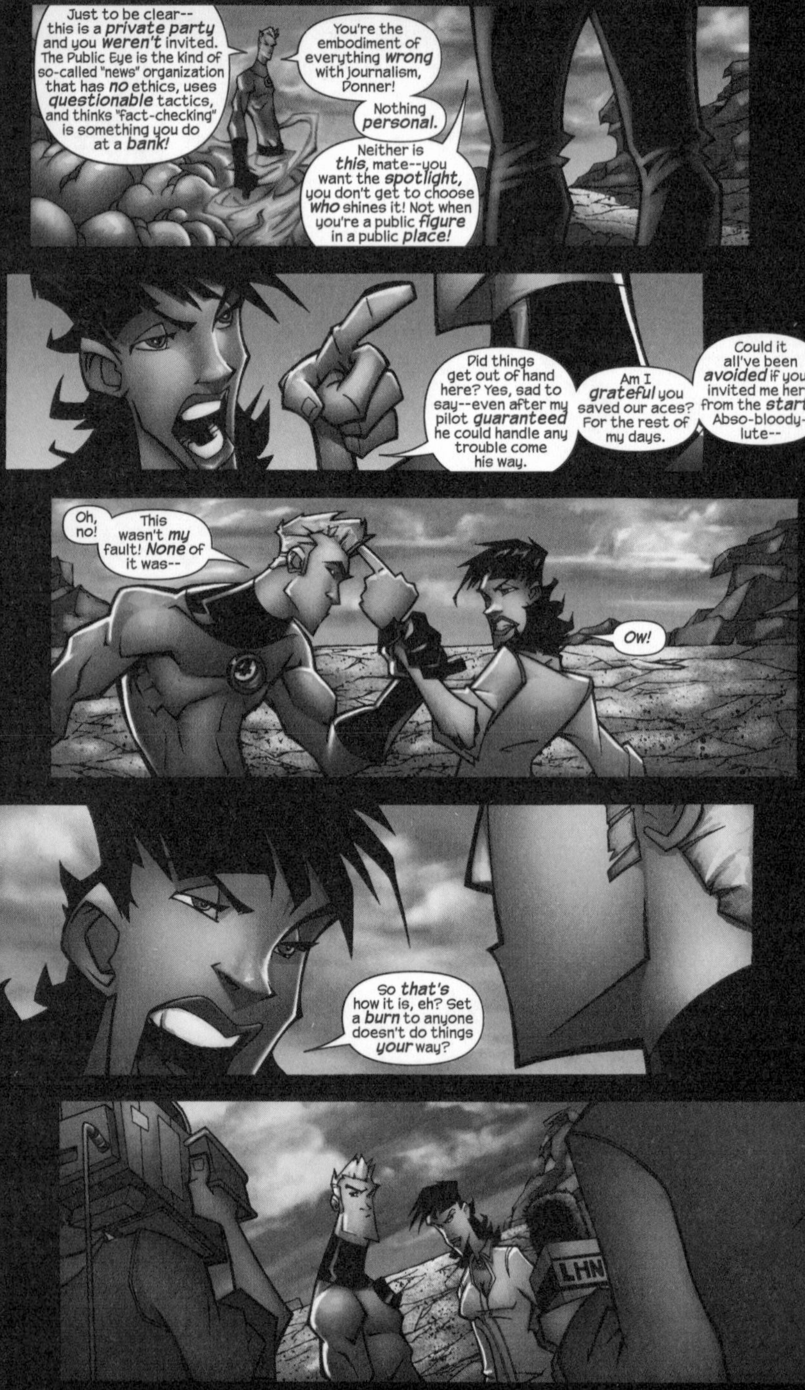
Just to be clear-- this is a private party and you weren't invited. The Public Eye is the kind of so-called "news" organization that has no ethics, uses questionable tactics, and thinks "fact-checking" is something you do at a bank!
You're the embodiment of everything wrong with journalism, Donner!
Nothing personal.
Neither is this, mate--you want the spotlight, you don't get to choose who shines it! Not when you're a public figure in a public place!
Did things get out of hand here? Yes, sad to say--even after my pilot guaranteed he could handle any trouble come his way.
Am I grateful you saved our aces? For the rest of my days.
Could it all've been avoided if you'd invited me here from the start? Abso-bloody-lute--
Oh, no!
This wasn't my fault! None of it was--
Ow!
So that's how it is, eh? Set a burn to anyone doesn't do things your way?
LHN

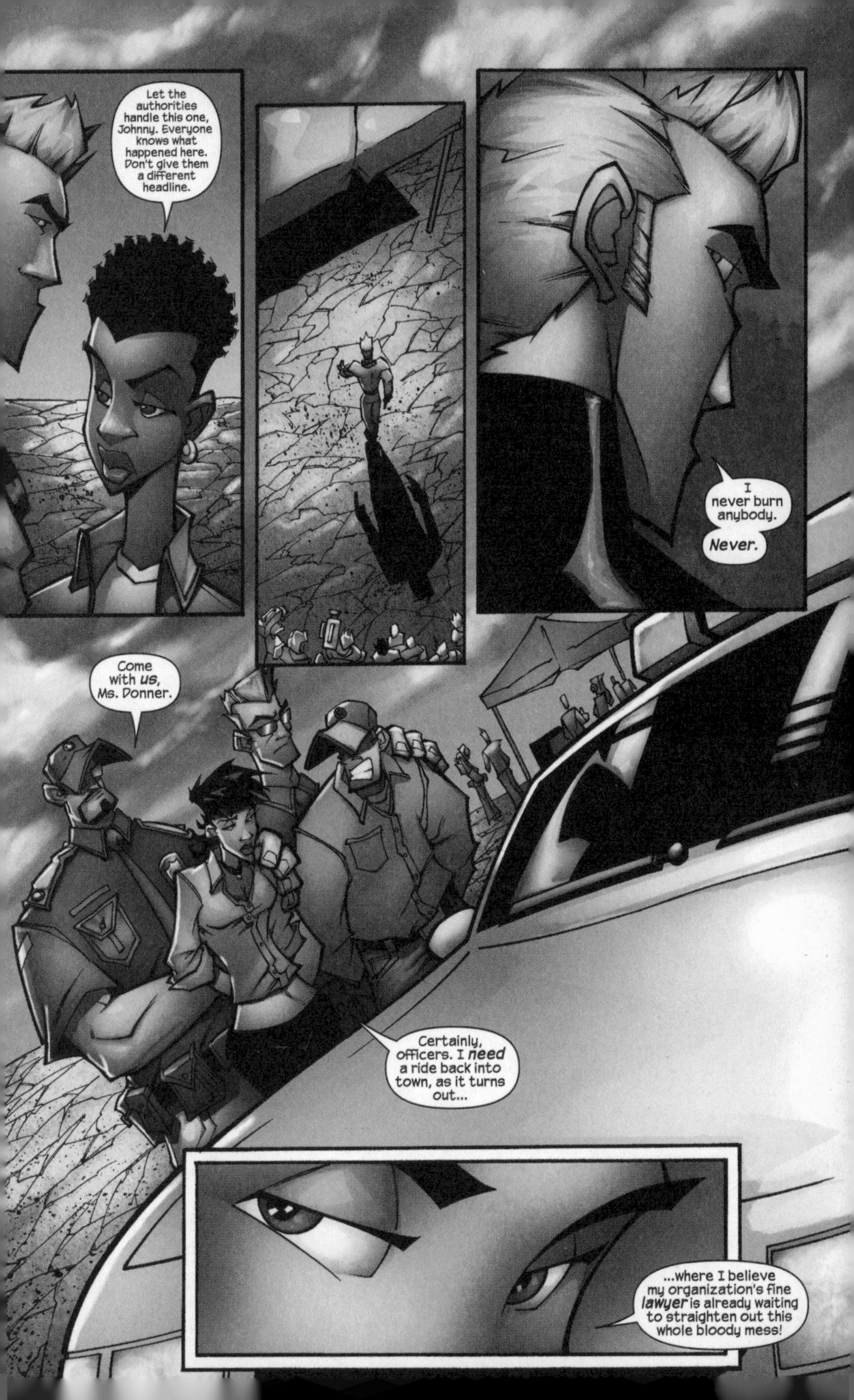
Let the authorities handle this one, Johnny. Everyone knows what happened here. Don't give them a different headline.
I never burn anybody.
Never.
Come with us, Ms. Donner.
Certainly, officers. I need a ride back into town, as it turns out...
...where I believe my organization's fine lawyer is already waiting to straighten out this whole bloody mess!

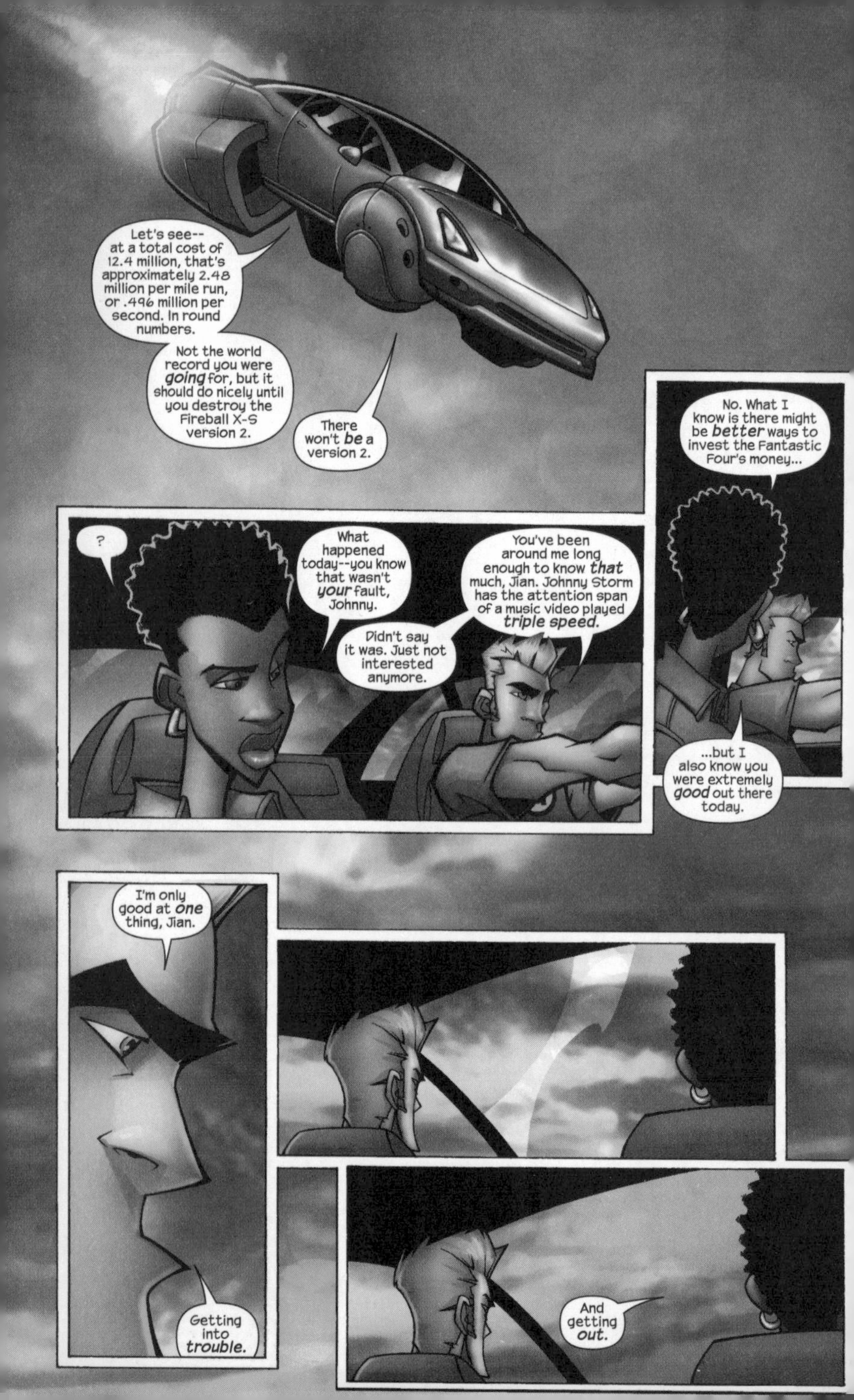

Let's see--at a total cost of 12.4 million, that's approximately 2.48 million per mile run, or .496 million per second. In round numbers.
Not the world record you were *going* for, but it should do nicely until you destroy the Fireball X-S version 2.
There won't *be* a version 2.
No. What I know is there might be *better* ways to invest the Fantastic Four's money...
?
What happened today--you know that wasn't *your* fault, Johnny.
Didn't say it was. Just not interested anymore.
You've been around me long enough to know *that* much, Jian. Johnny Storm has the attention span of a music video played *triple speed.*
...but I also know you were extremely *good* out there today.
I'm only good at *one* thing, Jian.
Getting into *trouble.*
And getting *out.*

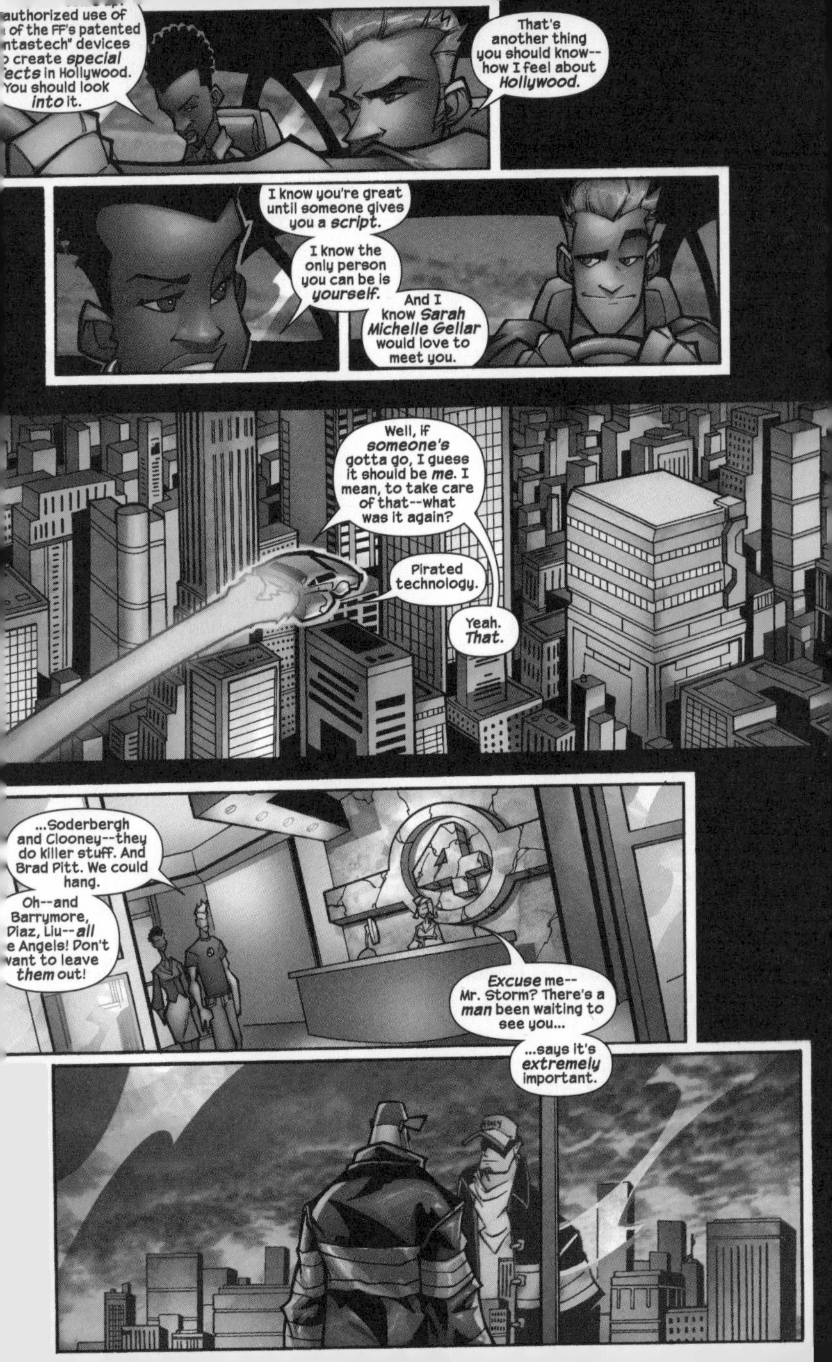

authorized use of
of the FF's patented
ntastech" devices
o create special
fects in Hollywood.
You should look
into it.
That's another thing you should know--how I feel about Hollywood.
I know you're great until someone gives you a script.
I know the only person you can be is yourself.
And I know Sarah Michelle Gellar would love to meet you.
Well, if someone's gotta go, I guess it should be me. I mean, to take care of that--what was it again?
Pirated technology.
Yeah. That.
...Soderbergh and Clooney--they do killer stuff. And Brad Pitt. We could hang.
Oh--and Barrymore, Diaz, Liu--all
e Angels! Don't
want to leave
them out!
Excuse me--Mr. Storm? There's a man been waiting to see you...
...says it's extremely important.

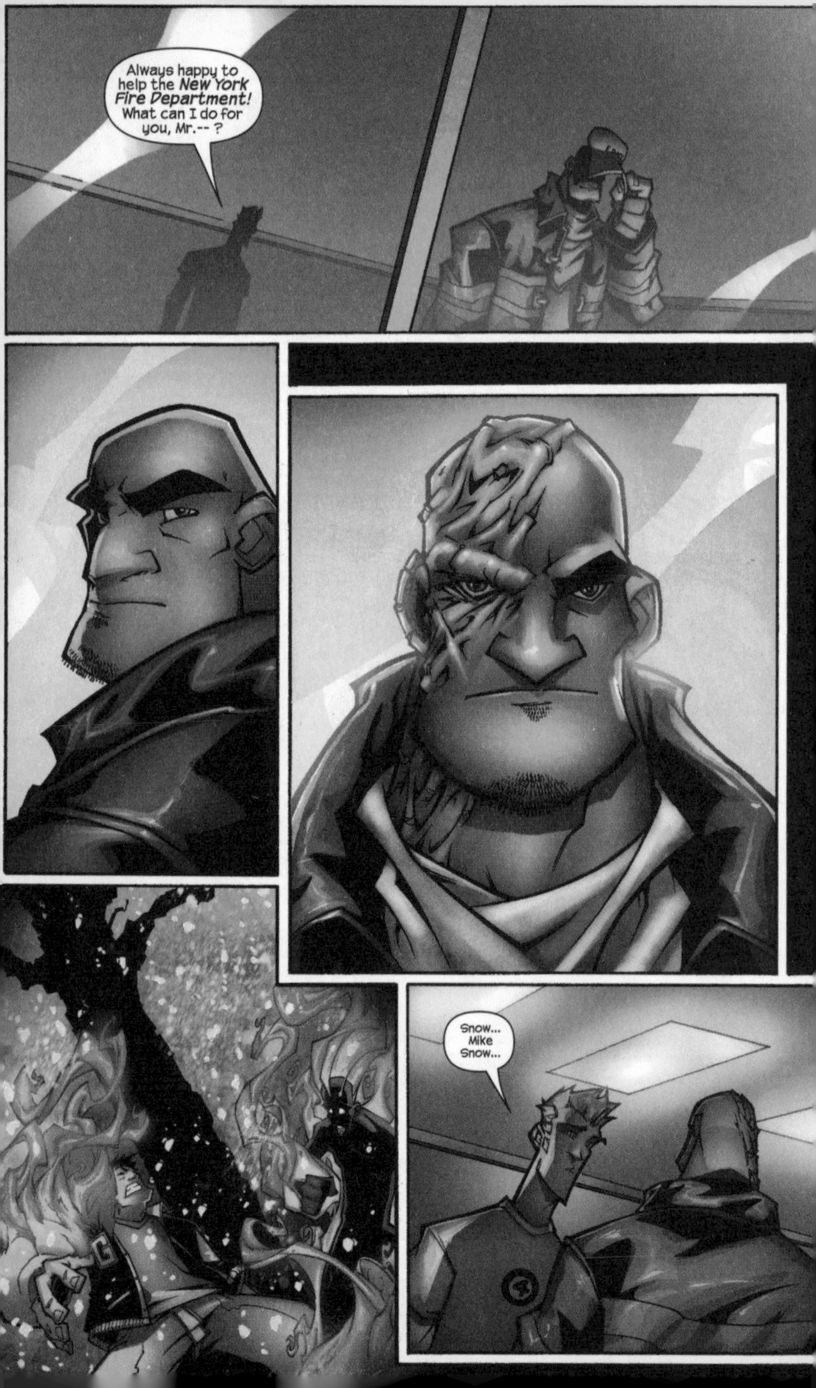
Always happy to help the *New York Fire Department!* What can I do for you, Mr.-- ?
Snow... Mike Snow...

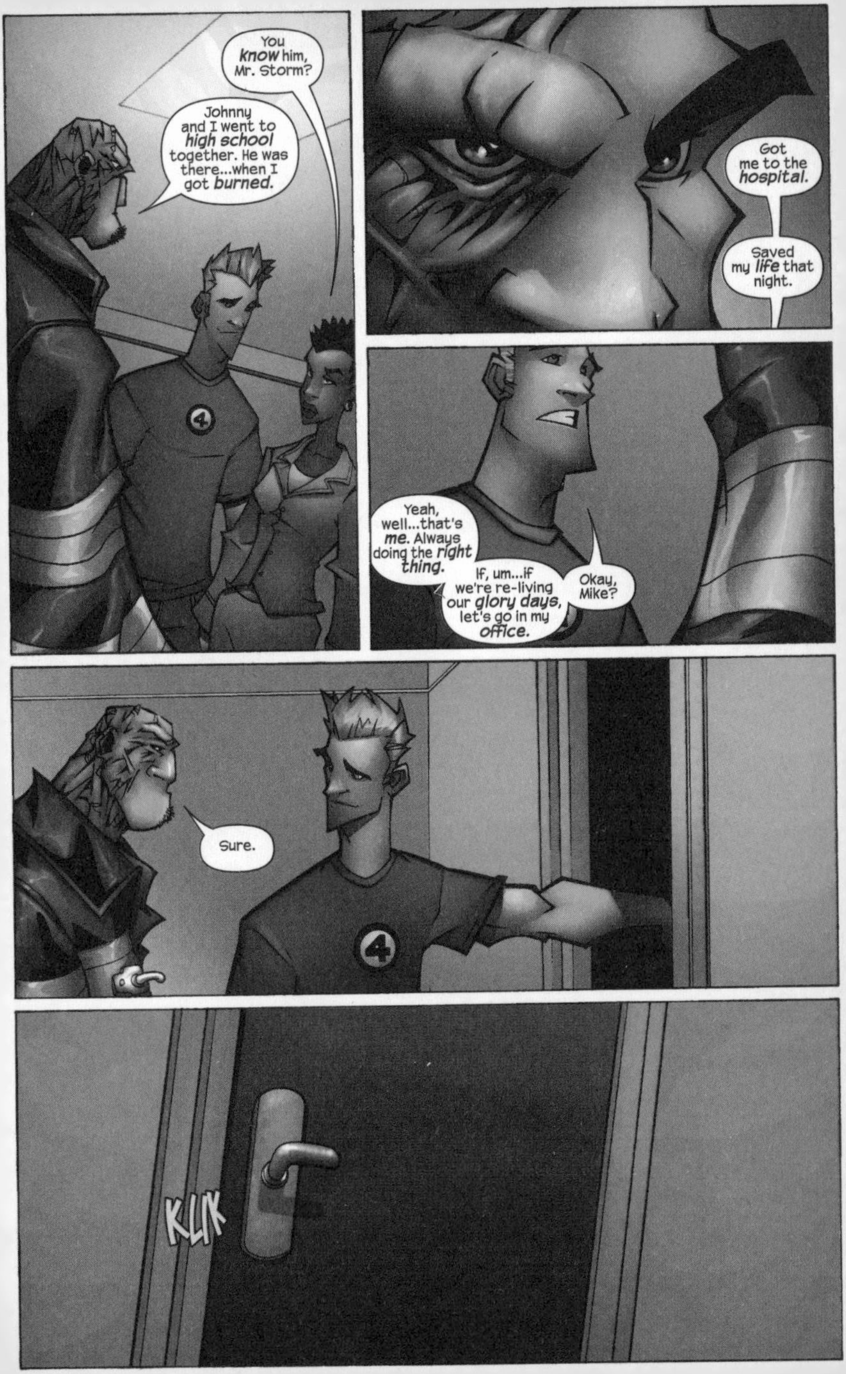
Johnny and I went to high school together. He was there...when I got burned.
You know him, Mr. Storm?
Got me to the hospital.
Saved my life that night.
Yeah, well...that's me. Always doing the right thing.
If, um...if we're re-living our glory days, let's go in my office.
Okay, Mike?
Sure.
KLIK

Don't worry...

I wouldn't have *told* them. I've never told *anyone*. That was our agreement.

Our secret.

What... *do* you tell people?

That I was waiting to *prank* you. Another in a long line of stunts that our classmates enjoyed and *encouraged*.

But this one blew up in my face. *Literally.*

Flash powder.

Good thing *you* were there.

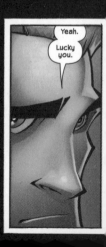

Yeah. Lucky *you*.

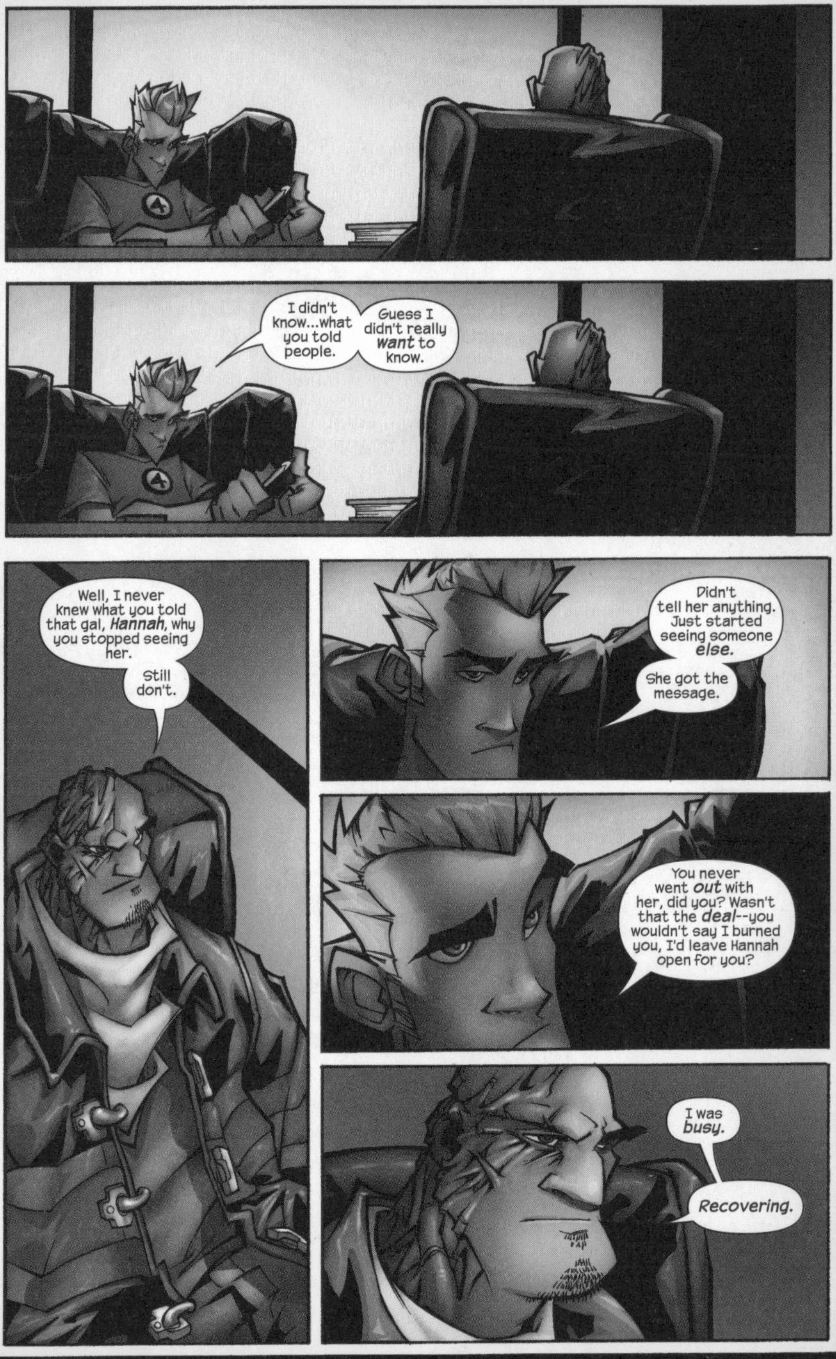
I didn't know...what you told people.
Guess I didn't really *want* to know.
Well, I never knew what you told that gal, *Hannah*, why you stopped seeing her.
Still don't.
Didn't tell her anything. Just started seeing someone *else.*
She got the message.
You never went *out* with her, did you? Wasn't that the *deal*--you wouldn't say I burned you, I'd leave Hannah open for you?
I was *busy.*
Recovering.

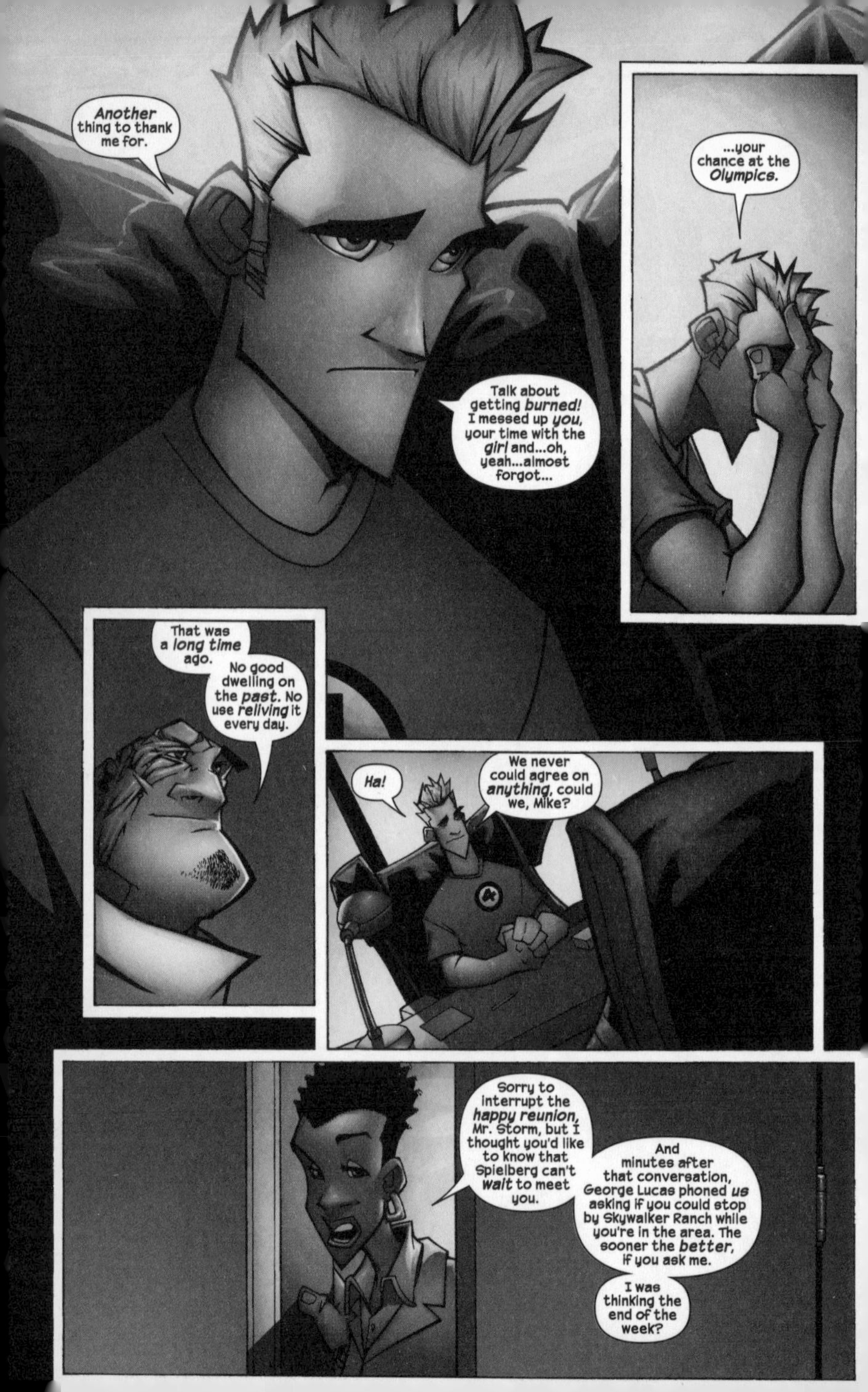

Another thing to thank me for.
Talk about getting burned! I messed up you, your time with the girl and...oh, yeah...almost forgot...
...your chance at the Olympics.
That was a long time ago.
No good dwelling on the past. No use reliving it every day.
Ha!
We never could agree on anything, could we, Mike?
Sorry to interrupt the happy reunion, Mr. Storm, but I thought you'd like to know that Spielberg can't wait to meet you.
And minutes after that conversation, George Lucas phoned us asking if you could stop by Skywalker Ranch while you're in the area. The sooner the better, if you ask me.
I was thinking the end of the week?

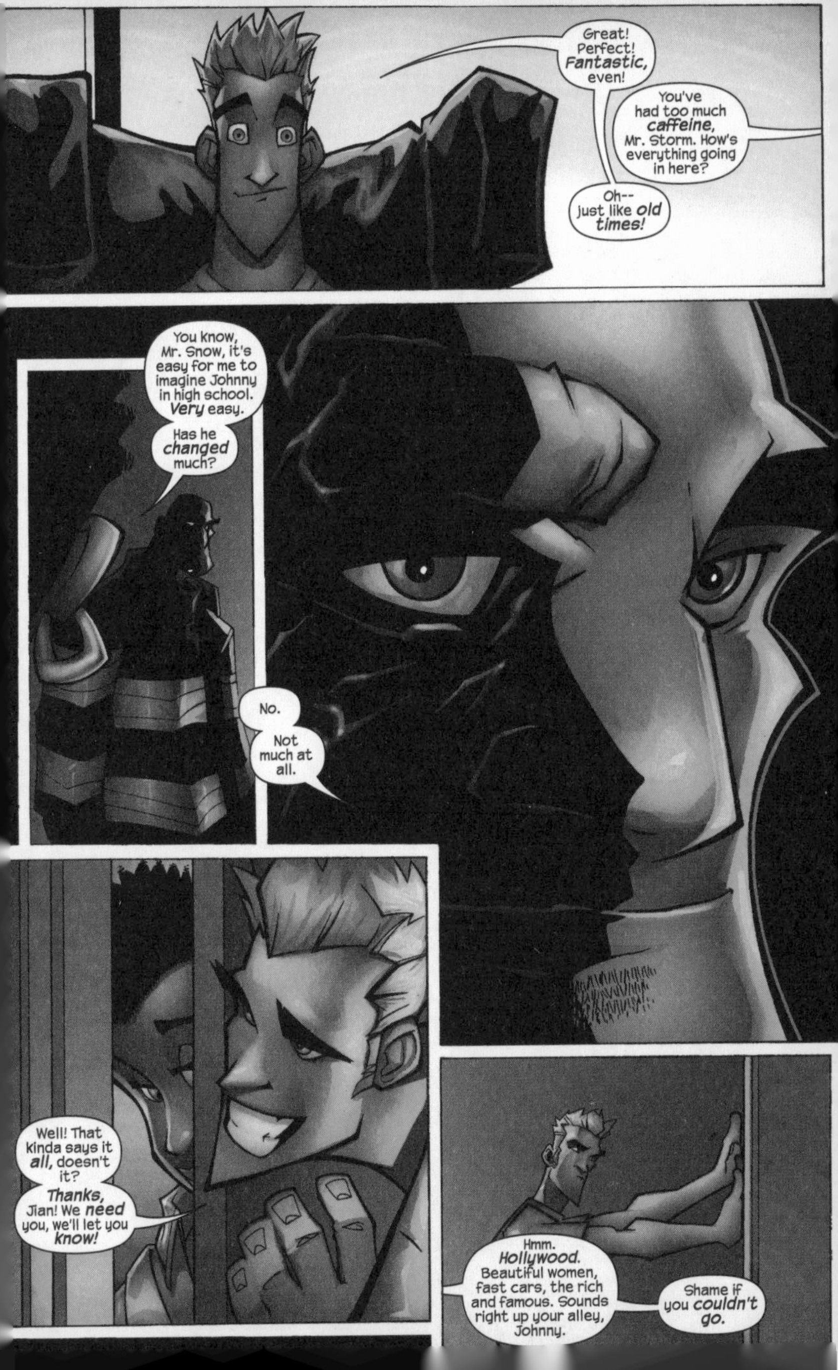
Great! Perfect! Fantastic, even!
You've had too much caffeine, Mr. Storm. How's everything going in here?
Oh-- just like old times!
You know, Mr. Snow, it's easy for me to imagine Johnny in high school. Very easy.
Has he changed much?
No.
Not much at all.
Well! That kinda says it all, doesn't it?
Thanks, Jian! We need you, we'll let you know!
Hmm. Hollywood. Beautiful women, fast cars, the rich and famous. Sounds right up your alley, Johnny.
Shame if you couldn't go.

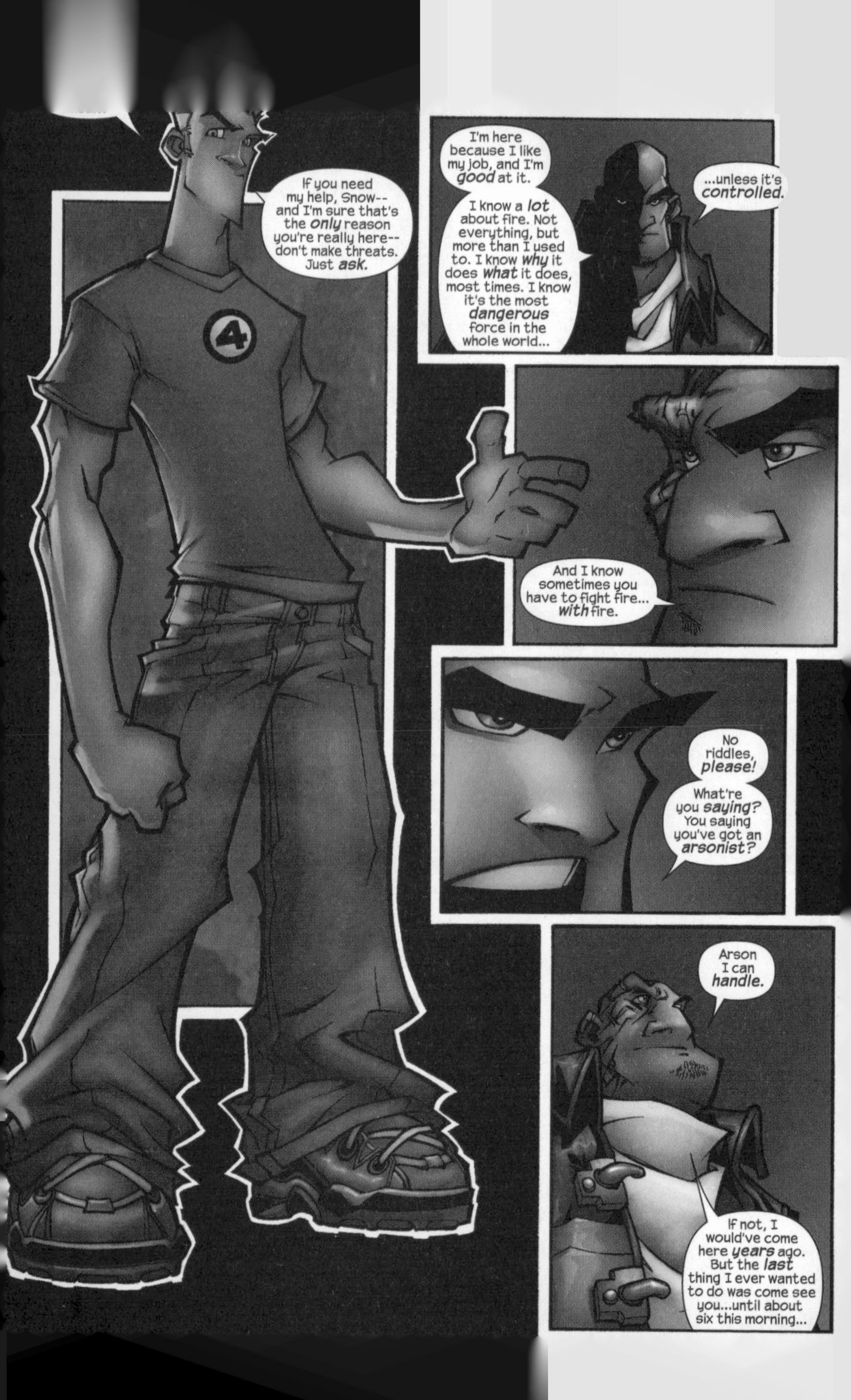
If you need my help, Snow--and I'm sure that's the only reason you're really here--don't make threats. Just ask.
I'm here because I like my job, and I'm good at it.
I know a lot about fire. Not everything, but more than I used to. I know why it does what it does, most times. I know it's the most dangerous force in the whole world...
...unless it's controlled.
And I know sometimes you have to fight fire... with fire.
No riddles, please!
What're you saying? You saying you've got an arsonist?
Arson I can handle.
If not, I would've come here years ago. But the last thing I ever wanted to do was come see you...until about six this morning...

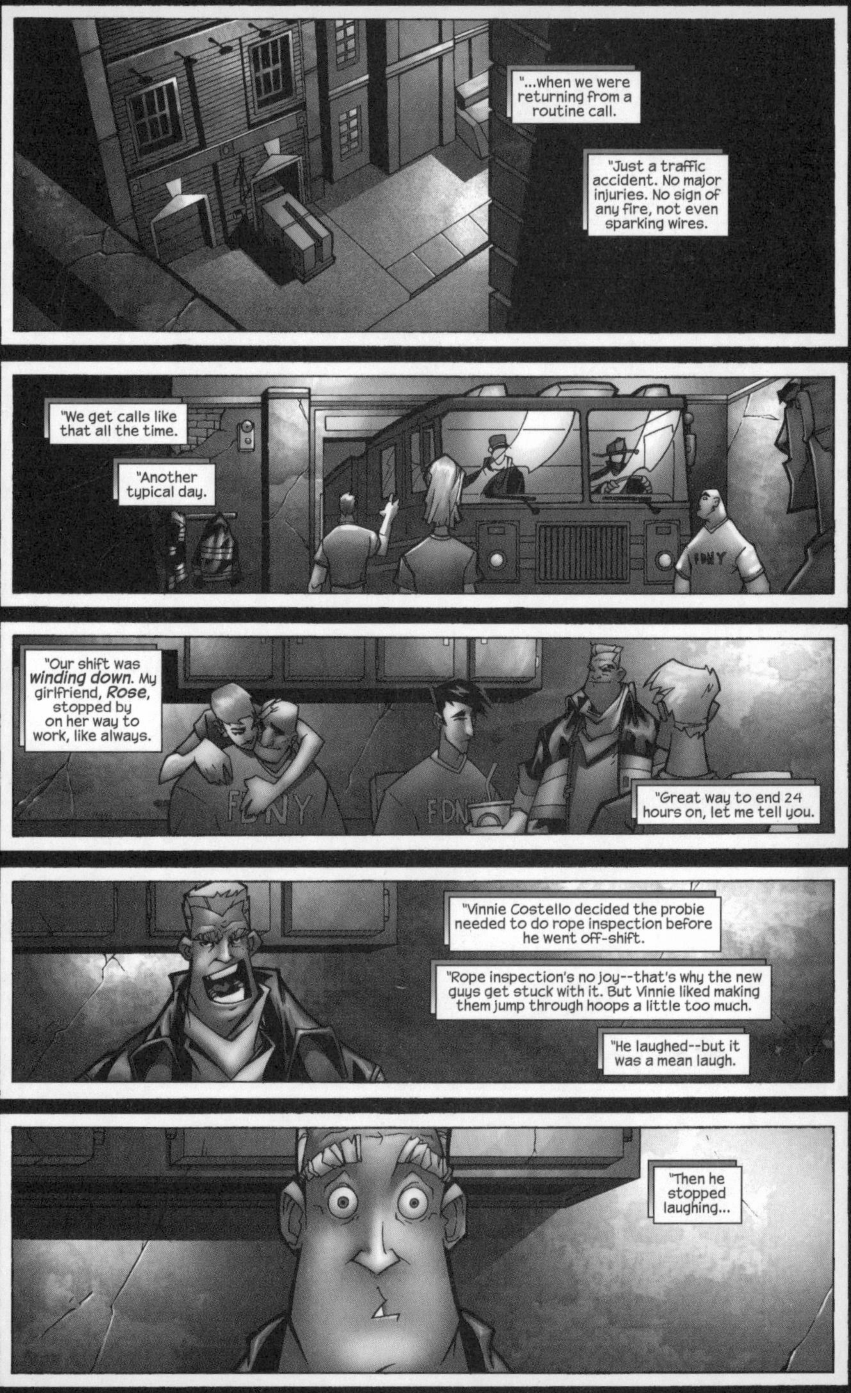
"...when we were returning from a routine call.
"Just a traffic accident. No major injuries. No sign of any fire, not even sparking wires.
"We get calls like that all the time.
"Another typical day.
FDNY
"Our shift was *winding down*. My girlfriend, *Rose*, stopped by on her way to work, like always.
FDNY
FDNY
"Great way to end 24 hours on, let me tell you.
"Vinnie Costello decided the probie needed to do rope inspection before he went off-shift.
"Rope inspection's no joy--that's why the new guys get stuck with it. But Vinnie liked making them jump through hoops a little too much.
"He laughed--but it was a mean laugh.
"Then he stopped laughing...

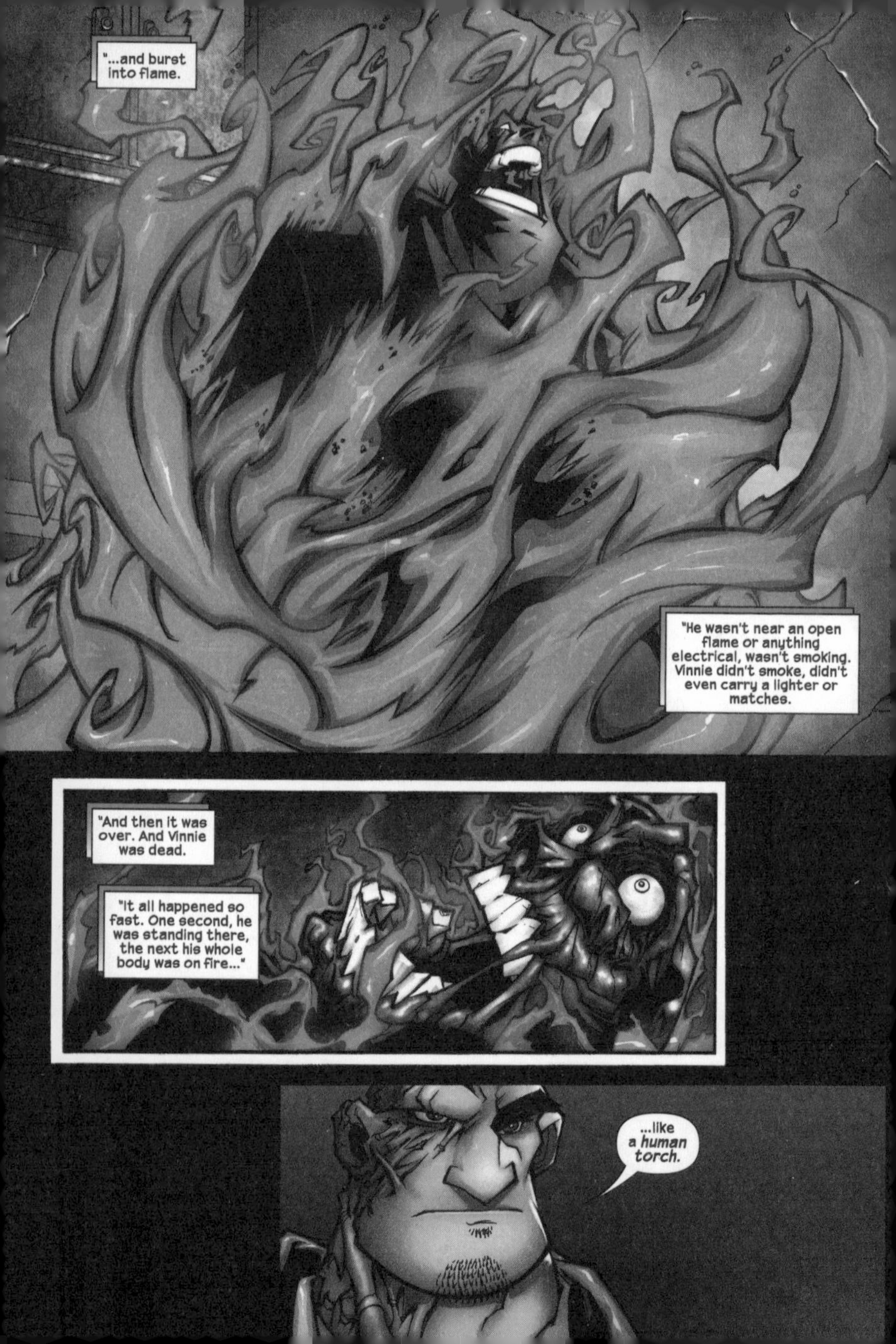
"...and burst into flame.
"He wasn't near an open flame or anything electrical, wasn't smoking. Vinnie didn't smoke, didn't even carry a lighter or matches.
"And then it was over. And Vinnie was dead.
"It all happened so fast. One second, he was standing there, the next his whole body was on fire..."
...like a *human torch.*

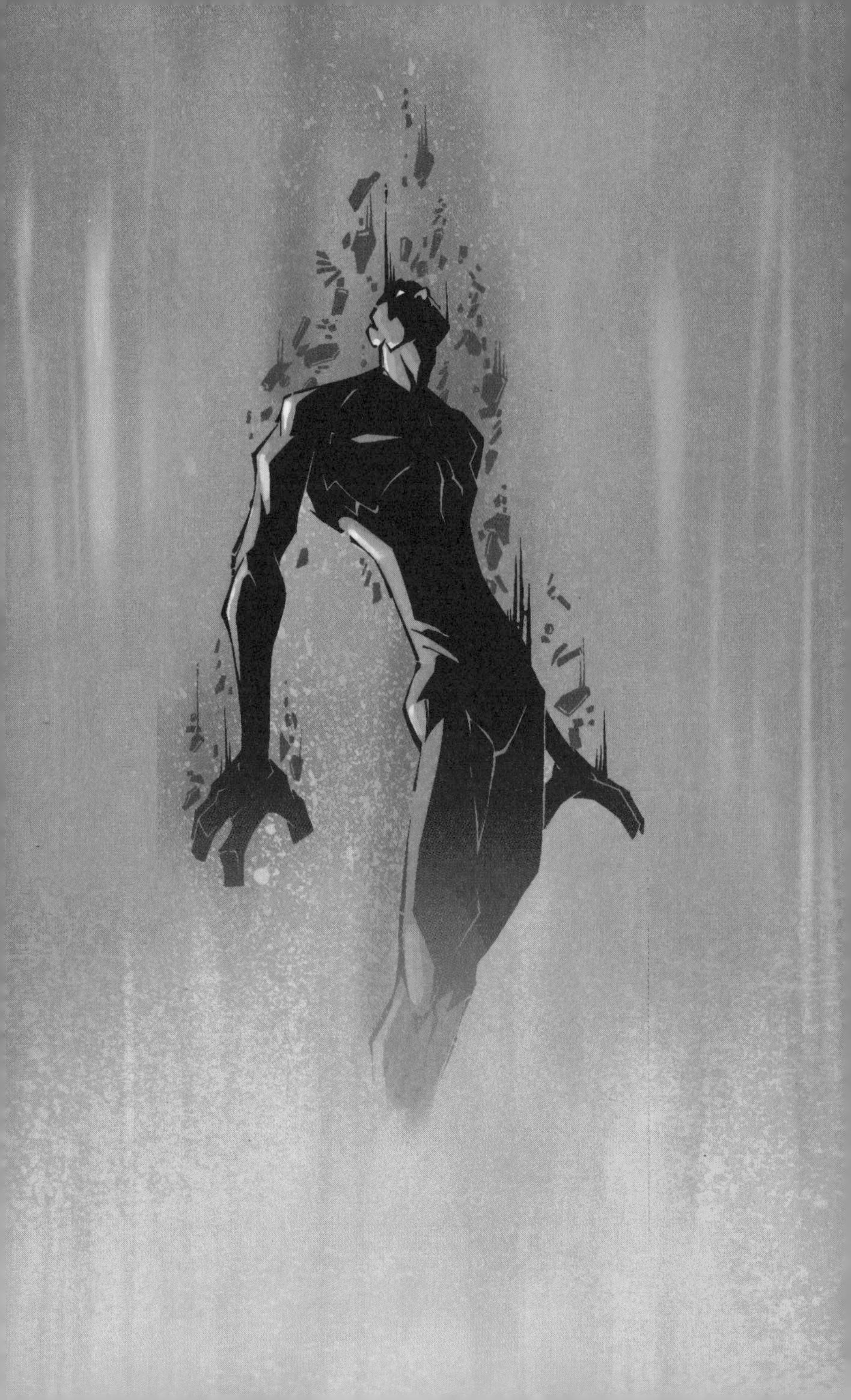

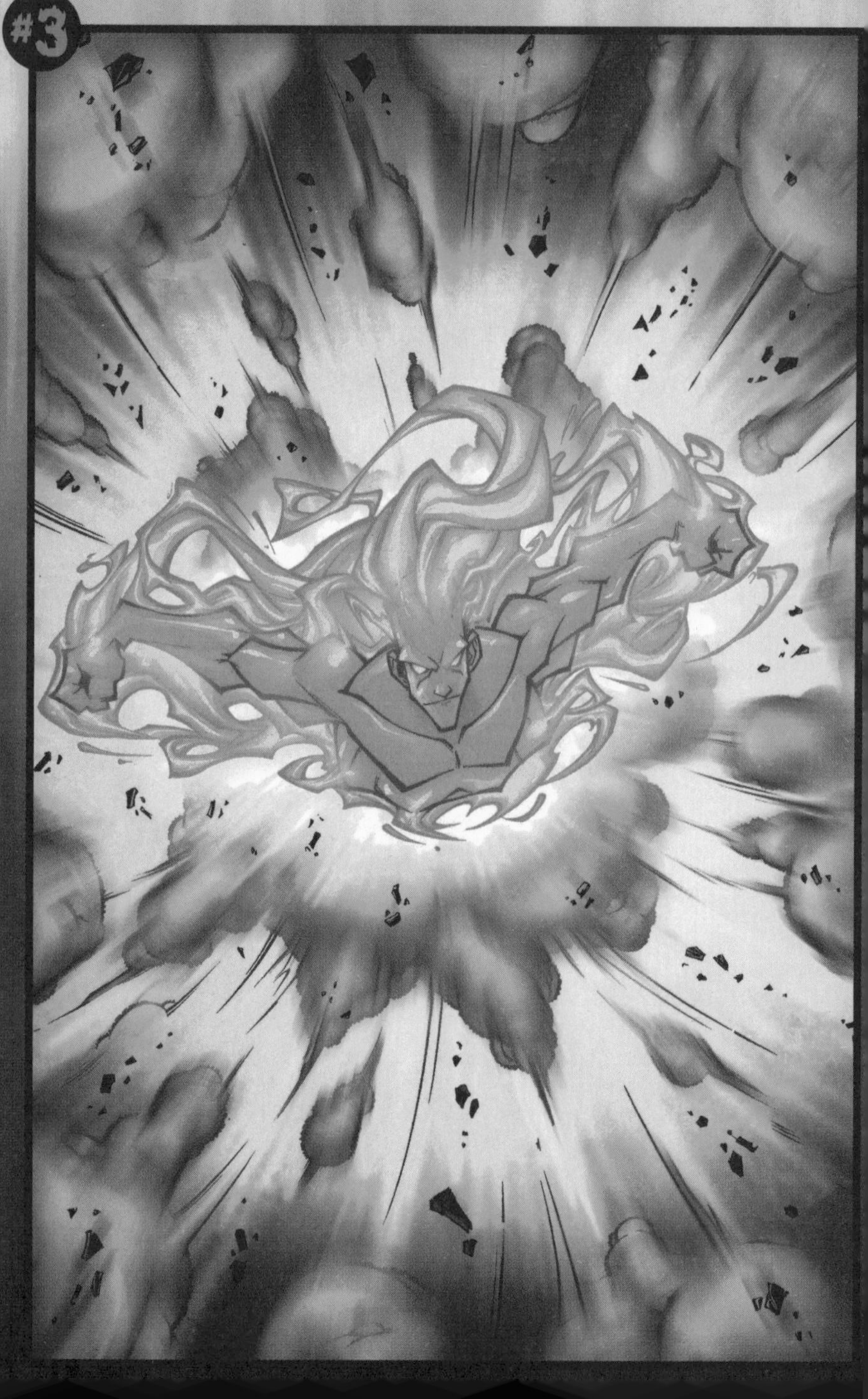
#3

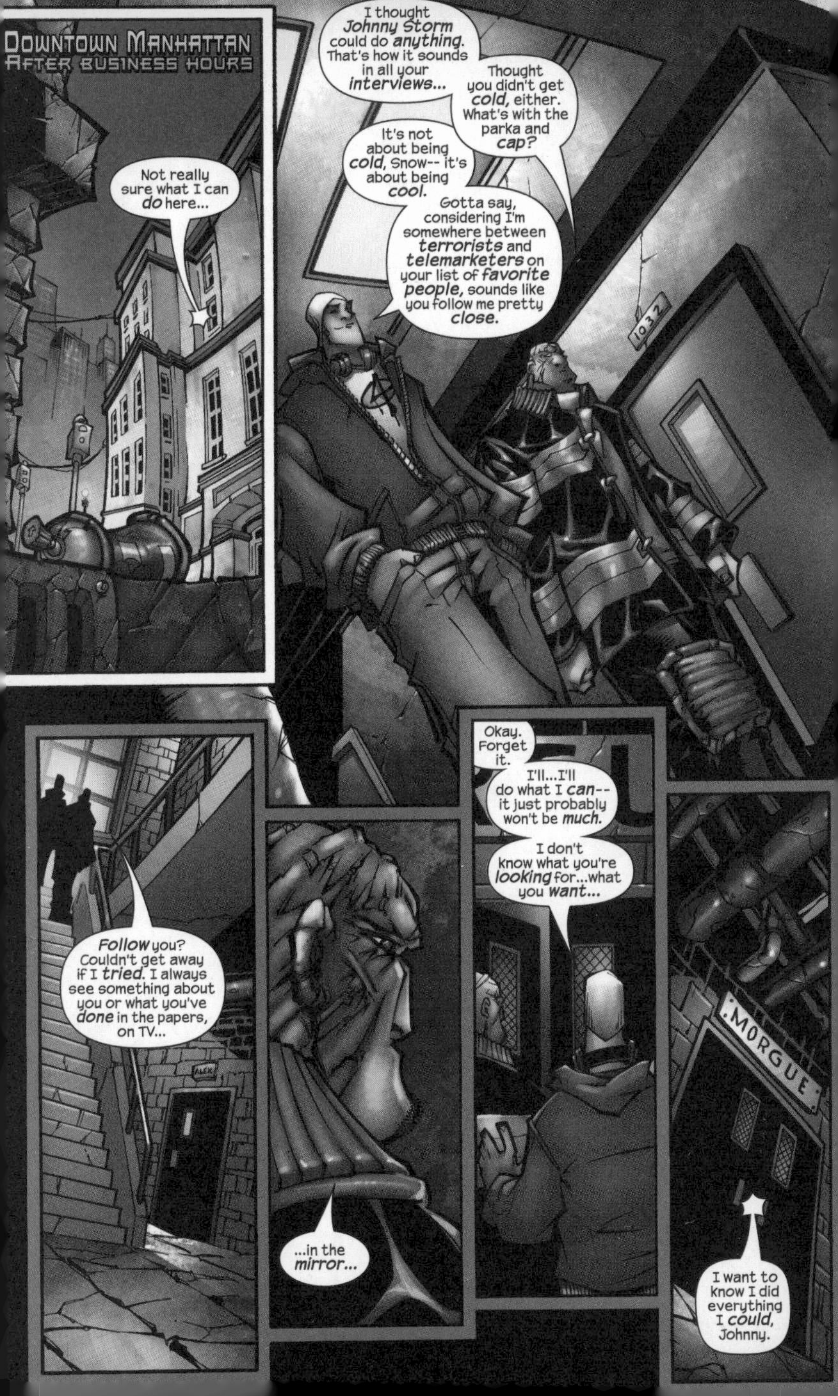
DOWNTOWN MANHATTAN
AFTER BUSINESS HOURS
Not really sure what I can *do* here...
I thought *Johnny Storm* could do *anything*. That's how it sounds in all your *interviews*...
Thought you didn't get *cold,* either. What's with the parka and *cap?*
It's not about being *cold,* Snow-- it's about being *cool.*
Gotta say, considering I'm somewhere between *terrorists* and *telemarketers* on your list of *favorite people,* sounds like you follow me pretty *close.*
1032
Follow you? Couldn't get away if I *tried.* I always see something about you or what you've *done* in the papers, on TV...
...in the *mirror...*
Okay. Forget it.
I'll...I'll do what I *can*-- it just probably won't be *much.*
I don't know what you're *looking* for...what you *want*...
MORGUE
I want to know I did everything I *could,* Johnny.

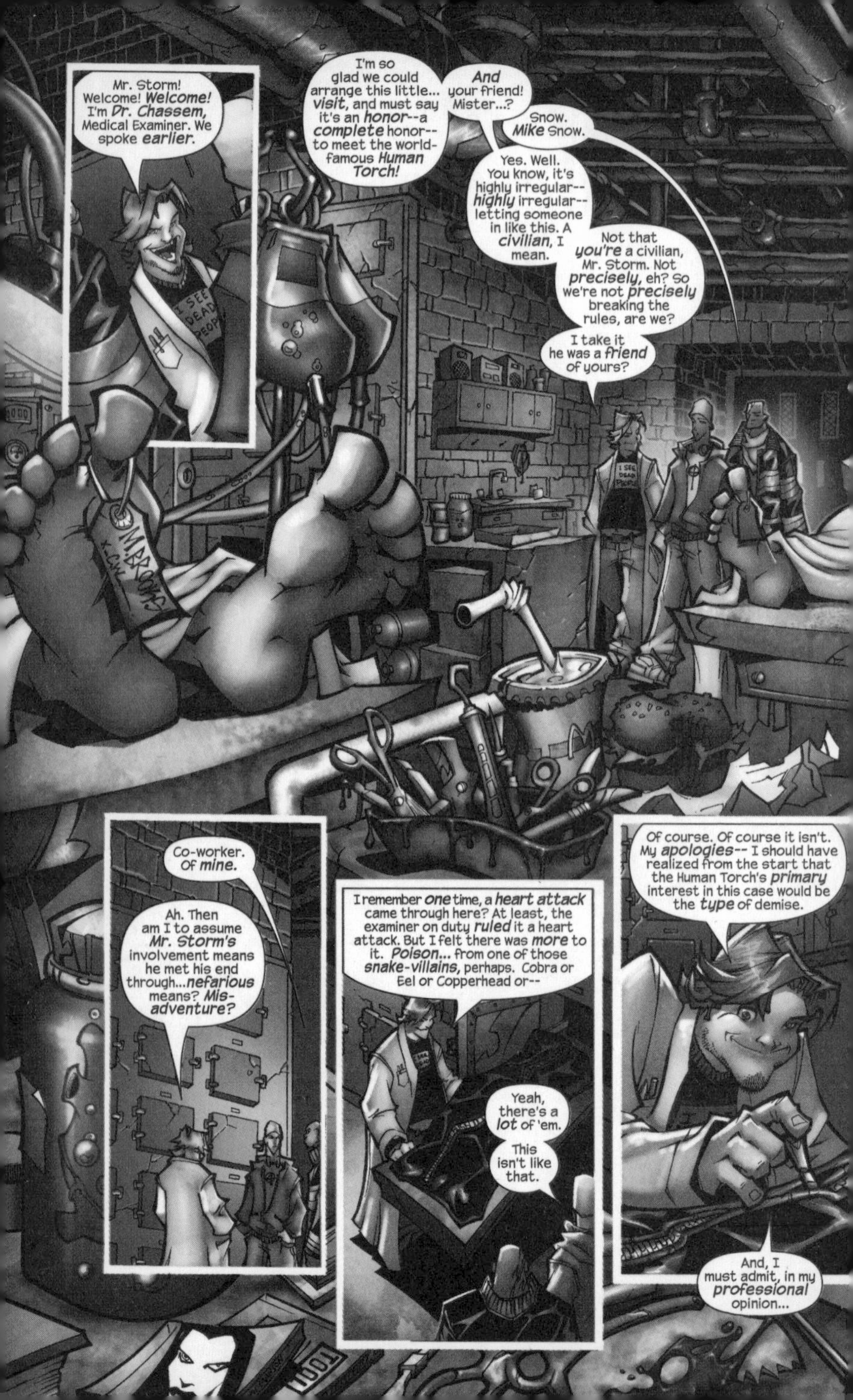
Mr. Storm! Welcome! Welcome! I'm Dr. Chassem, Medical Examiner. We spoke earlier.
I'm so glad we could arrange this little... visit, and must say it's an honor--a complete honor--to meet the world-famous Human Torch!
And your friend! Mister...?
Snow. Mike Snow.
Yes. Well. You know, it's highly irregular--highly irregular--letting someone in like this. A civilian, I mean.
Not that you're a civilian, Mr. Storm. Not precisely, eh? So we're not precisely breaking the rules, are we?
I take it he was a friend of yours?
Co-worker. Of mine.
Ah. Then am I to assume Mr. Storm's involvement means he met his end through...nefarious means? Misadventure?
I remember one time, a heart attack came through here? At least, the examiner on duty ruled it a heart attack. But I felt there was more to it. Poison... from one of those snake-villains, perhaps. Cobra or Eel or Copperhead or--
Yeah, there's a lot of 'em.
This isn't like that.
Of course. Of course it isn't. My apologies-- I should have realized from the start that the Human Torch's primary interest in this case would be the type of demise.
And, I must admit, in my professional opinion...

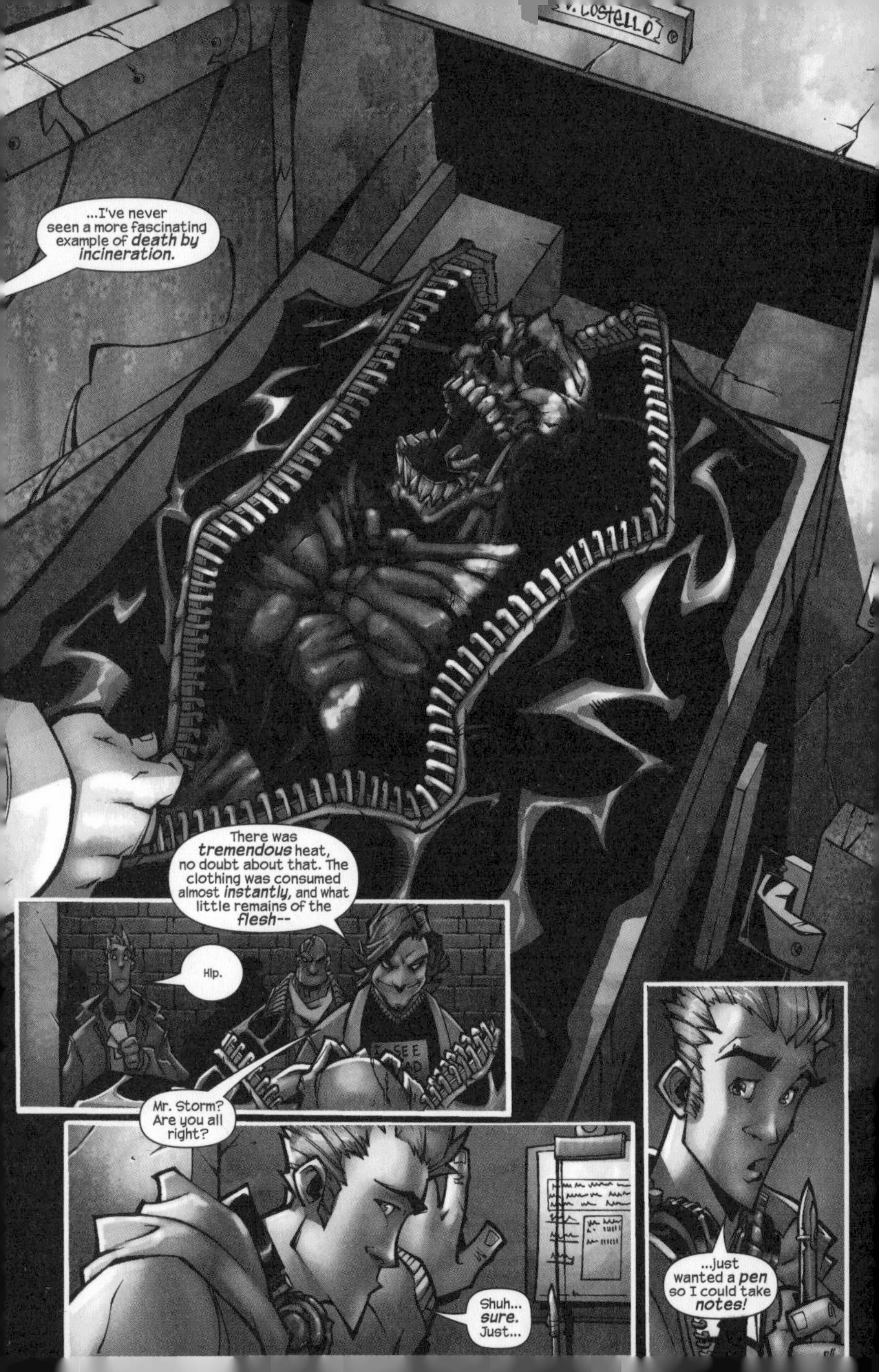
V. COSTELLO
...I've never seen a more fascinating example of *death by incineration.*
There was *tremendous* heat, no doubt about that. The clothing was consumed almost *instantly,* and what little remains of the *flesh--*
Hlp.
Mr. Storm? Are you all right?
Shuh... *sure.* Just...
...just wanted a *pen* so I could take *notes!*

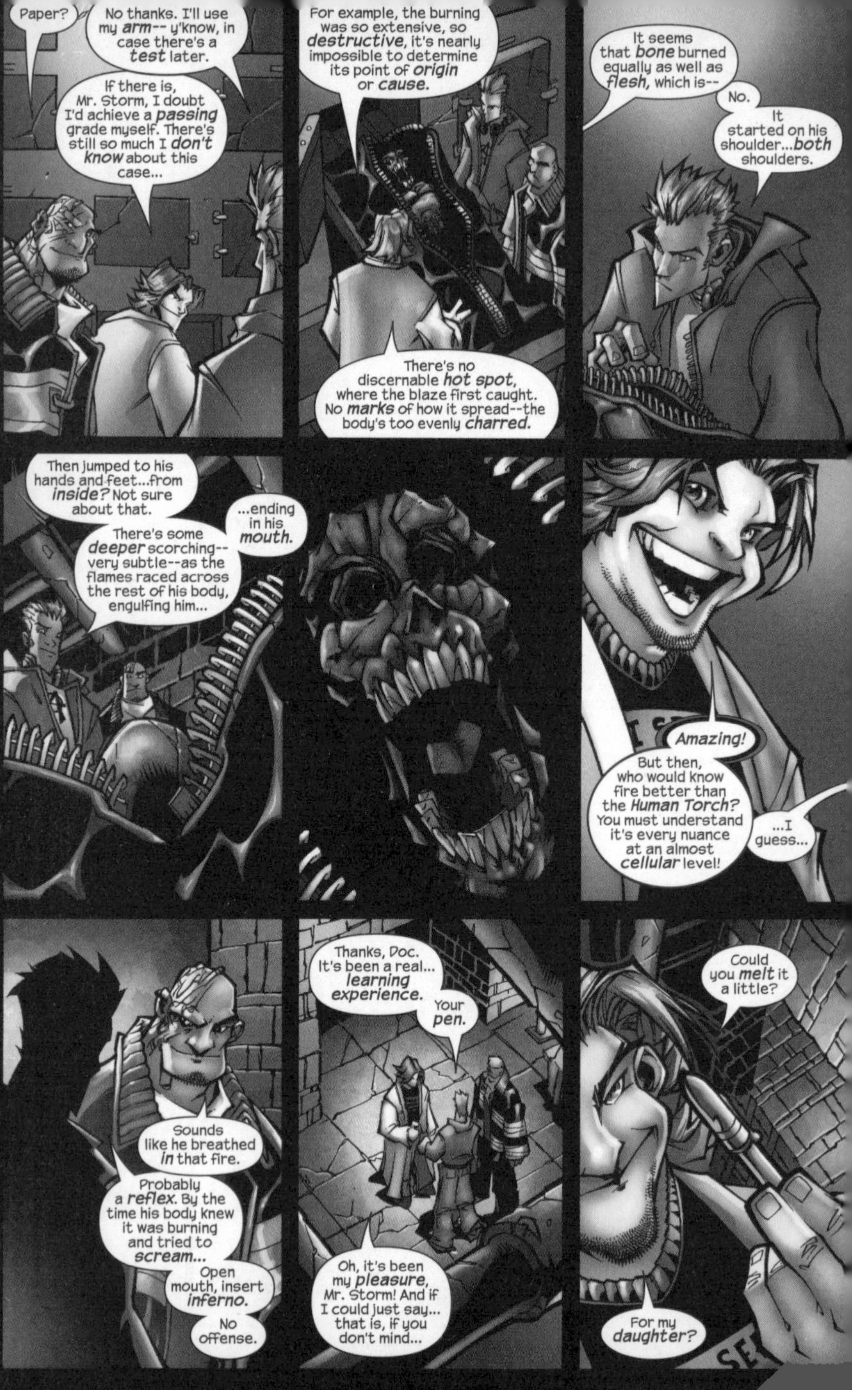
Paper?
No thanks. I'll use my arm-- y'know, in case there's a test later.
If there is, Mr. Storm, I doubt I'd achieve a passing grade myself. There's still so much I don't know about this case...
For example, the burning was so extensive, so destructive, it's nearly impossible to determine its point of origin or cause.
There's no discernable hot spot, where the blaze first caught. No marks of how it spread--the body's too evenly charred.
It seems that bone burned equally as well as flesh, which is--
No.
It started on his shoulder...both shoulders.
Then jumped to his hands and feet...from inside? Not sure about that.
There's some deeper scorching--very subtle--as the flames raced across the rest of his body, engulfing him...
...ending in his mouth.
Amazing!
But then, who would know fire better than the Human Torch? You must understand it's every nuance at an almost cellular level!
...I guess...
Sounds like he breathed in that fire.
Probably a reflex. By the time his body knew it was burning and tried to scream...
Open mouth, insert inferno.
No offense.
Thanks, Doc. It's been a real... learning experience.
Your pen.
Oh, it's been my pleasure, Mr. Storm! And if I could just say... that is, if you don't mind...
Could you melt it a little?
For my daughter?

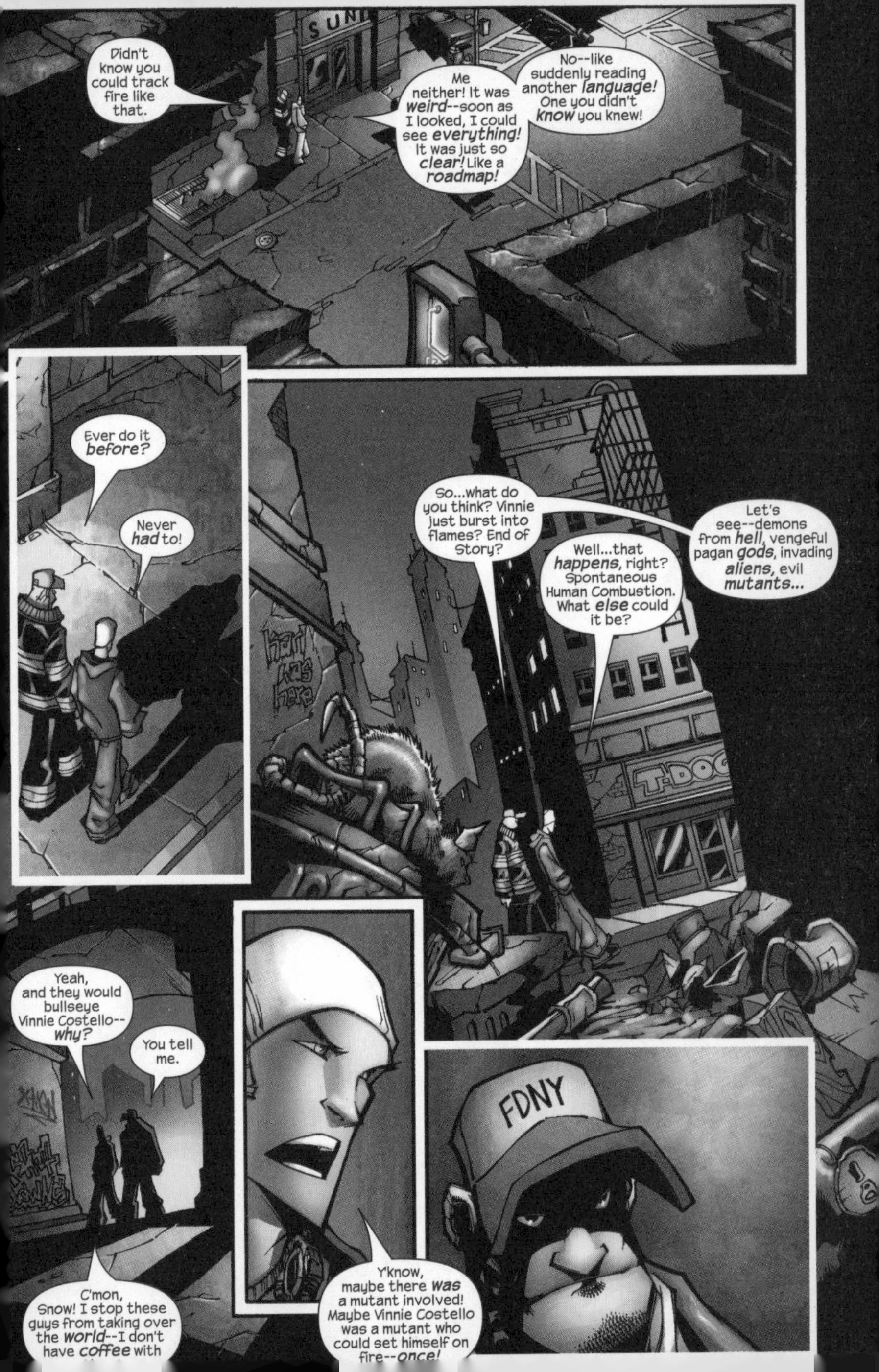
SUN
Didn't know you could track fire like that.
Me neither! It was weird--soon as I looked, I could see everything! It was just so clear! Like a roadmap!
No--like suddenly reading another language! One you didn't know you knew!
Ever do it before?
Never had to!
So...what do you think? Vinnie just burst into flames? End of story?
Well...that happens, right? Spontaneous Human Combustion. What else could it be?
Let's see--demons from hell, vengeful pagan gods, invading aliens, evil mutants...
T-DOG
Yeah, and they would bullseye Vinnie Costello--why?
You tell me.
C'mon, Snow! I stop these guys from taking over the world--I don't have coffee with
Y'know, maybe there was a mutant involved! Maybe Vinnie Costello was a mutant who could set himself on fire--once!
FDNY

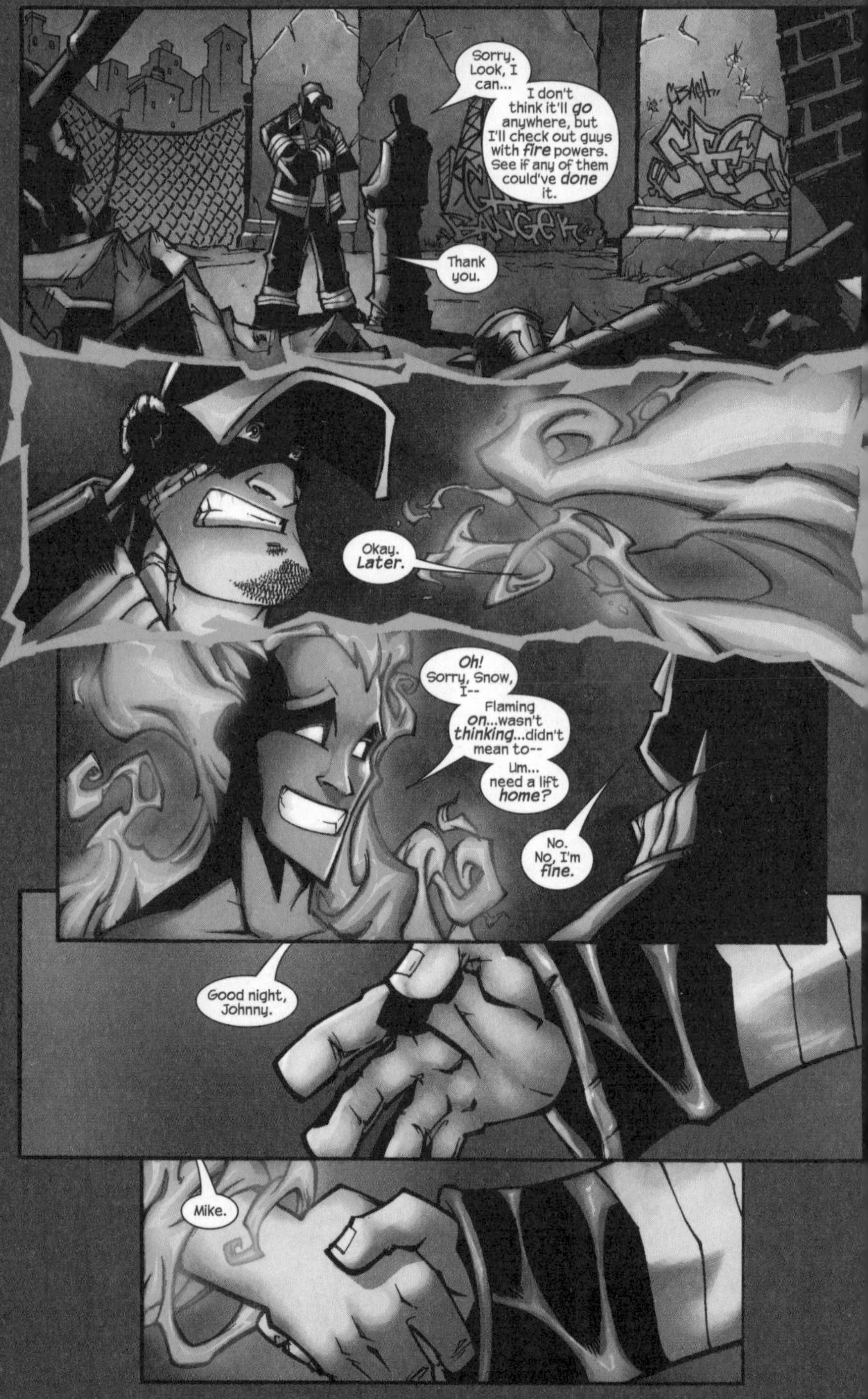
Sorry. Look, I can...
I don't think it'll *go* anywhere, but I'll check out guys with *fire* powers. See if any of them could've *done* it.
Thank you.
Okay. **Later.**
Oh! Sorry, Snow, I--
Flaming *on*...wasn't *thinking*...didn't mean to--
Um... need a lift *home?*
No. No, I'm *fine.*
Good night, Johnny.
Mike.

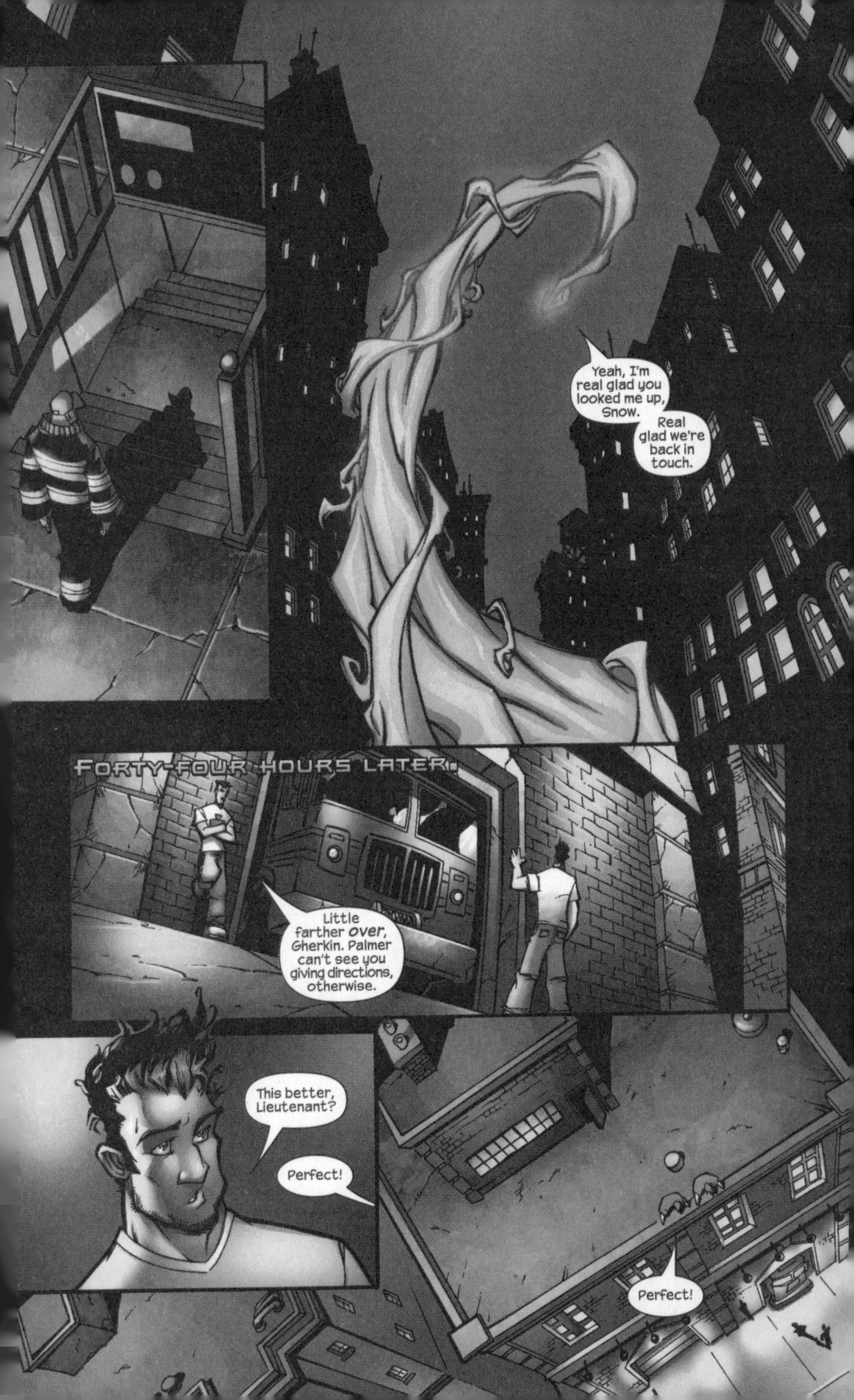

Yeah, I'm real glad you looked me up, Snow.
Real glad we're back in touch.
FORTY-FOUR HOURS LATER.
Little farther *over*, Gherkin. Palmer can't see you giving directions, otherwise.
This better, Lieutenant?
Perfect!
Perfect!

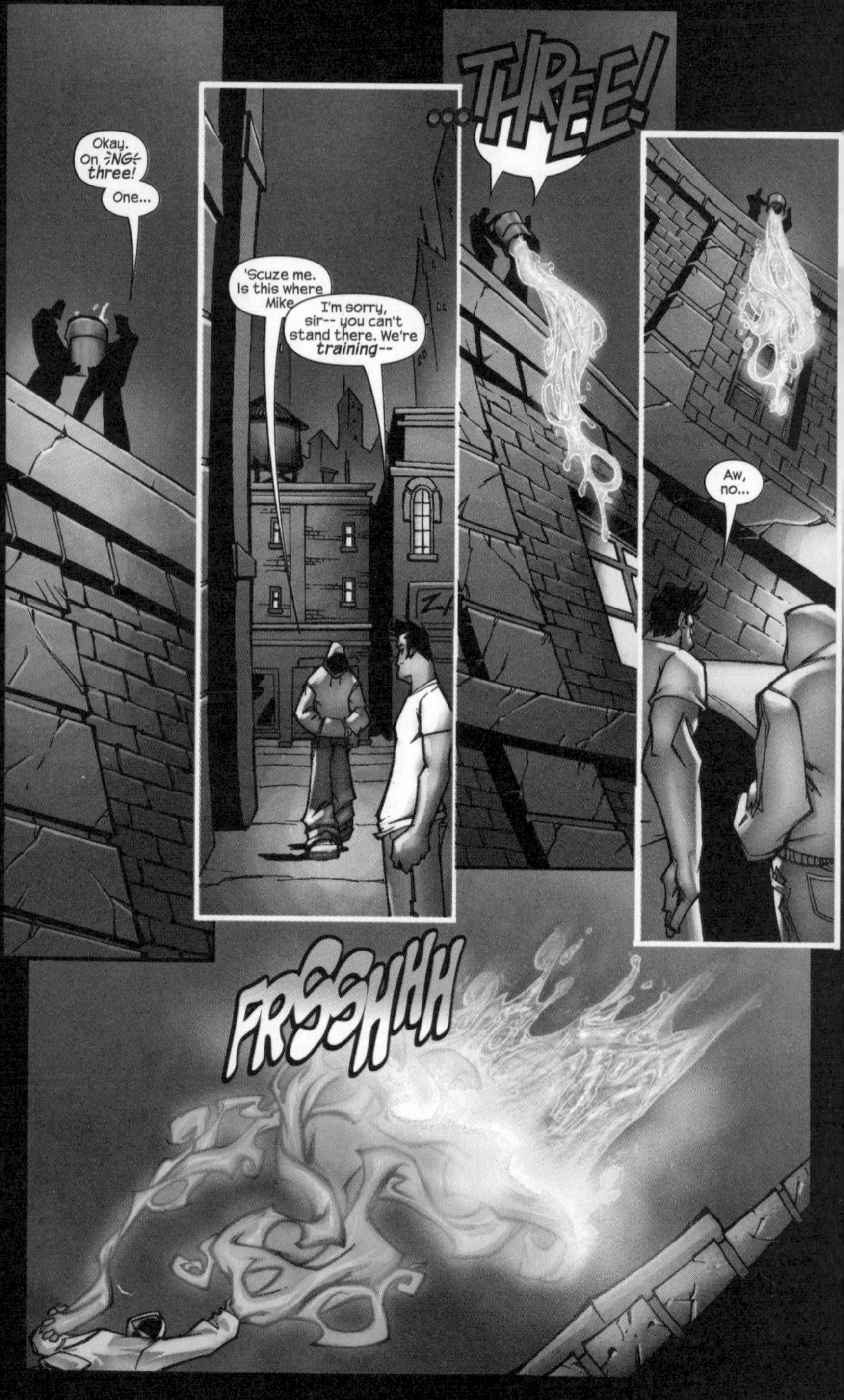
Okay. On ≷NG≶ three!
One...
'Scuze me. Is this where Mike
I'm sorry, sir-- you can't stand there. We're *training*--
...THREE!
Aw, no...
FRSSHHH

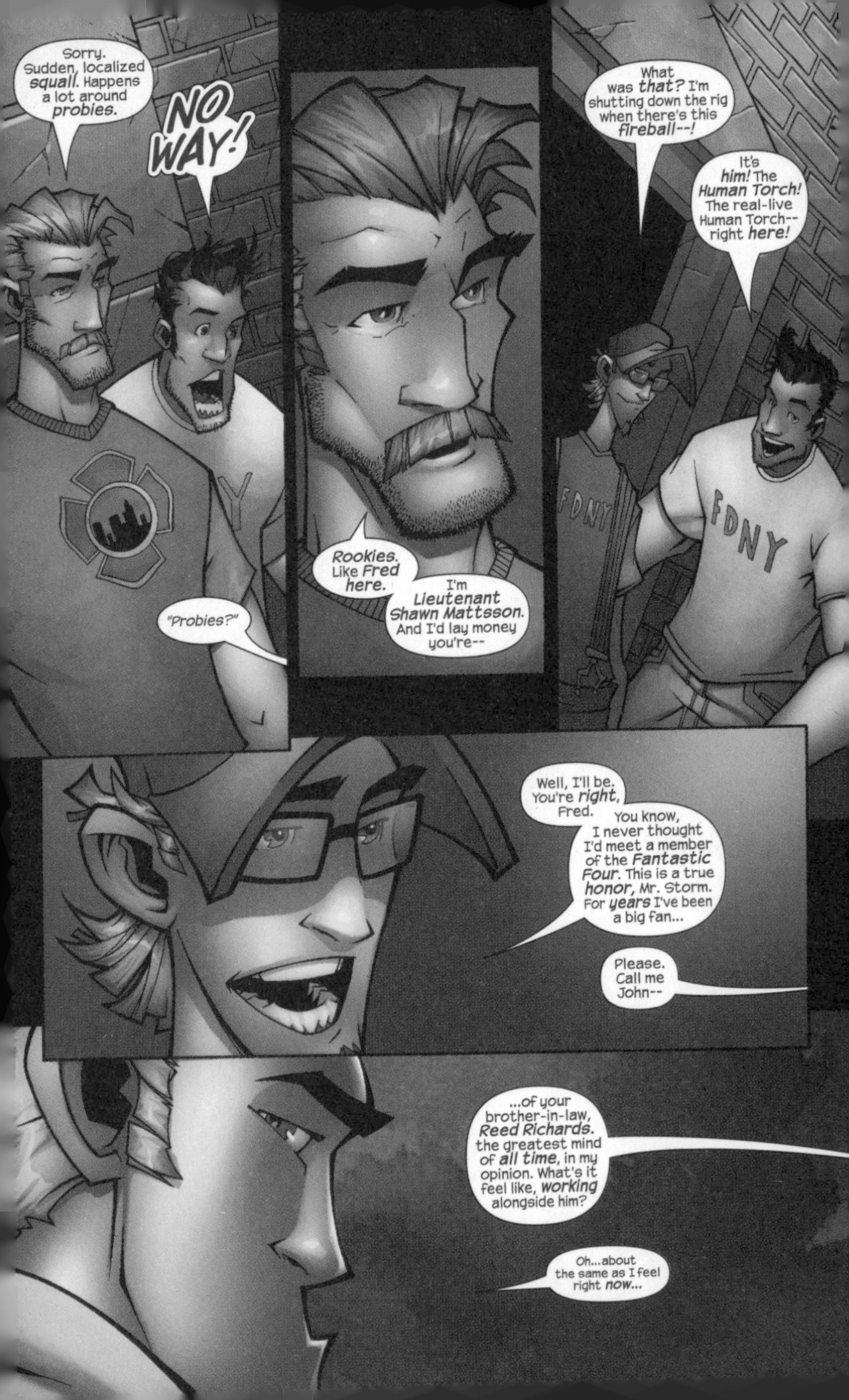

Sorry. Sudden, localized squall. Happens a lot around probies.
NO WAY!
"Probies?"
Rookies. Like Fred here.
I'm Lieutenant Shawn Mattsson. And I'd lay money you're--
What was that? I'm shutting down the rig when there's this fireball--!
It's him! The Human Torch! The real-live Human Torch--right here!
FDNY
FDNY
Well, I'll be. You're right, Fred.
You know, I never thought I'd meet a member of the Fantastic Four. This is a true honor, Mr. Storm. For years I've been a big fan...
Please. Call me John--
...of your brother-in-law, Reed Richards. the greatest mind of all time, in my opinion. What's it feel like, working alongside him?
Oh...about the same as I feel right now...

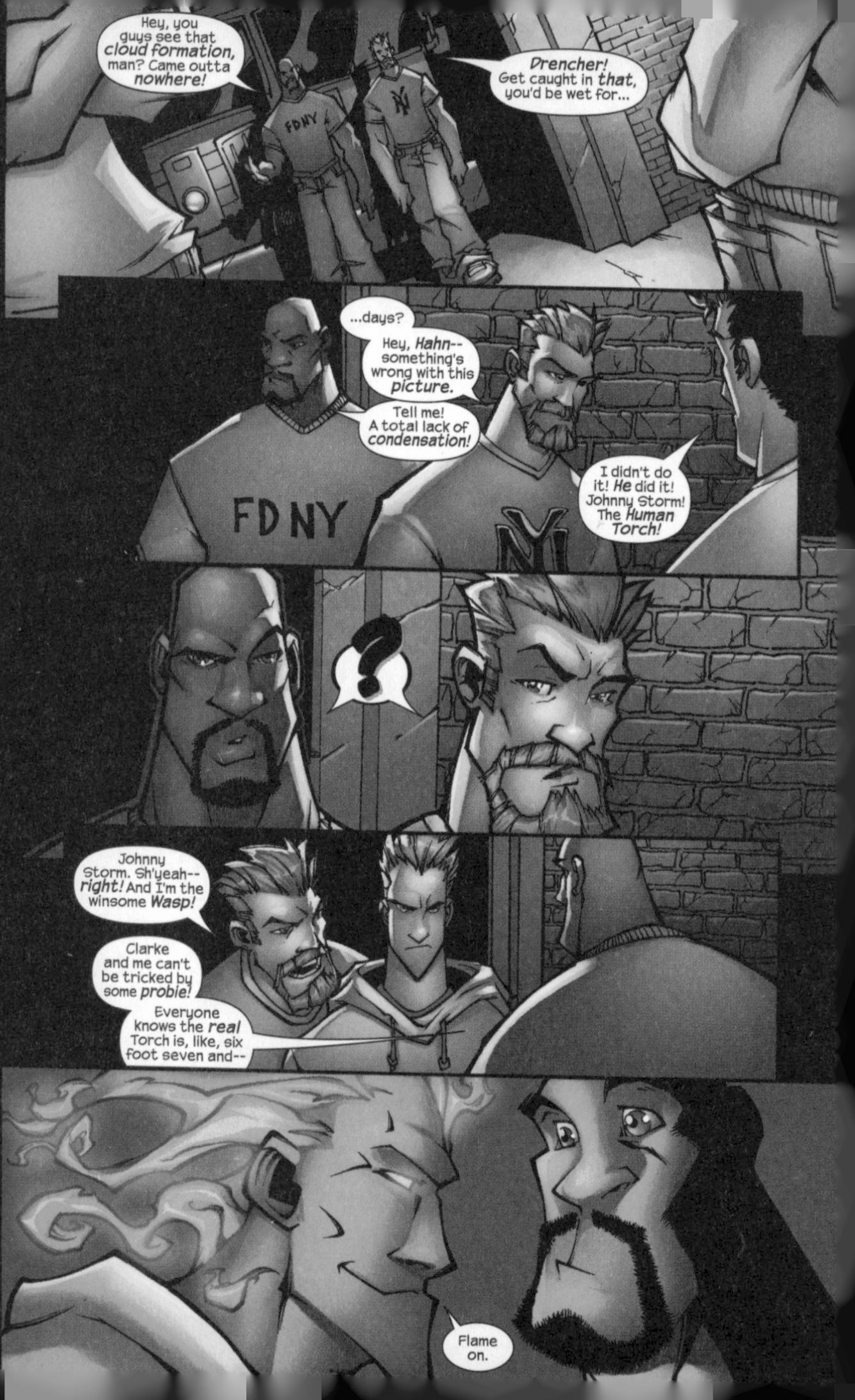

Hey, you guys see that *cloud formation*, man? Came outta *nowhere!*
Drencher! Get caught in *that*, you'd be wet for...
...days?
Hey, *Hahn*-- something's wrong with this *picture.*
Tell me! A total lack of *condensation!*
I didn't do it! *He* did it! Johnny Storm! The *Human Torch!*
?
Johnny Storm. Sh'yeah-- *right!* And I'm the winsome *Wasp!*
Clarke and me can't be tricked by some *probie!*
Everyone knows the *real* Torch is, like, six foot seven and--
Flame on.

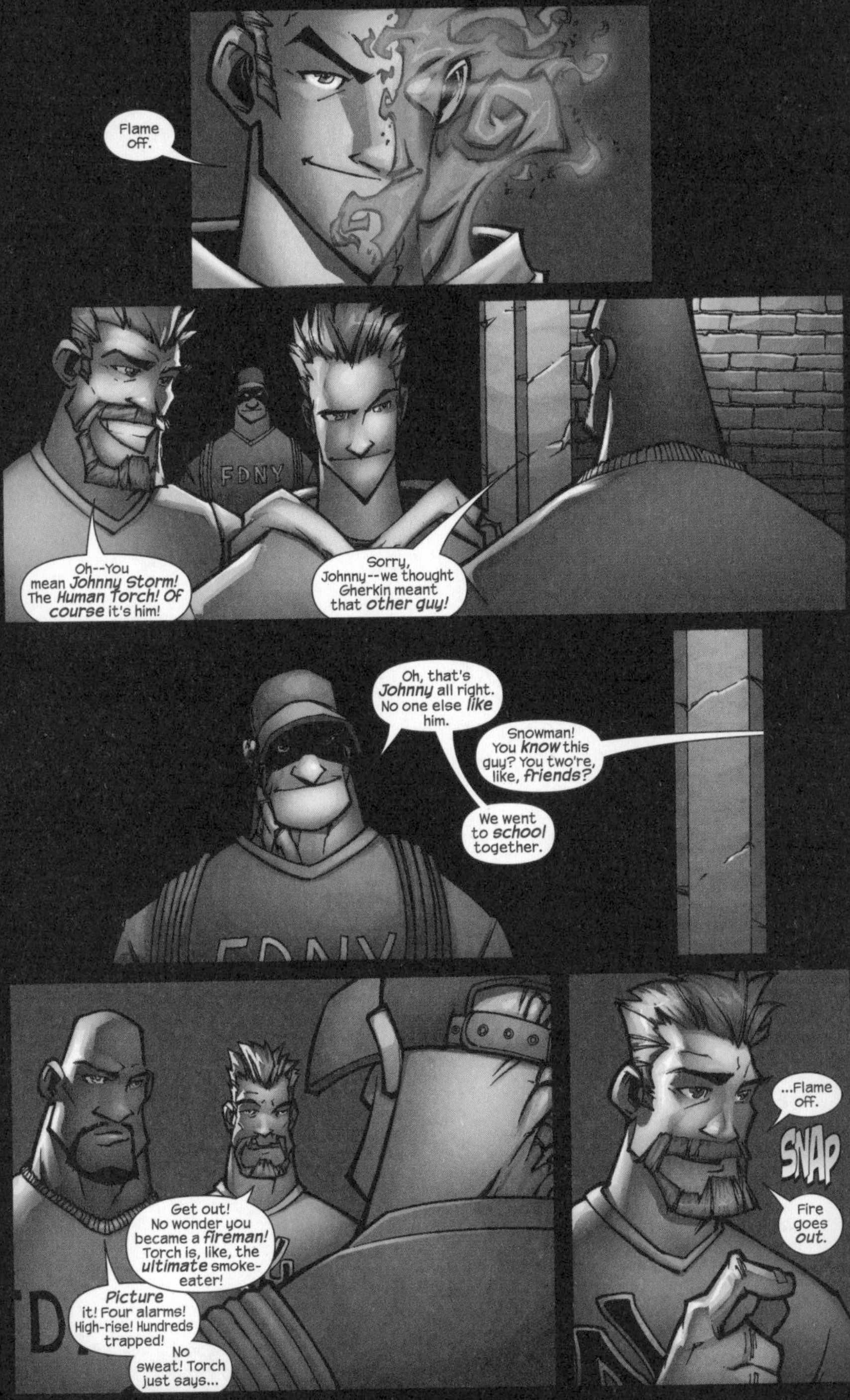
Flame off.
Oh--You mean Johnny Storm! The Human Torch! Of course it's him!
Sorry, Johnny--we thought Gherkin meant that other guy!
Oh, that's Johnny all right. No one else like him.
Snowman! You know this guy? You two're, like, friends?
We went to school together.
Get out! No wonder you became a fireman! Torch is, like, the ultimate smoke-eater!
Picture it! Four alarms! High-rise! Hundreds trapped!
No sweat! Torch just says...
...Flame off.
SNAP
Fire goes out.

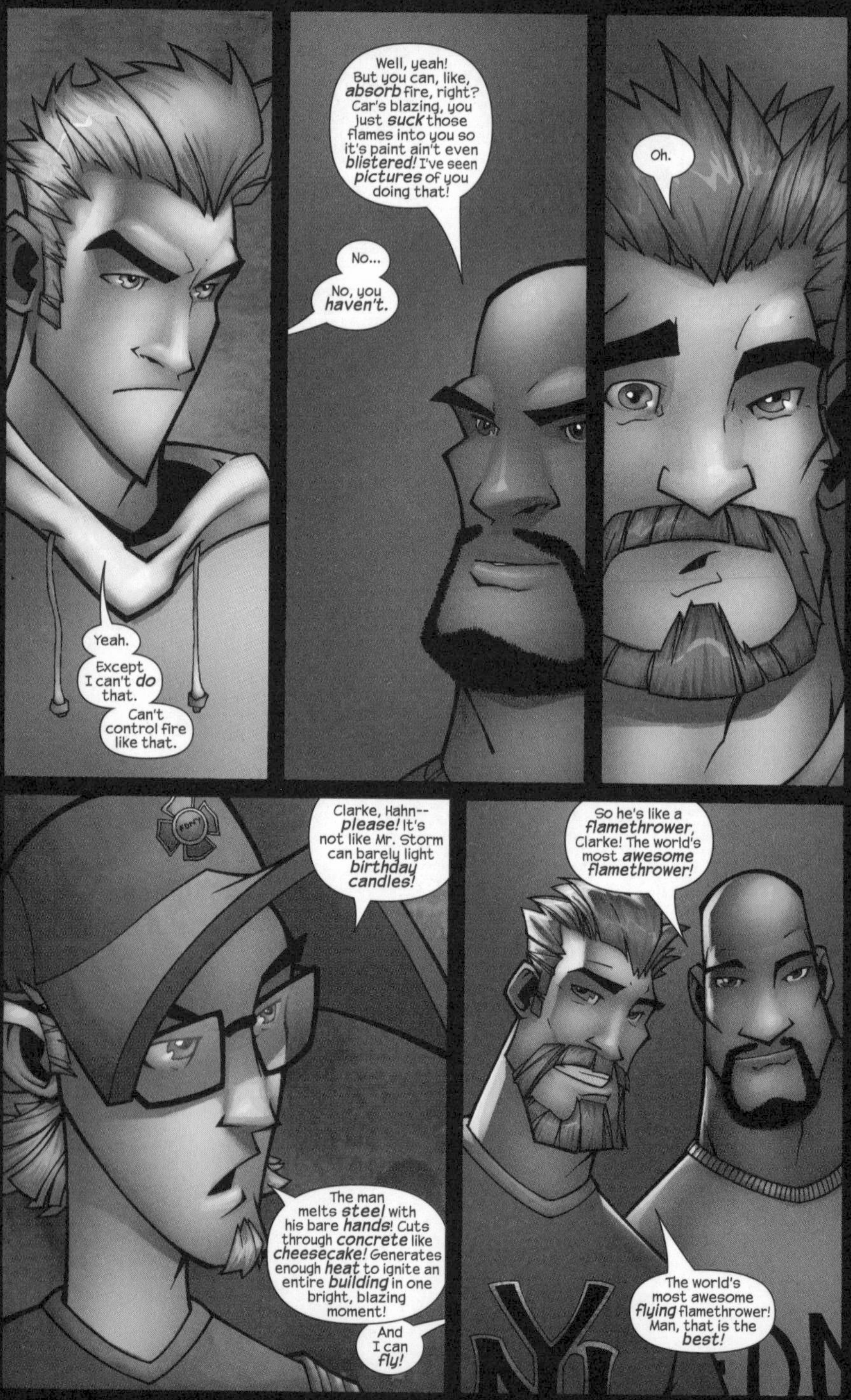

Yeah.
Except I can't do that.
Can't control fire like that.
Well, yeah! But you can, like, absorb fire, right? Car's blazing, you just suck those flames into you so it's paint ain't even blistered! I've seen pictures of you doing that!
No...
No, you haven't.
Oh.
Clarke, Hahn-- please! It's not like Mr. Storm can barely light birthday candles!
The man melts steel with his bare hands! Cuts through concrete like cheesecake! Generates enough heat to ignite an entire building in one bright, blazing moment!
And I can fly!
So he's like a flamethrower, Clarke! The world's most awesome flamethrower!
The world's most awesome flying flamethrower! Man, that is the best!

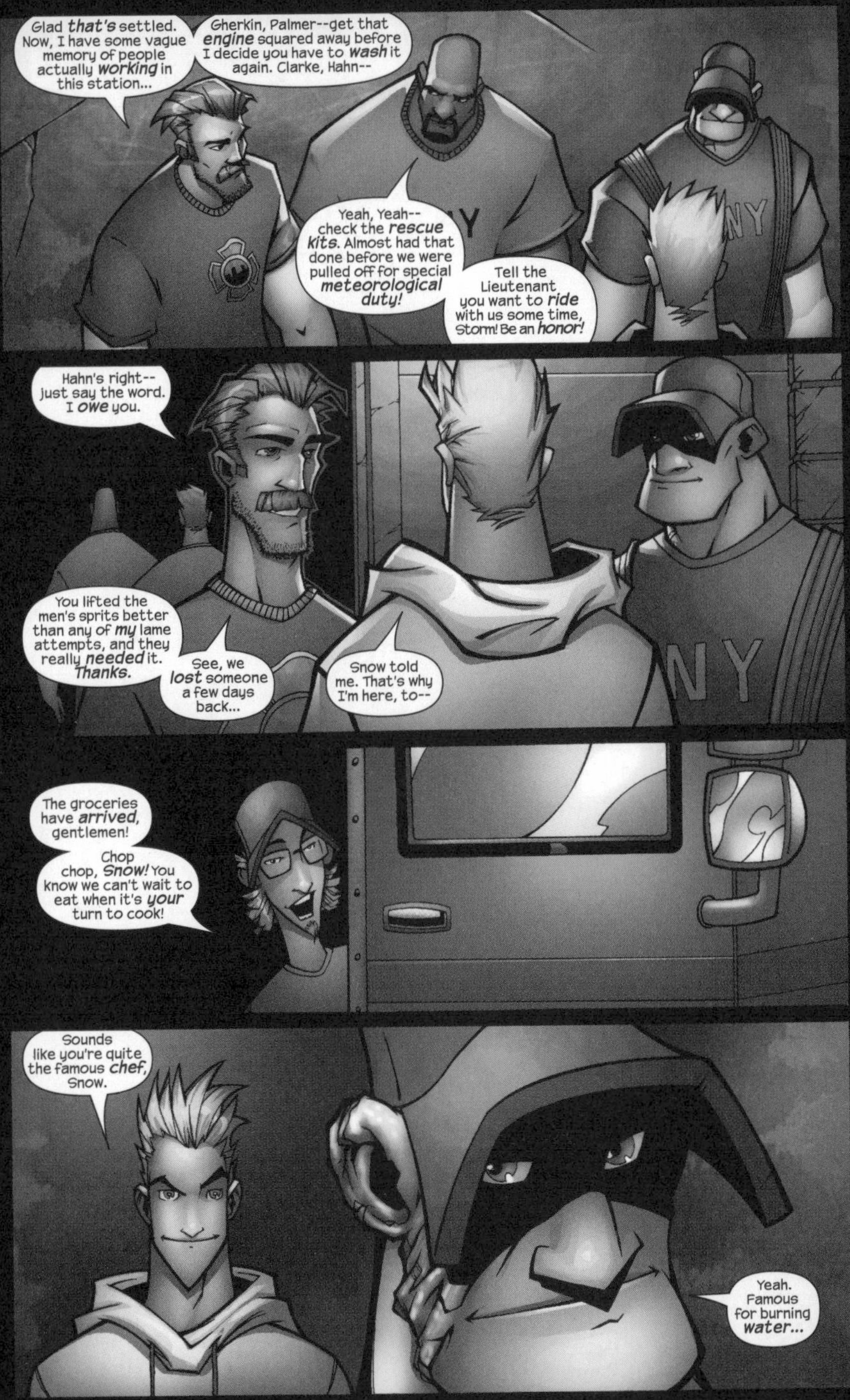
Glad that's settled. Now, I have some vague memory of people actually working in this station...
Gherkin, Palmer--get that engine squared away before I decide you have to wash it again. Clarke, Hahn--
Yeah, Yeah--check the rescue kits. Almost had that done before we were pulled off for special meteorological duty!
Tell the Lieutenant you want to ride with us some time, Storm! Be an honor!
Hahn's right--just say the word. I owe you.
You lifted the men's sprits better than any of my lame attempts, and they really needed it. Thanks.
See, we lost someone a few days back...
Snow told me. That's why I'm here, to--
The groceries have arrived, gentlemen!
Chop chop, Snow! You know we can't wait to eat when it's your turn to cook!
Sounds like you're quite the famous chef, Snow.
Yeah. Famous for burning water...

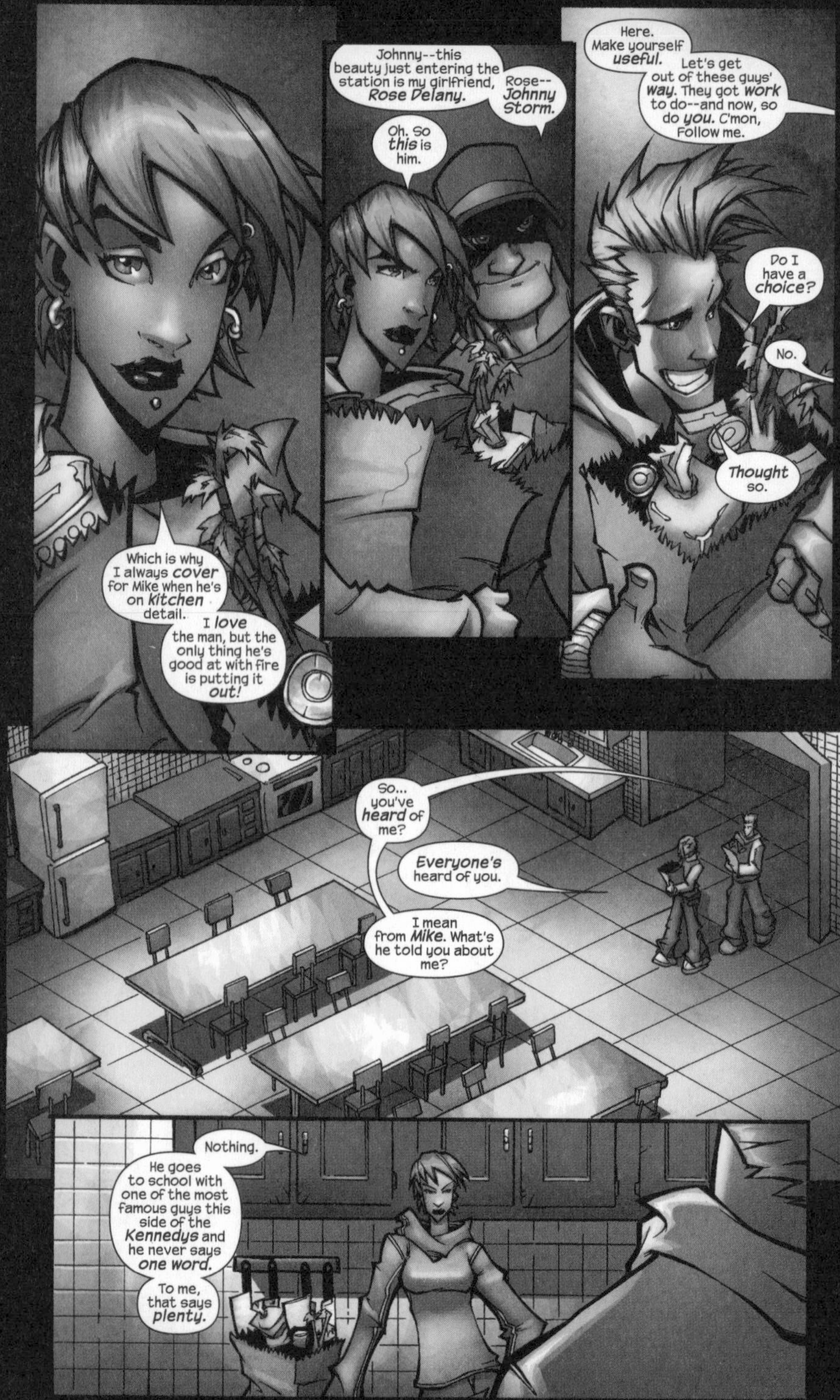
Which is why I always cover for Mike when he's on kitchen detail.
I love the man, but the only thing he's good at with fire is putting it out!
Johnny--this beauty just entering the station is my girlfriend, Rose Delany.
Rose-- Johnny Storm.
Oh. So this is him.
Here. Make yourself useful.
Let's get out of these guys' way. They got work to do--and now, so do you. C'mon, Follow me.
Do I have a choice?
No.
Thought so.
So... you've heard of me?
Everyone's heard of you.
I mean from Mike. What's he told you about me?
Nothing.
He goes to school with one of the most famous guys this side of the Kennedys and he never says one word.
To me, that says plenty.

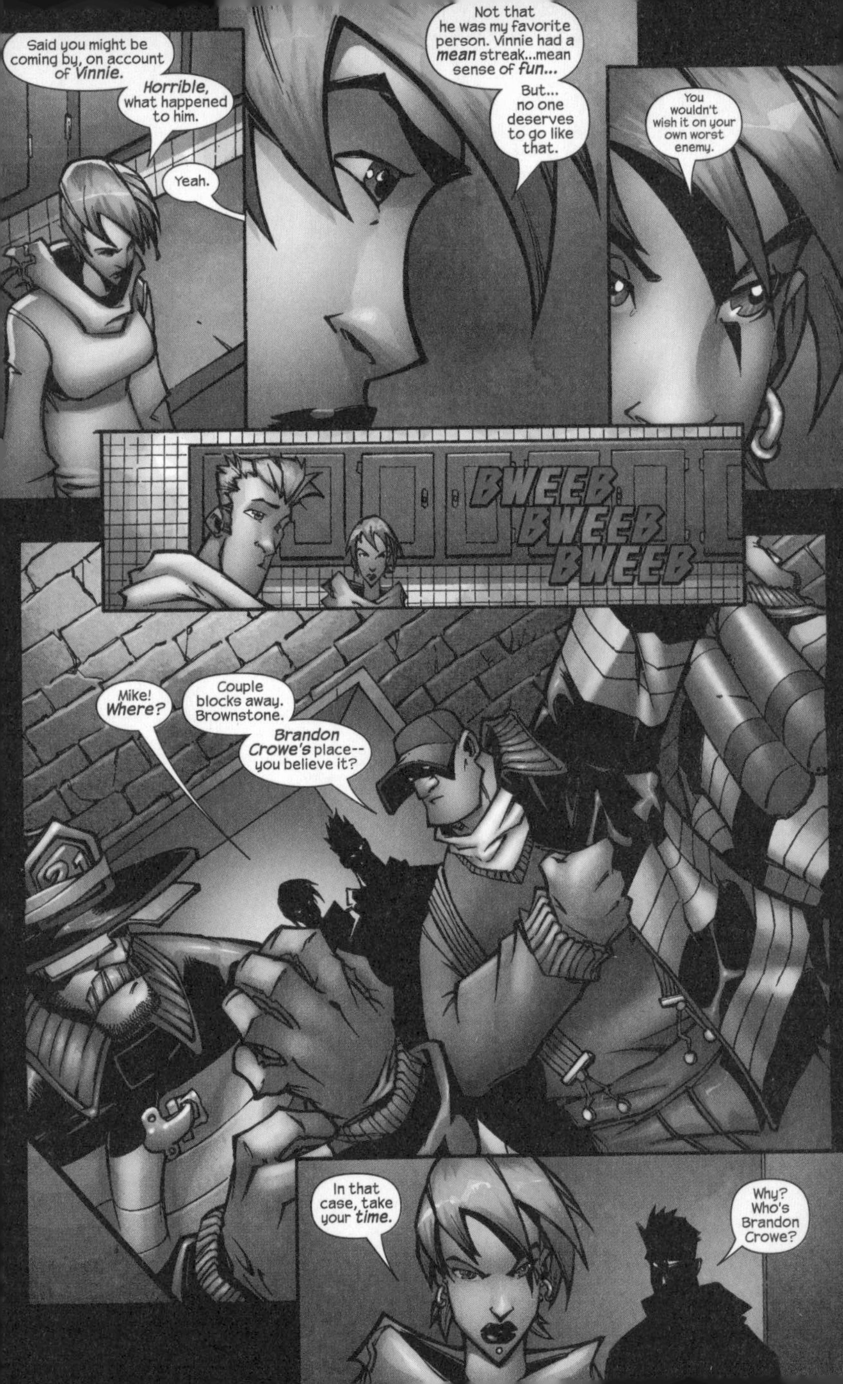
Said you might be coming by, on account of *Vinnie*.
Horrible, what happened to him.
Yeah.
Not that he was my favorite person. Vinnie had a *mean* streak...mean sense of *fun*...
But... no one deserves to go like that.
You wouldn't wish it on your own worst enemy.
BWEEB BWEEB BWEEB
Mike! *Where?*
Couple blocks away. Brownstone.
Brandon Crowe's place-- you believe it?
In that case, take your *time*.
Why? Who's Brandon Crowe?

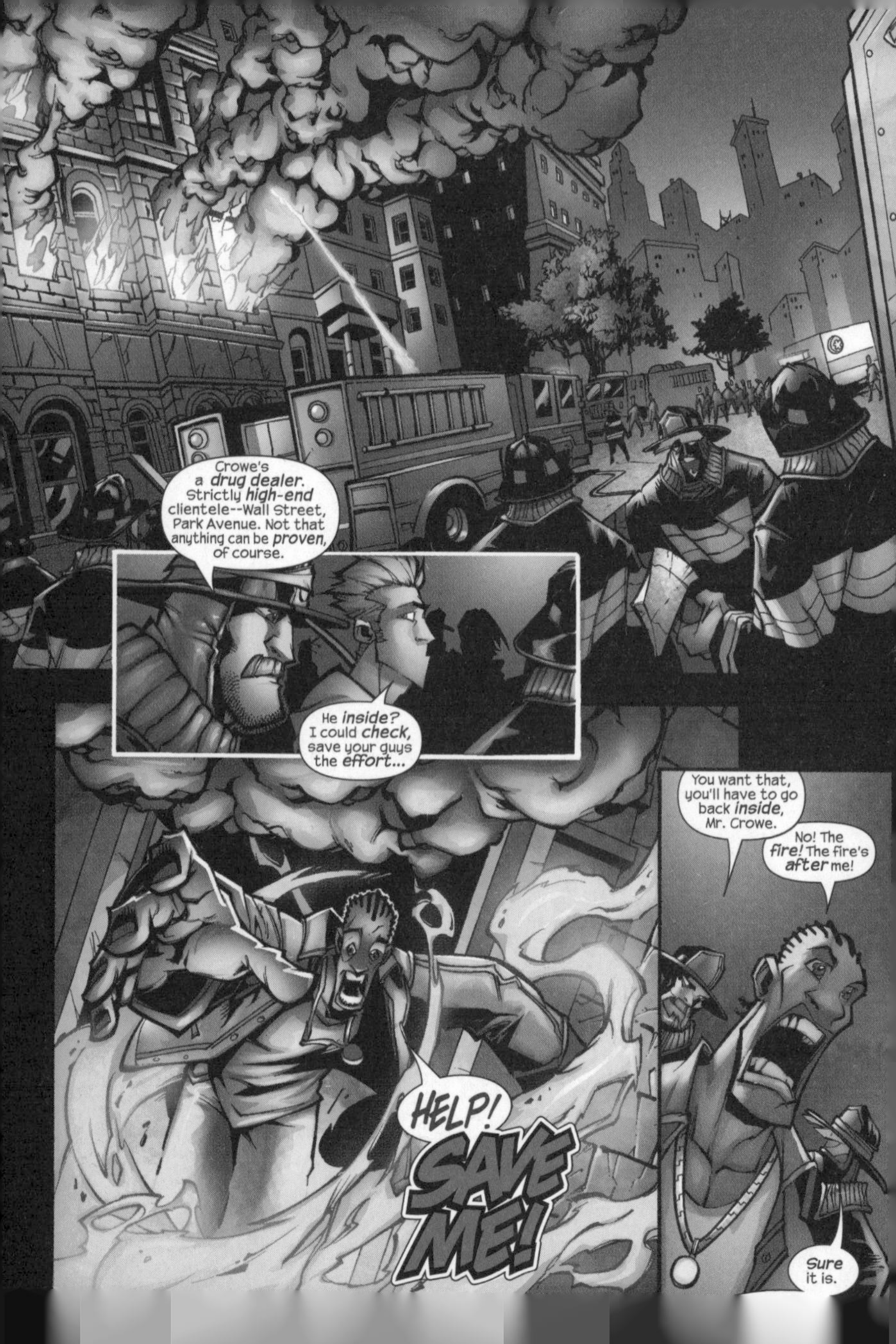
Crowe's a drug dealer. Strictly high-end clientele--Wall Street, Park Avenue. Not that anything can be proven, of course.
He inside? I could check, save your guys the effort...
HELP!
SAVE ME!
You want that, you'll have to go back inside, Mr. Crowe.
No! The fire! The fire's after me!
Sure it is.

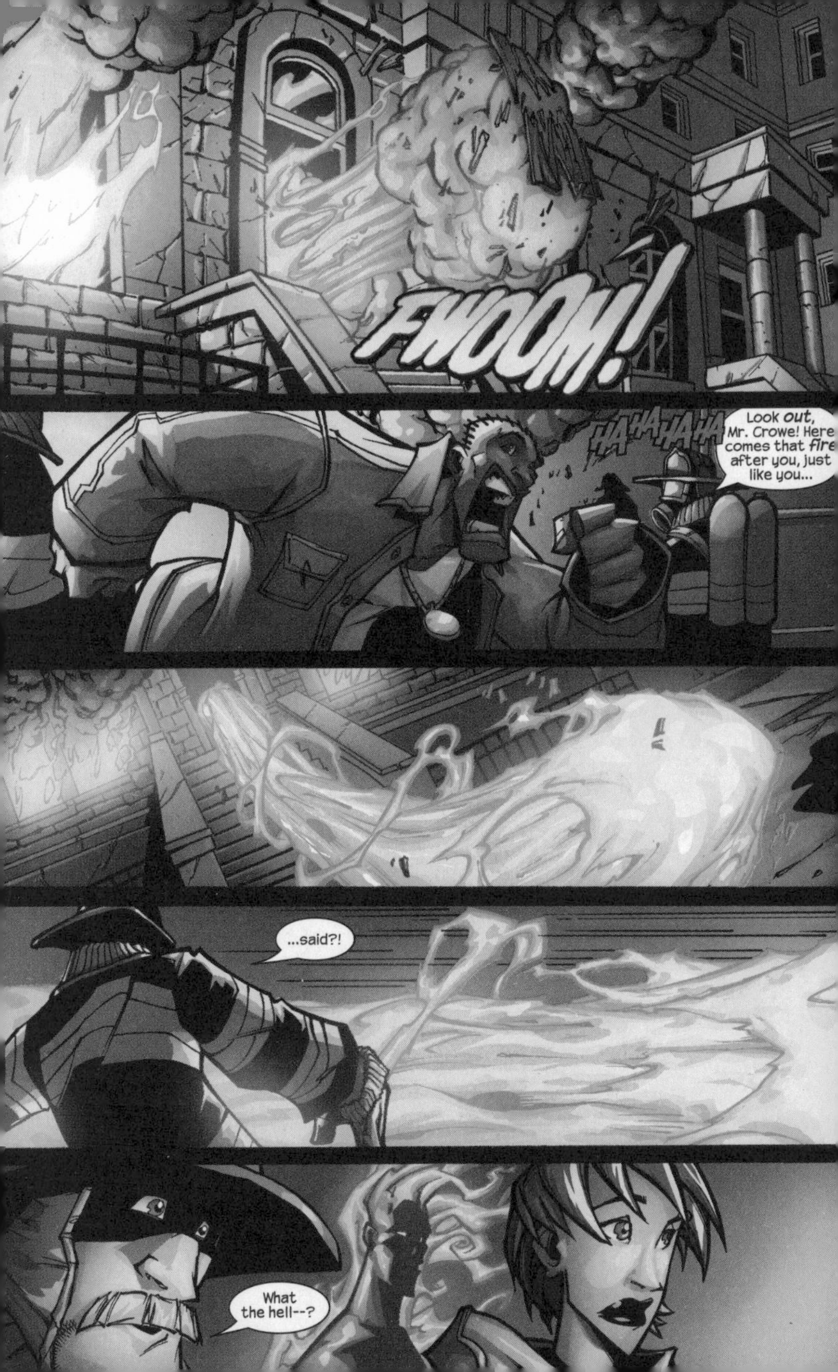
FWOOM!
HAHAHAHA
Look out, Mr. Crowe! Here comes that fire after you, just like you...
...said?!
What the hell--?

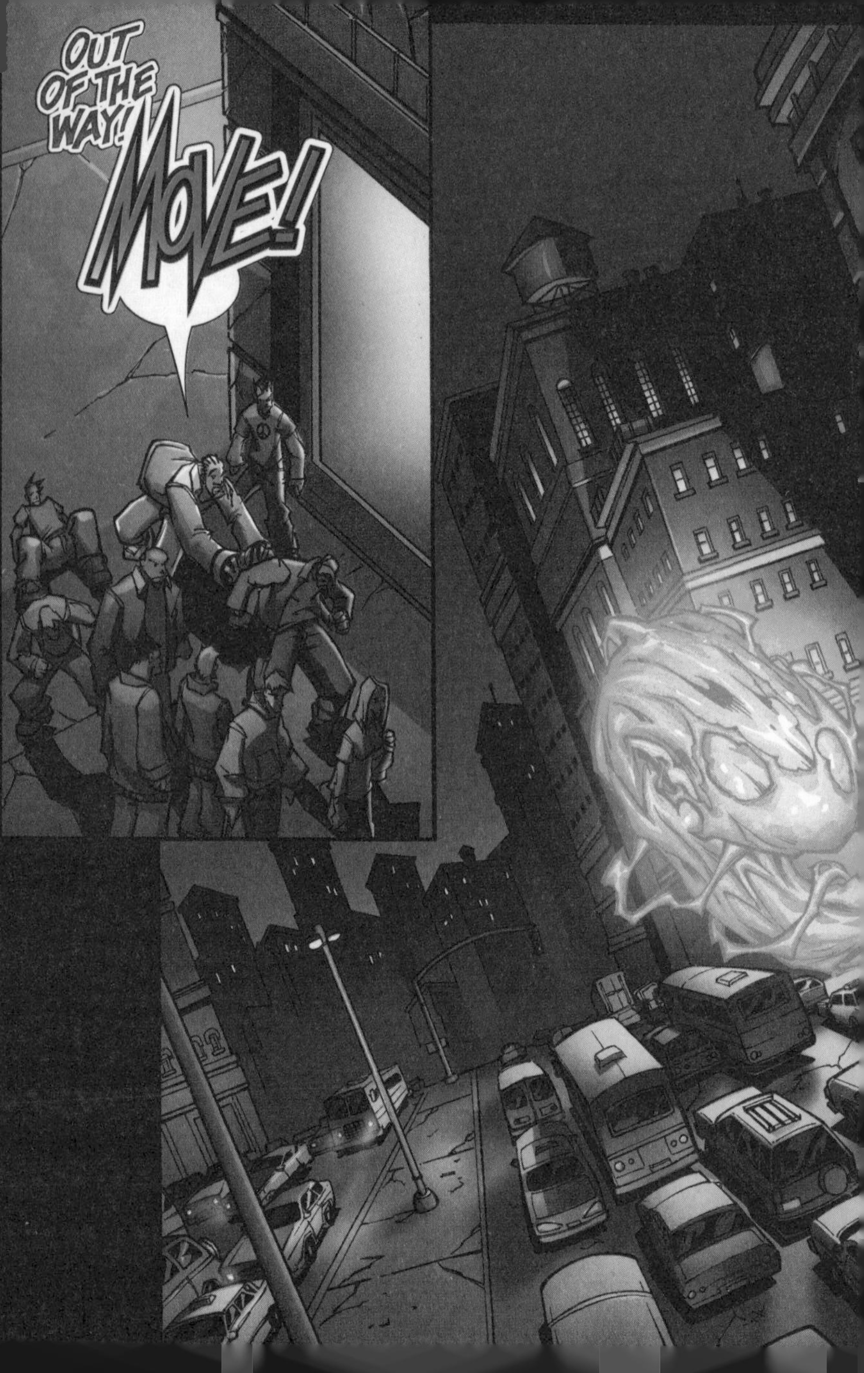
OUT OF THE WAY!
MOVE!

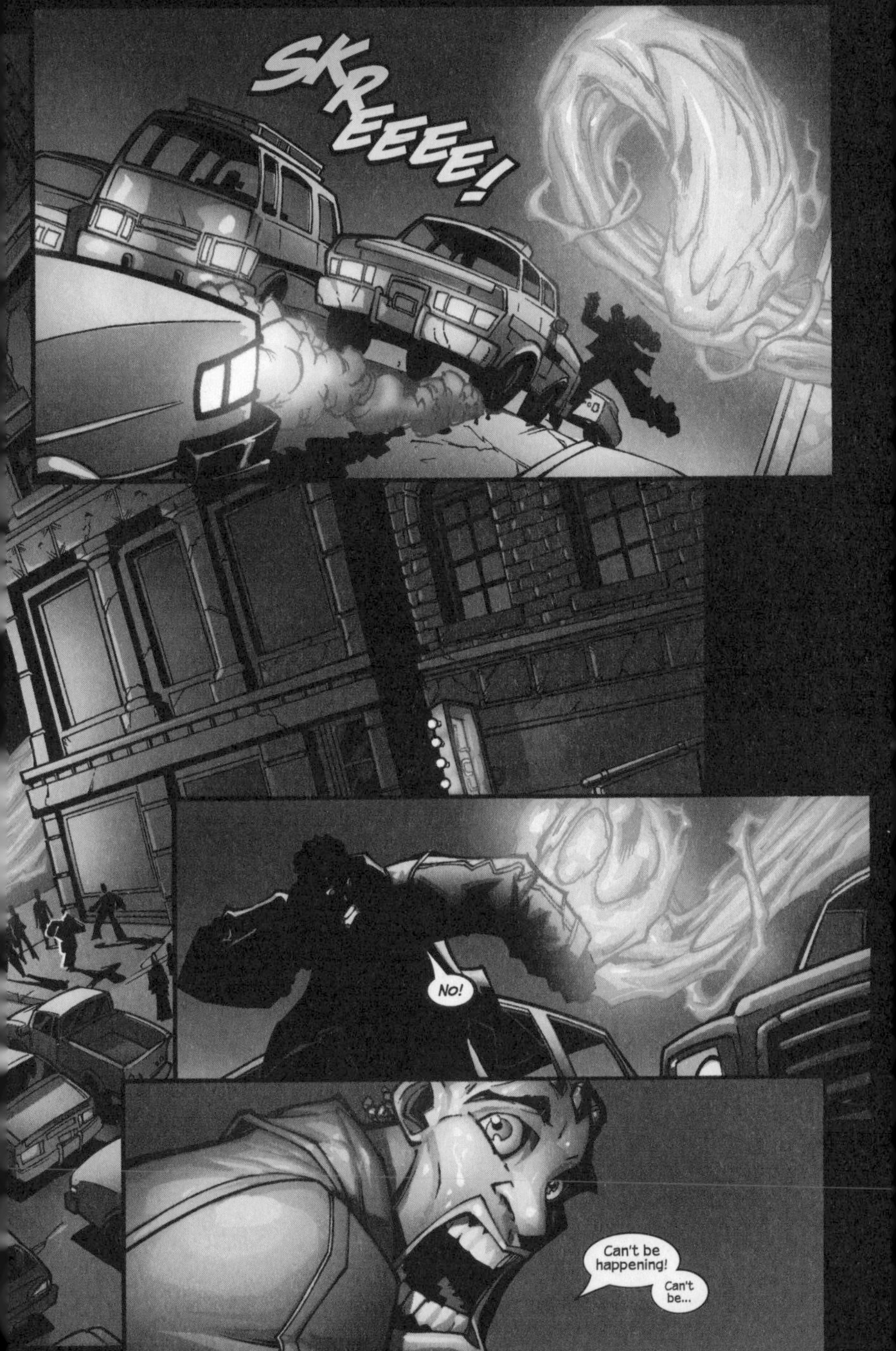

SKREEEEE!
No!
Can't be happening!
Can't be...

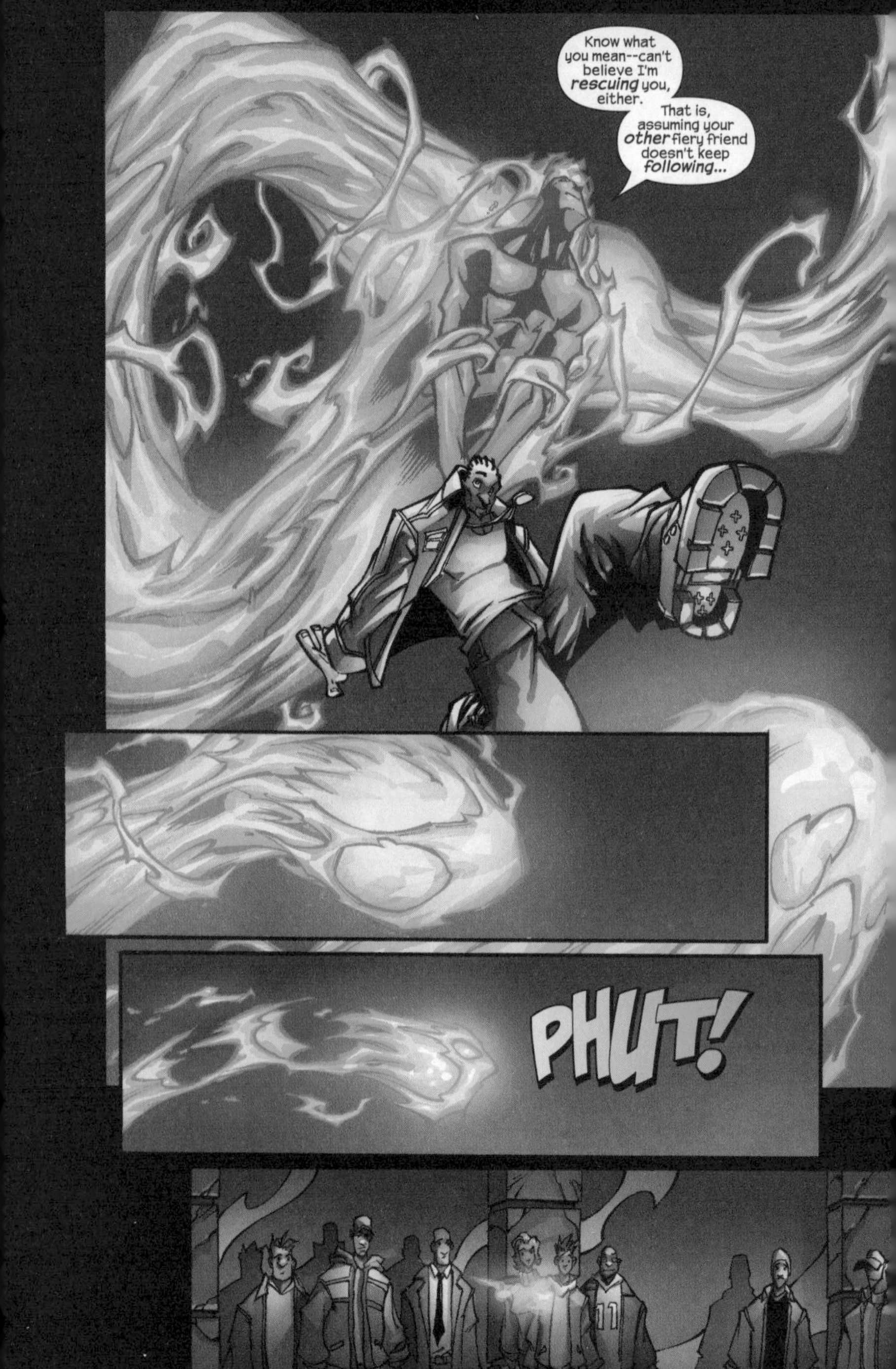
Know what you mean--can't believe I'm *rescuing* you, either.
That is, assuming your *other* fiery friend doesn't keep *following*...
PHUT!

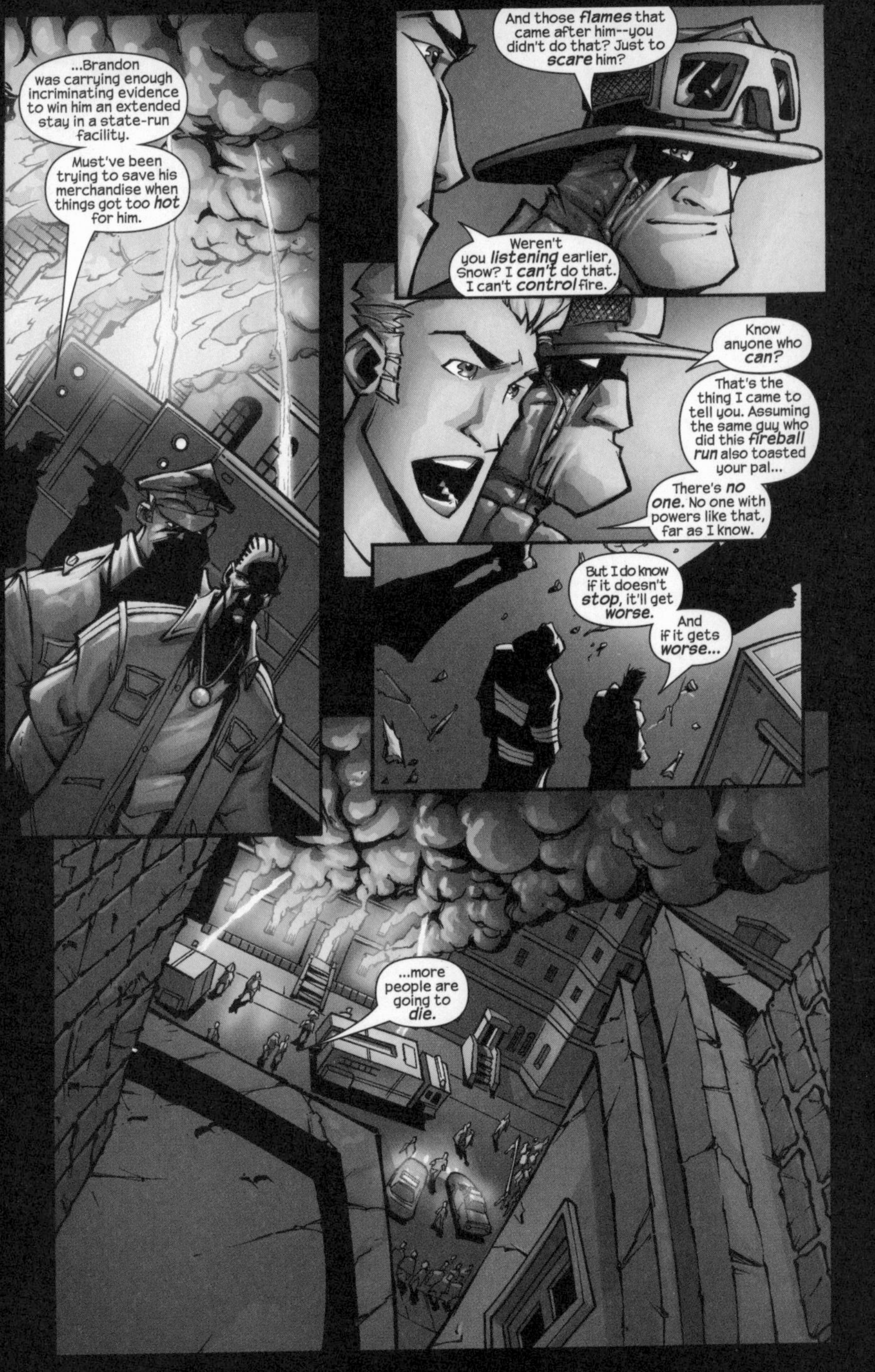
...Brandon was carrying enough incriminating evidence to win him an extended stay in a state-run facility.
Must've been trying to save his merchandise when things got too *hot* for him.
And those *flames* that came after him--you didn't do that? Just to *scare* him?
Weren't you *listening* earlier, Snow? I *can't* do that. I can't *control* fire.
Know anyone who *can?*
That's the thing I came to tell you. Assuming the same guy who did this *fireball run* also toasted your pal...
There's *no one.* No one with powers like that, far as I know.
But I do know if it doesn't *stop,* it'll get *worse.*
And if it gets *worse...*
...more people are going to *die.*

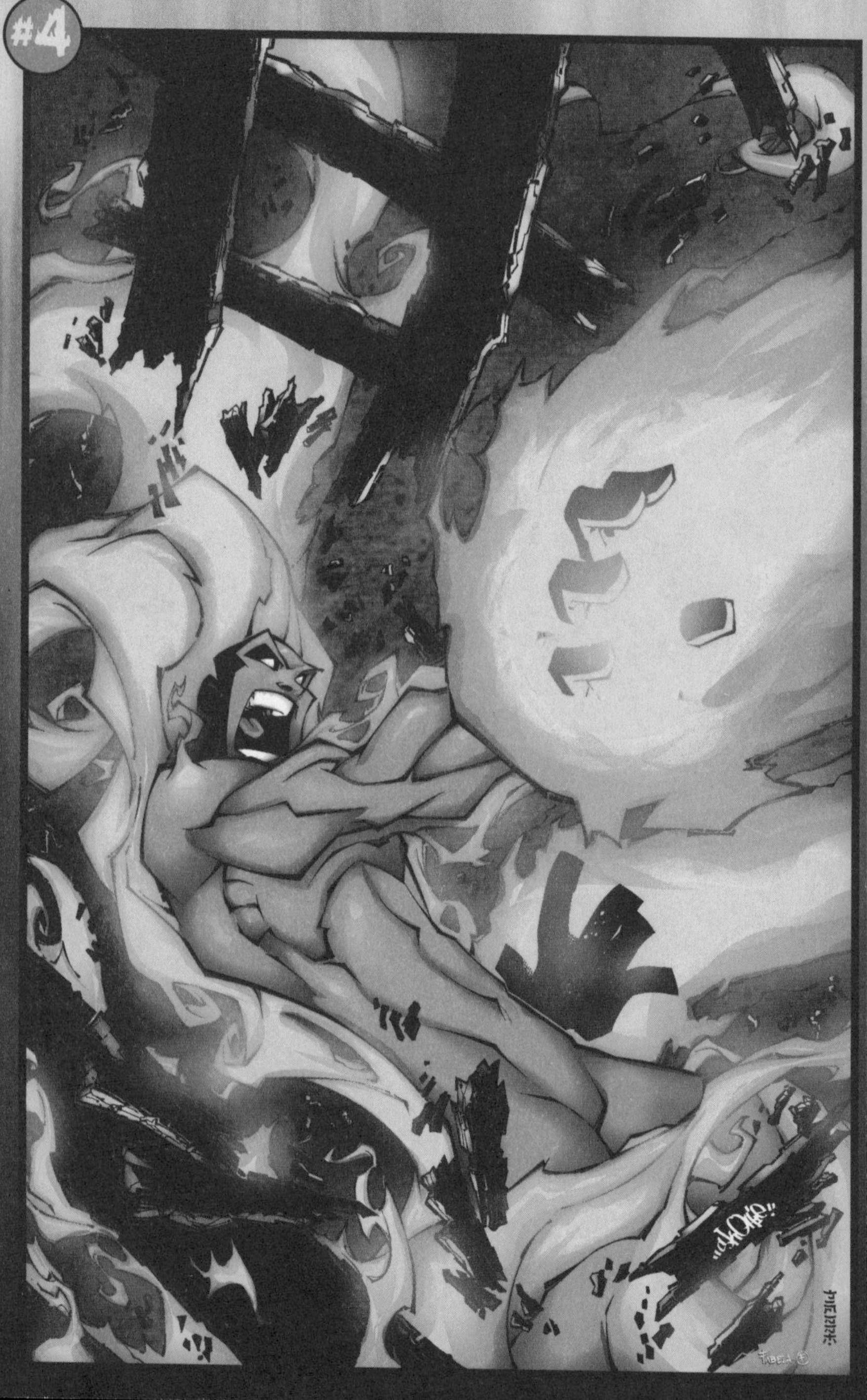
#4

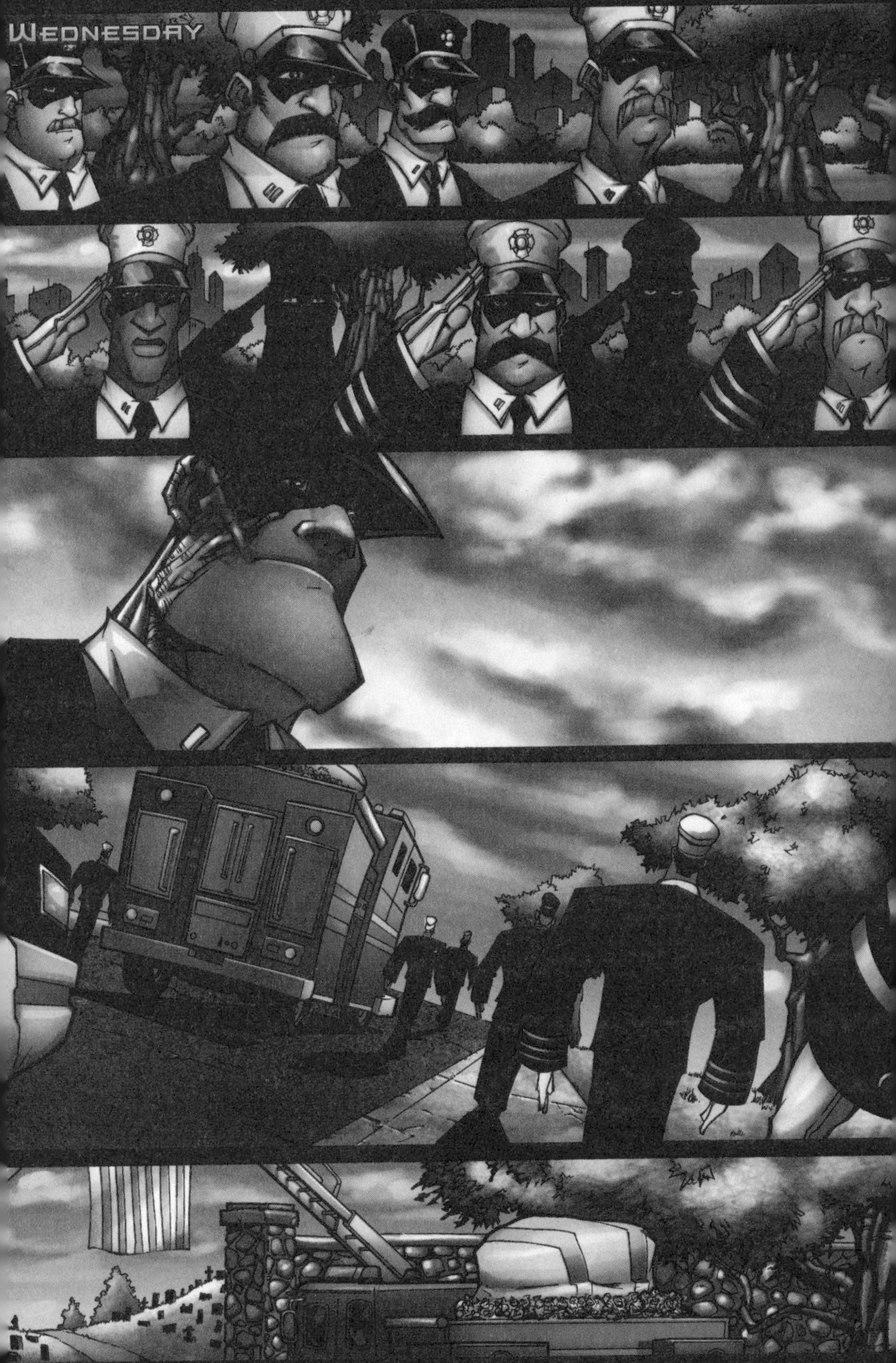
WEDNESDAY

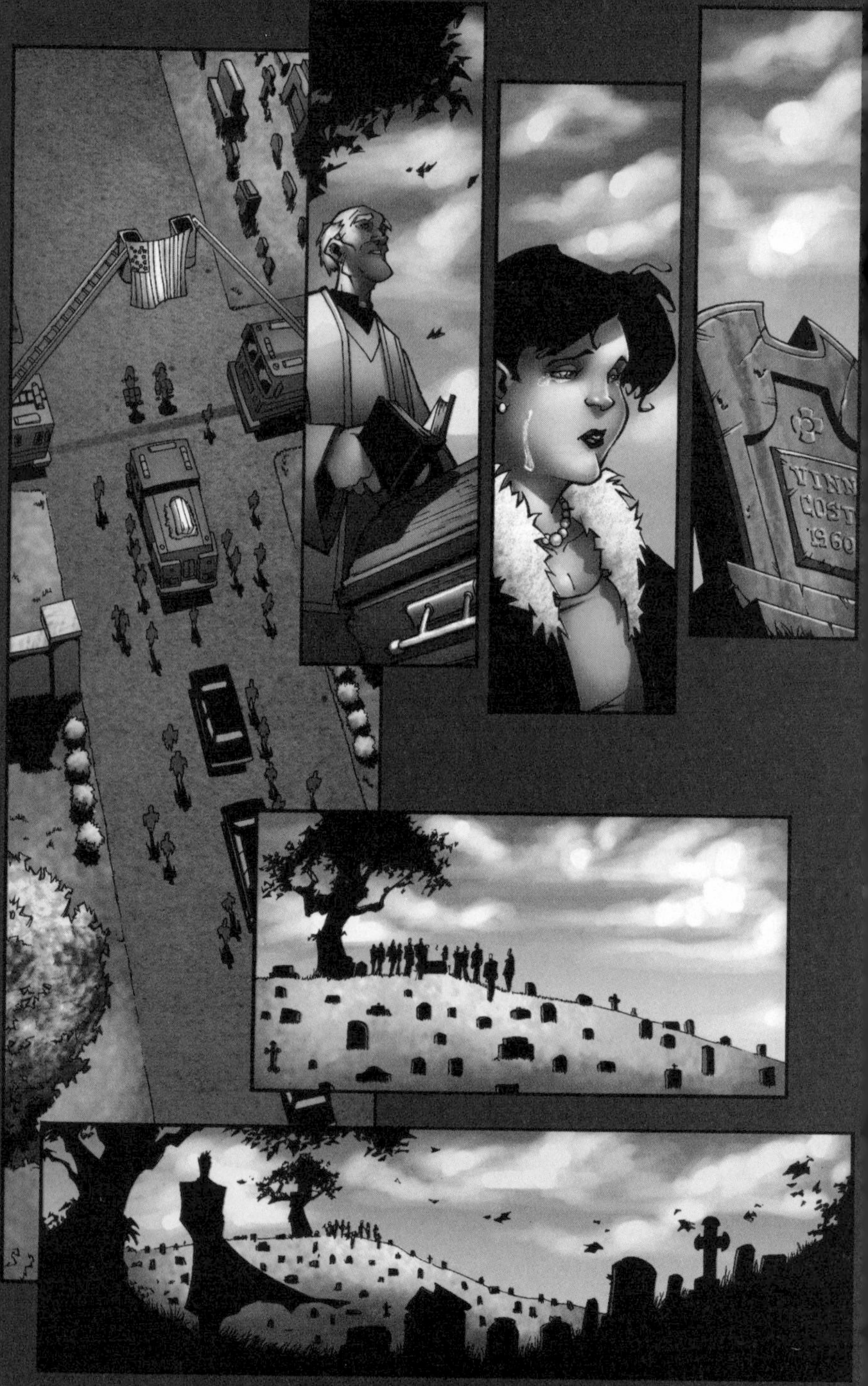
VINN
COST
1960

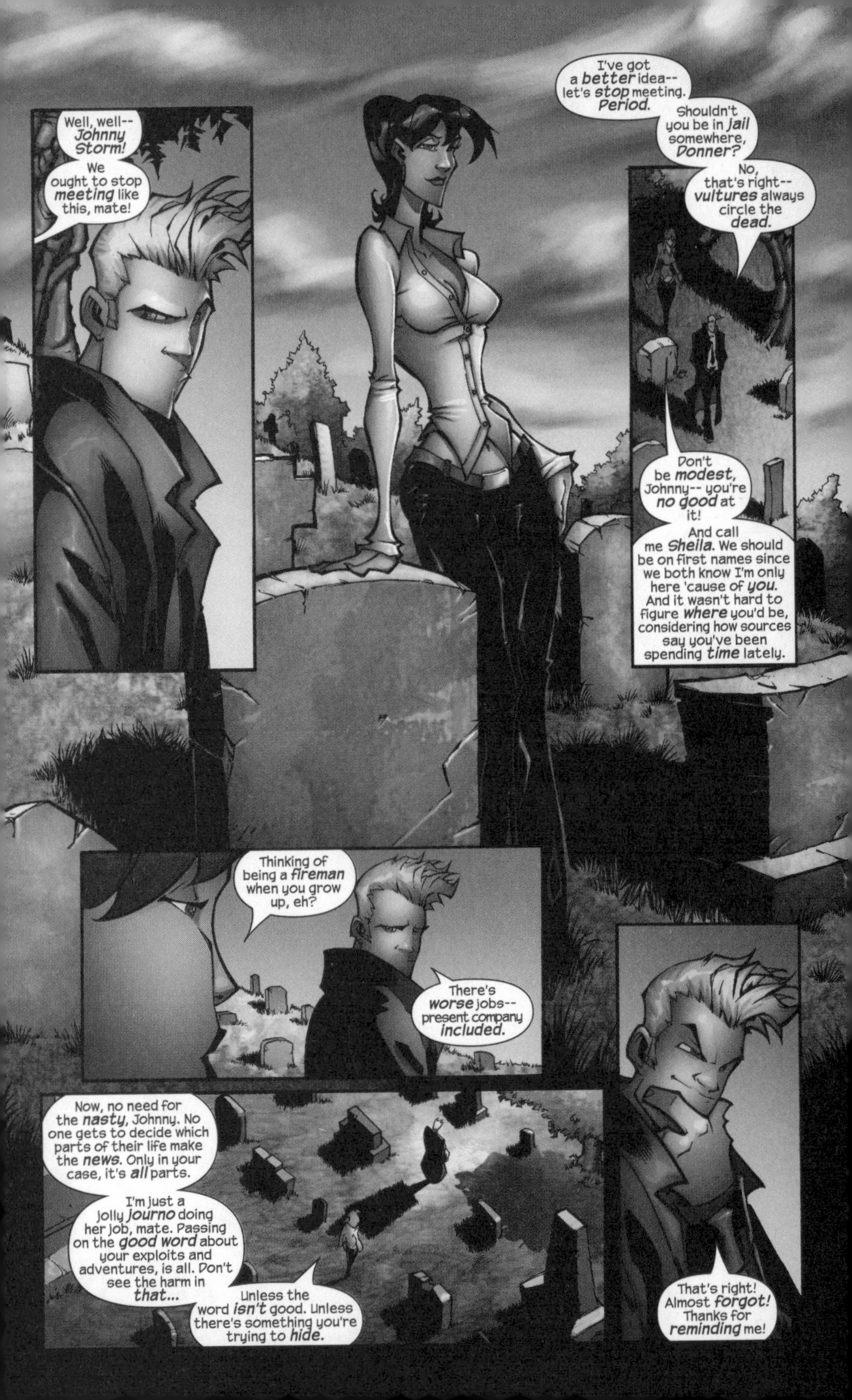
Well, well-- Johnny Storm!
We ought to stop meeting like this, mate!
I've got a better idea-- let's stop meeting. Period.
Shouldn't you be in jail somewhere, Donner?
No, that's right-- vultures always circle the dead.
Don't be modest, Johnny-- you're no good at it!
And call me Sheila. We should be on first names since we both know I'm only here 'cause of you. And it wasn't hard to figure where you'd be, considering how sources say you've been spending time lately.
Thinking of being a fireman when you grow up, eh?
There's worse jobs-- present company included.
Now, no need for the nasty, Johnny. No one gets to decide which parts of their life make the news. Only in your case, it's all parts.
I'm just a jolly journo doing her job, mate. Passing on the good word about your exploits and adventures, is all. Don't see the harm in that...
Unless the word isn't good. Unless there's something you're trying to hide.
That's right! Almost forgot! Thanks for reminding me!

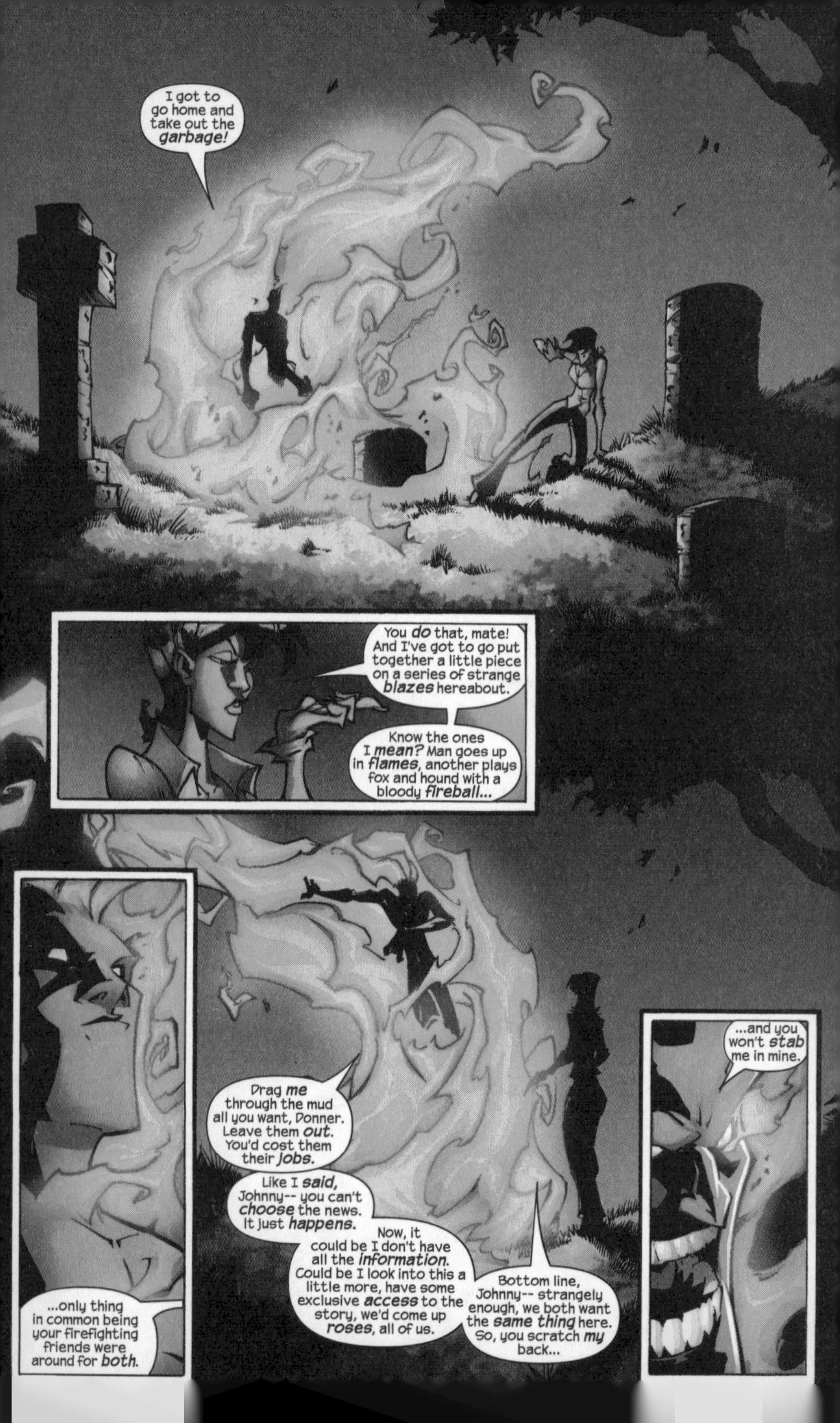
I got to go home and take out the garbage!
You do that, mate! And I've got to go put together a little piece on a series of strange blazes hereabout.
Know the ones I mean? Man goes up in flames, another plays fox and hound with a bloody fireball...
...only thing in common being your firefighting friends were around for both.
Drag me through the mud all you want, Donner. Leave them out. You'd cost them their jobs.
Like I said, Johnny-- you can't choose the news. It just happens.
Now, it could be I don't have all the information. Could be I look into this a little more, have some exclusive access to the story, we'd come up roses, all of us.
Bottom line, Johnny-- strangely enough, we both want the same thing here. So, you scratch my back...
...and you won't stab me in mine.

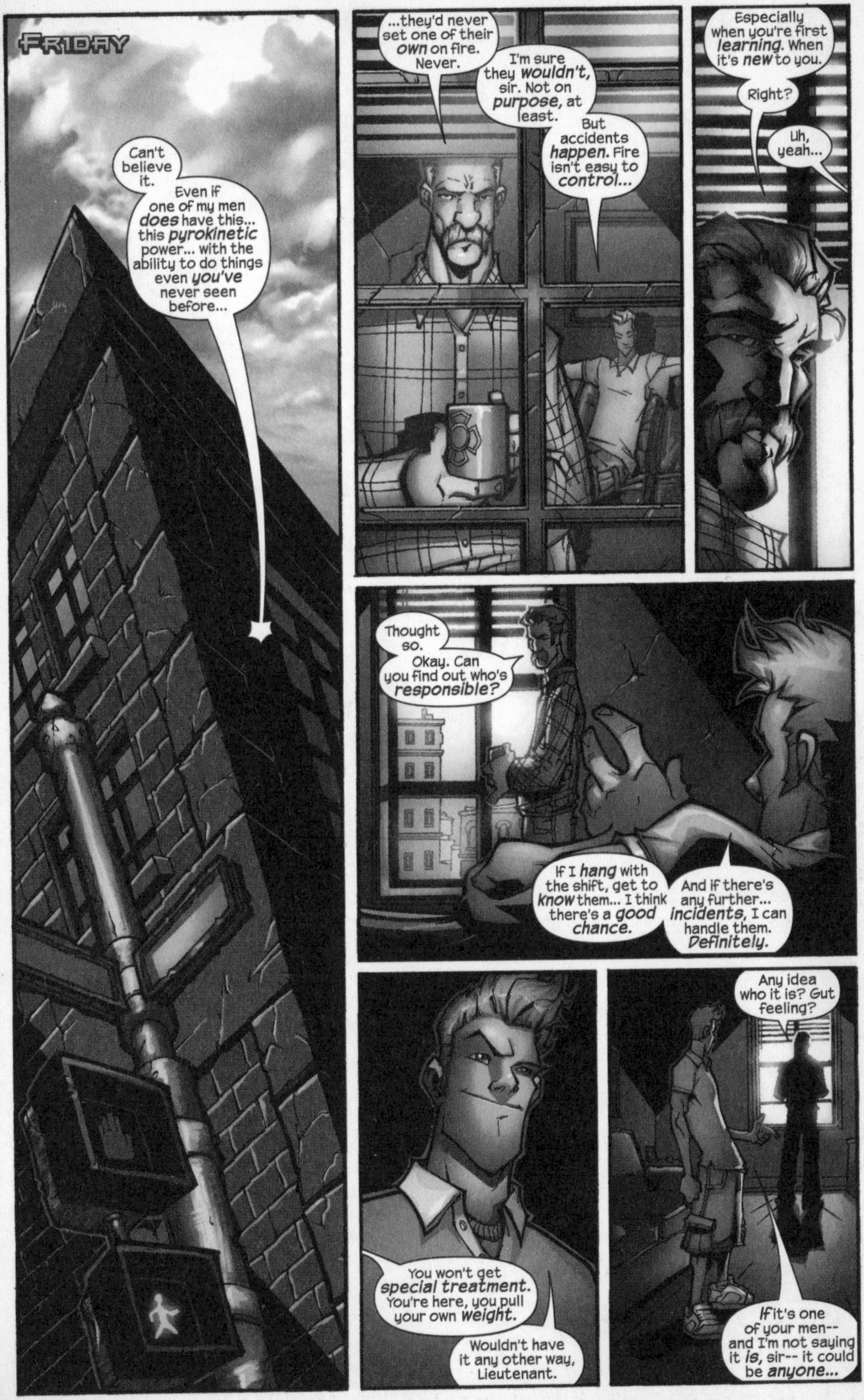
FRIDAY
Can't believe it.
Even if one of my men does have this... this pyrokinetic power... with the ability to do things even you've never seen before...
...they'd never set one of their own on fire. Never.
I'm sure they wouldn't, sir. Not on purpose, at least.
But accidents happen. Fire isn't easy to control...
Especially when you're first learning. When it's new to you.
Right?
Uh, yeah...
Thought so.
Okay. Can you find out who's responsible?
If I hang with the shift, get to know them... I think there's a good chance.
And if there's any further... incidents, I can handle them. Definitely.
You won't get special treatment. You're here, you pull your own weight.
Wouldn't have it any other way, Lieutenant.
Any idea who it is? Gut feeling?
If it's one of your men-- and I'm not saying it is, sir-- it could be anyone...

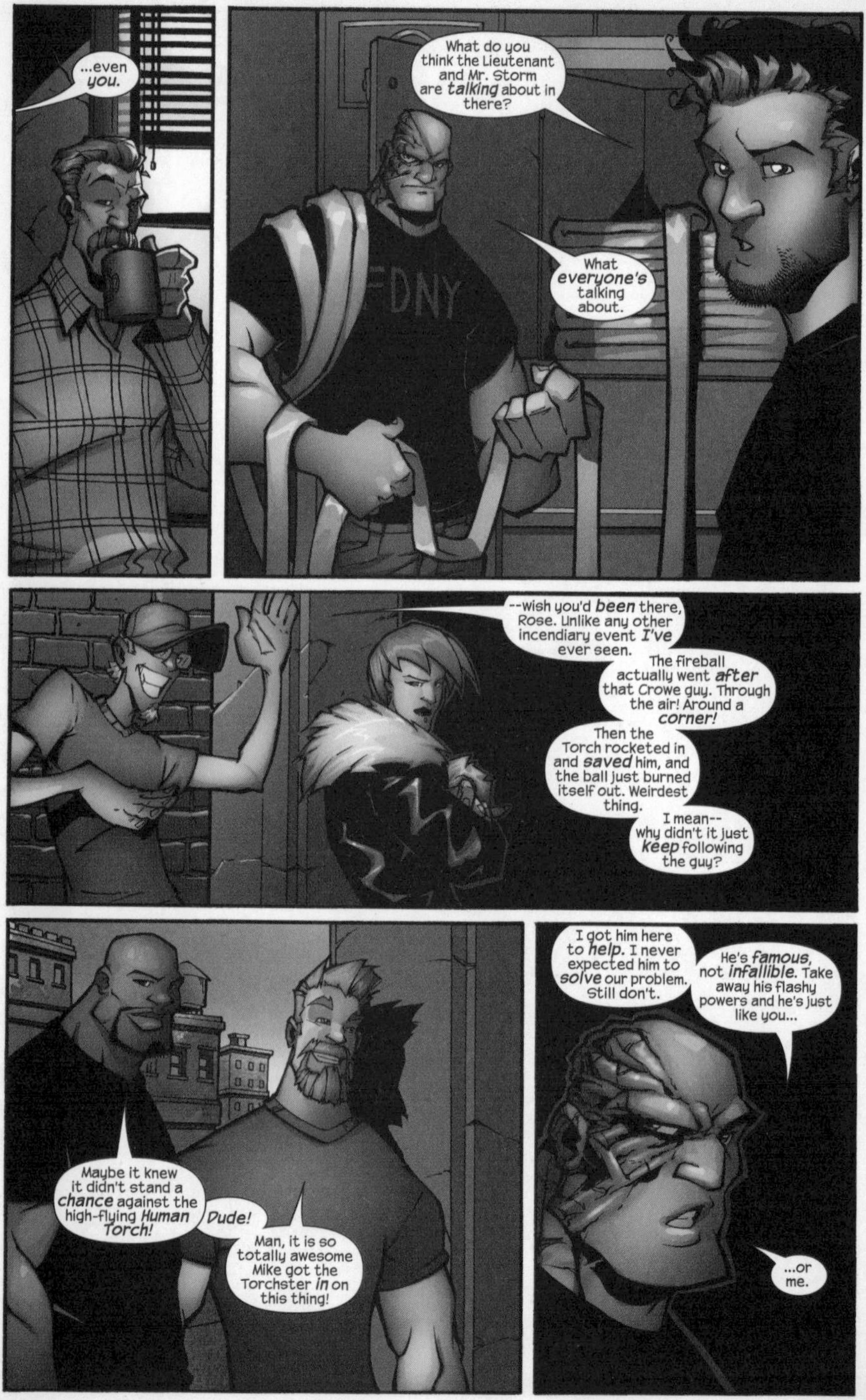
...even *you.*
What do you think the Lieutenant and Mr. Storm are *talking* about in there?
What *everyone's* talking about.
--wish you'd *been* there, Rose. Unlike any other incendiary event *I've* ever seen.
The fireball actually went *after* that Crowe guy. Through the air! Around a *corner!*
Then the Torch rocketed in and *saved* him, and the ball just burned itself out. Weirdest thing.
I mean-- why didn't it just *keep* following the guy?
Maybe it knew it didn't stand a *chance* against the high-flying *Human Torch!*
Dude!
Man, it is so totally awesome Mike got the Torchster *in* on this thing!
I got him here to *help.* I never expected him to *solve* our problem. Still don't.
He's *famous,* not *infallible.* Take away his flashy powers and he's just like you...
...or me.

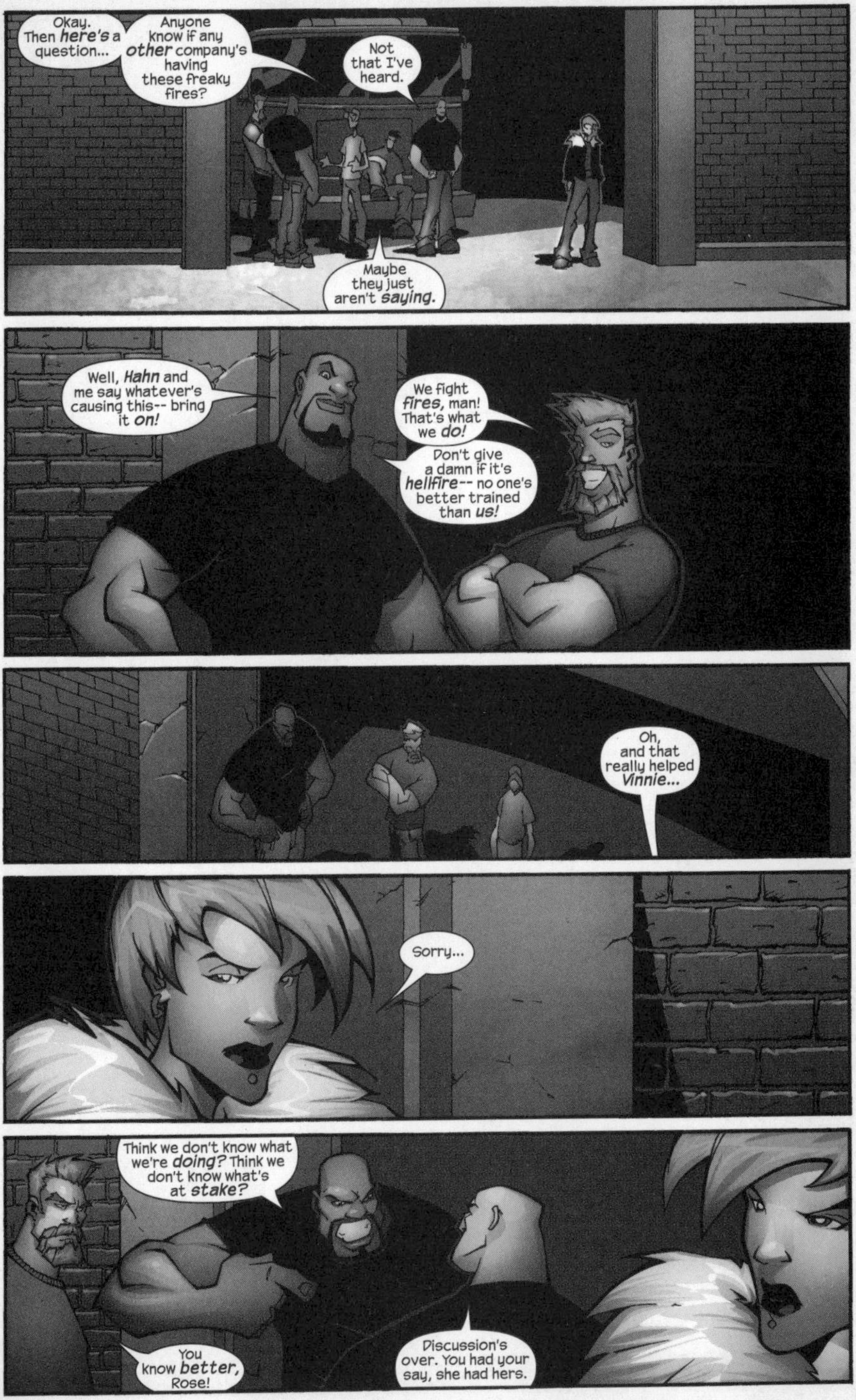

Okay. Then here's a question...
Anyone know if any other company's having these freaky fires?
Not that I've heard.
Maybe they just aren't saying.
Well, Hahn and me say whatever's causing this-- bring it on!
We fight fires, man! That's what we do!
Don't give a damn if it's hellfire-- no one's better trained than us!
Oh, and that really helped Vinnie...
Sorry...
Think we don't know what we're doing? Think we don't know what's at stake?
You know better, Rose!
Discussion's over. You had your say, she had hers.

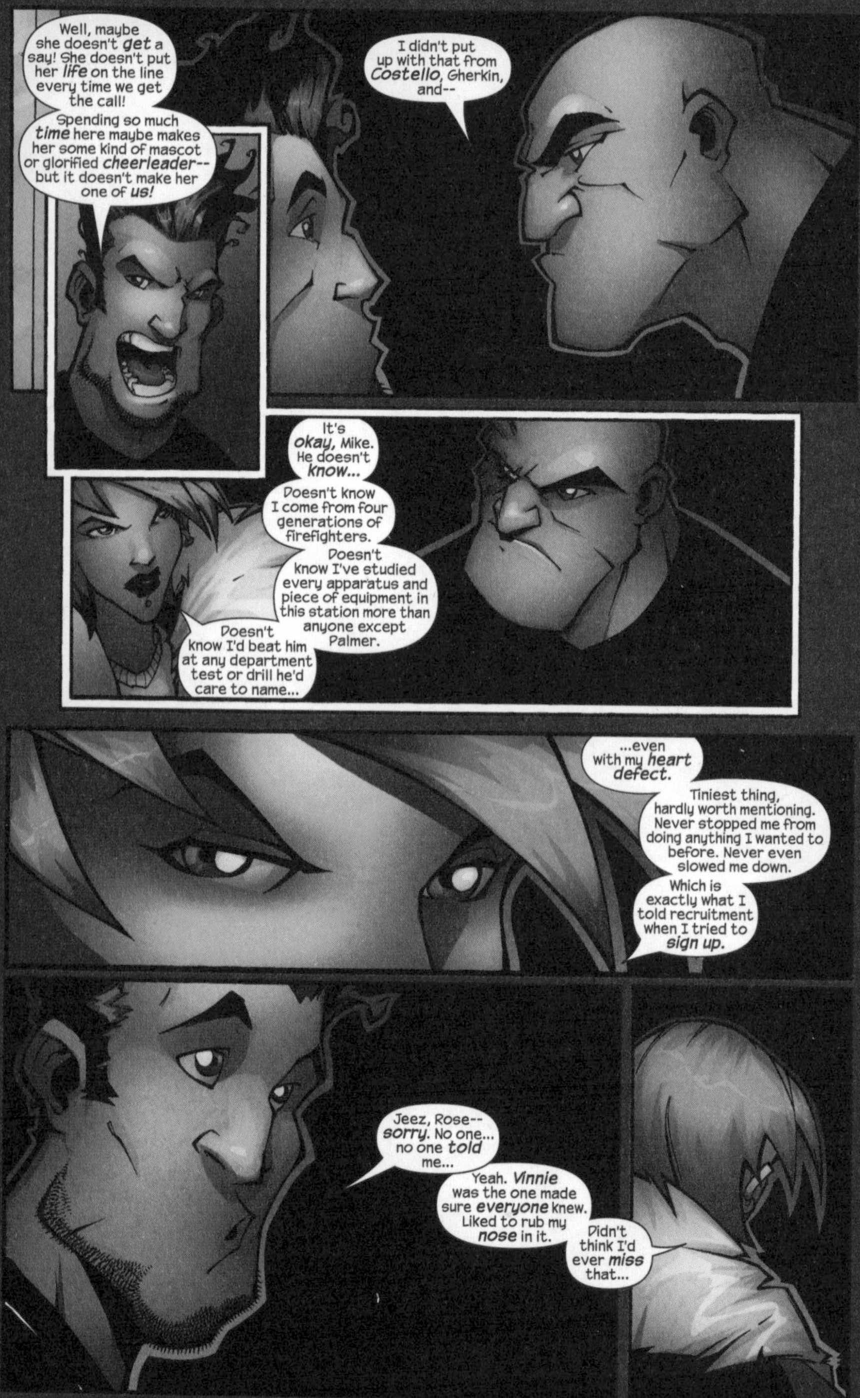
Well, maybe she doesn't get a say! She doesn't put her life on the line every time we get the call!
Spending so much time here maybe makes her some kind of mascot or glorified cheerleader-- but it doesn't make her one of us!
I didn't put up with that from Costello, Gherkin, and--
It's okay, Mike. He doesn't know...
Doesn't know I come from four generations of firefighters.
Doesn't know I've studied every apparatus and piece of equipment in this station more than anyone except Palmer.
Doesn't know I'd beat him at any department test or drill he'd care to name...
...even with my heart defect.
Tiniest thing, hardly worth mentioning. Never stopped me from doing anything I wanted to before. Never even slowed me down.
Which is exactly what I told recruitment when I tried to sign up.
Jeez, Rose-- sorry. No one... no one told me...
Yeah. Vinnie was the one made sure everyone knew. Liked to rub my nose in it.
Didn't think I'd ever miss that...

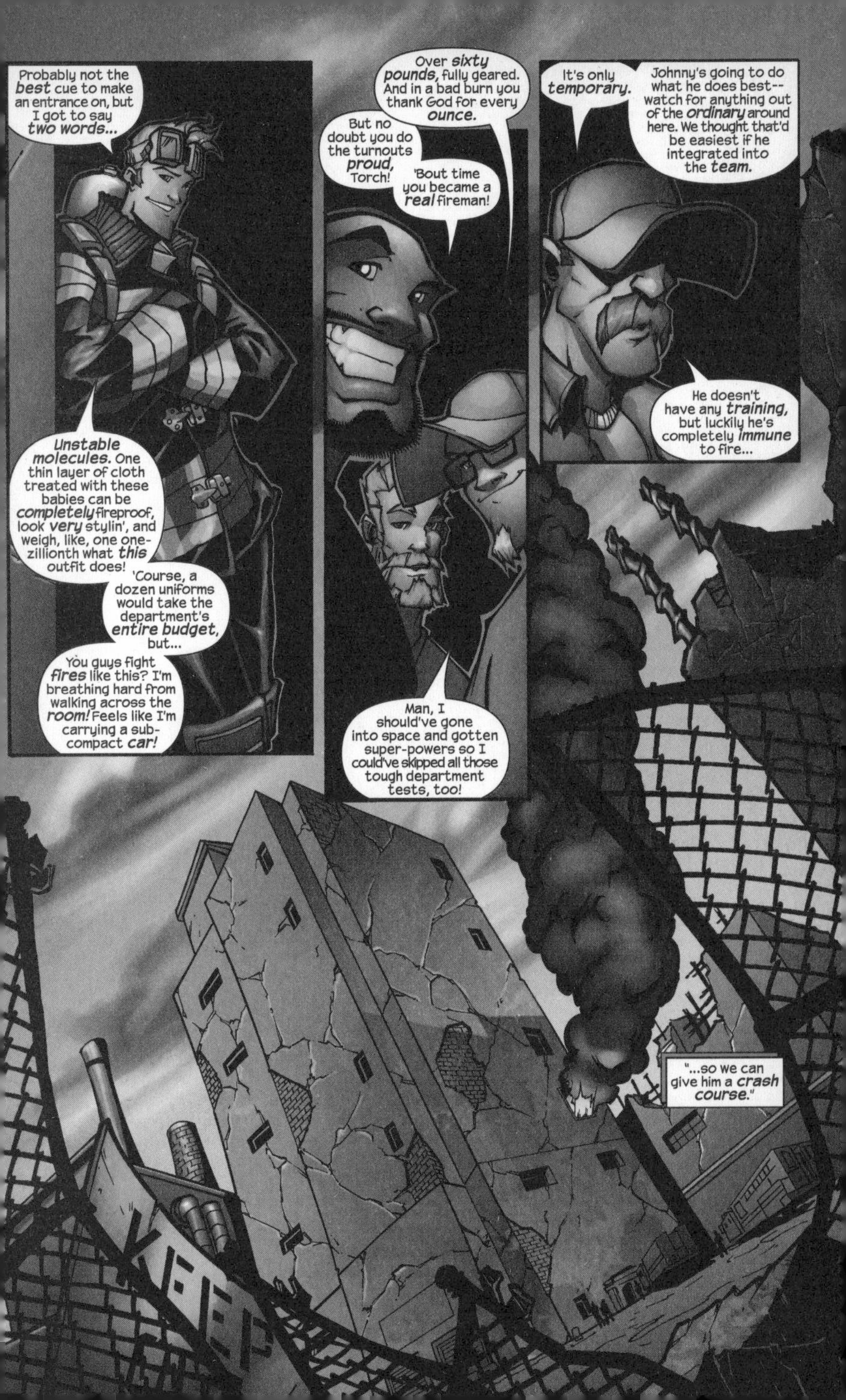
Probably not the best cue to make an entrance on, but I got to say two words...
Unstable molecules. One thin layer of cloth treated with these babies can be completely fireproof, look very stylin', and weigh, like, one one-zillionth what this outfit does!
'Course, a dozen uniforms would take the department's entire budget, but...
You guys fight fires like this? I'm breathing hard from walking across the room! Feels like I'm carrying a sub-compact car!
Over sixty pounds, fully geared. And in a bad burn you thank God for every ounce.
But no doubt you do the turnouts proud, Torch!
'Bout time you became a real fireman!
Man, I should've gone into space and gotten super-powers so I could've skipped all those tough department tests, too!
It's only temporary.
Johnny's going to do what he does best--watch for anything out of the ordinary around here. We thought that'd be easiest if he integrated into the team.
He doesn't have any training, but luckily he's completely immune to fire...
"...so we can give him a crash course."

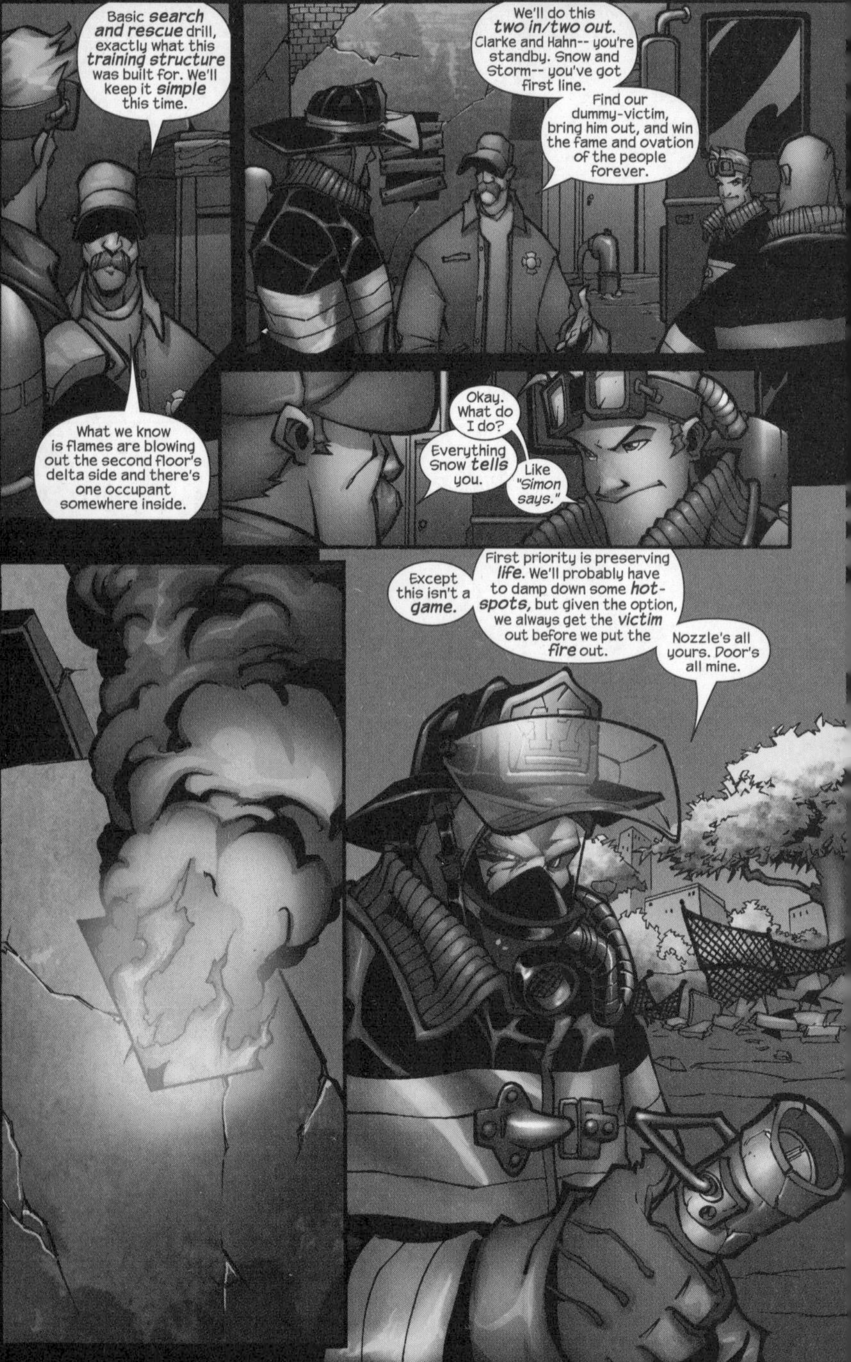
Basic search and rescue drill, exactly what this training structure was built for. We'll keep it simple this time.
We'll do this two in/two out. Clarke and Hahn-- you're standby. Snow and Storm-- you've got first line.
Find our dummy-victim, bring him out, and win the fame and ovation of the people forever.
What we know is flames are blowing out the second floor's delta side and there's one occupant somewhere inside.
Okay. What do I do?
Everything Snow tells you.
Like "Simon says."
Except this isn't a game.
First priority is preserving life. We'll probably have to damp down some hot-spots, but given the option, we always get the victim out before we put the fire out.
Nozzle's all yours. Door's all mine.

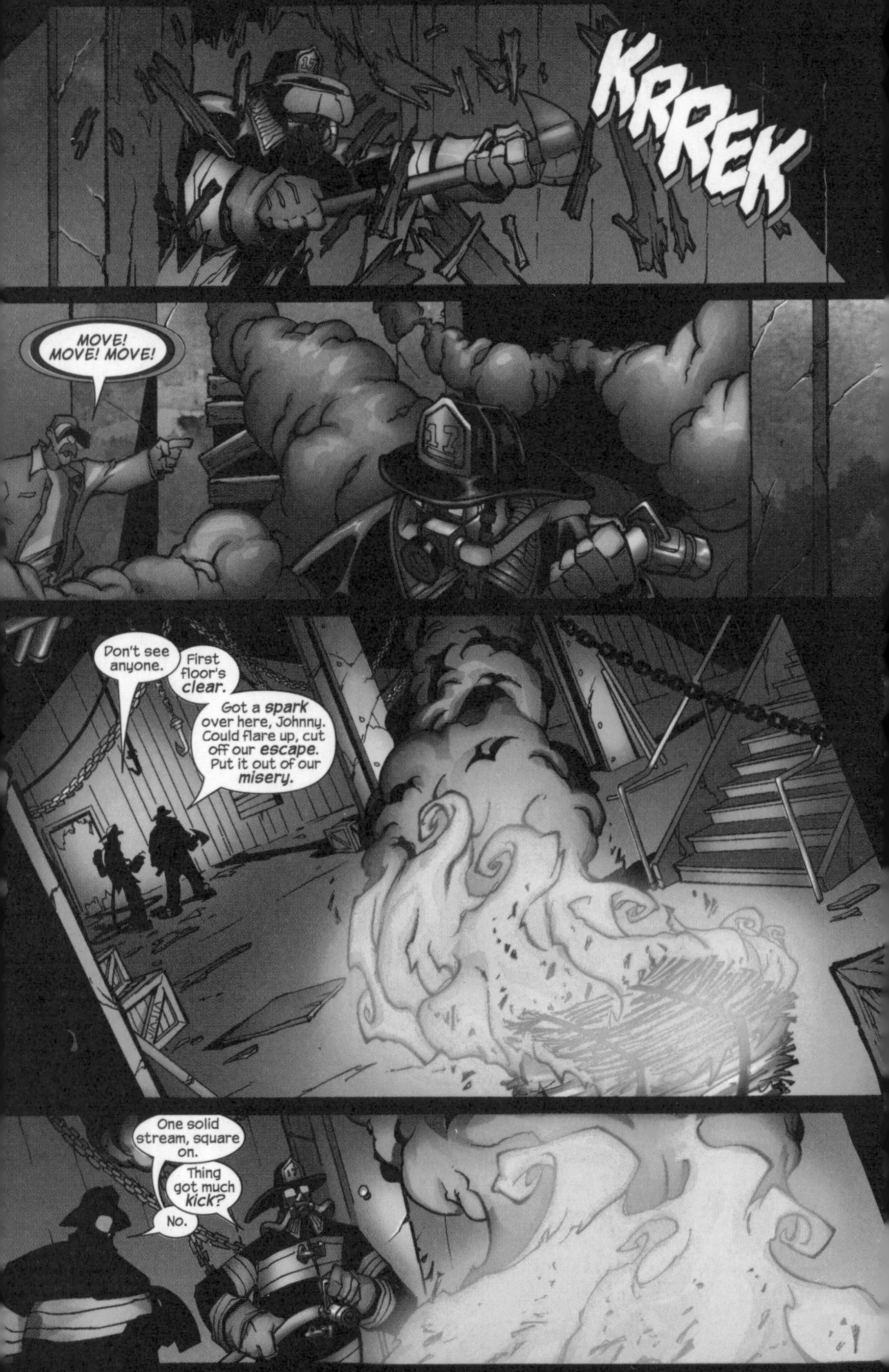
KRREK
MOVE! MOVE! MOVE!
Don't see anyone.
First floor's clear.
Got a spark over here, Johnny. Could flare up, cut off our escape. Put it out of our misery.
One solid stream, square on.
Thing got much kick?
No.

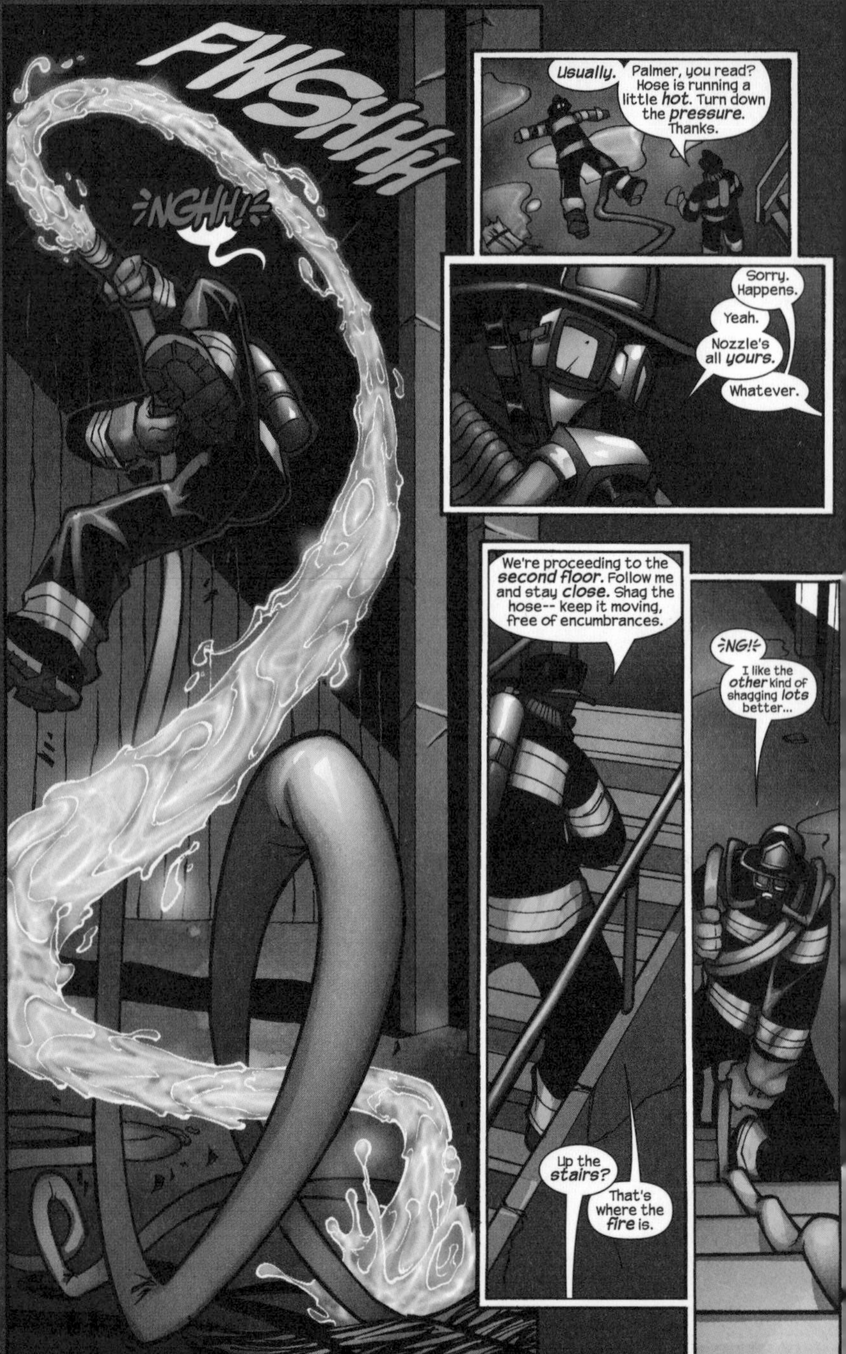
FWSHHH
NGHH!
Usually.
Palmer, you read? Hose is running a little hot. Turn down the pressure. Thanks.
Sorry. Happens.
Yeah.
Nozzle's all yours.
Whatever.
We're proceeding to the second floor. Follow me and stay close. Shag the hose-- keep it moving, free of encumbrances.
NG!
I like the other kind of shagging lots better...
Up the stairs?
That's where the fire is.

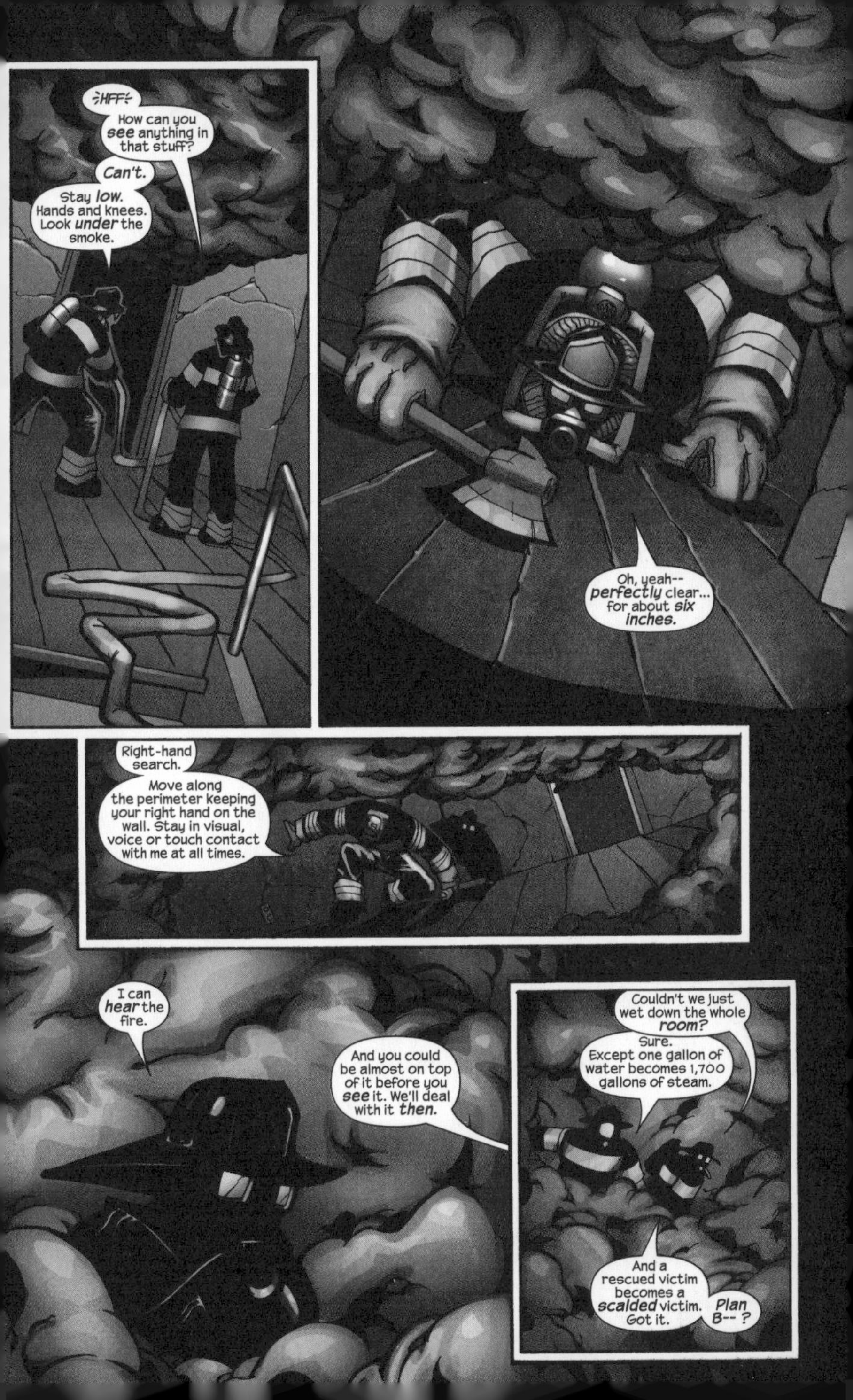

HFF
How can you see anything in that stuff?
Can't.
Stay low. Hands and knees. Look under the smoke.
Oh, yeah-- perfectly clear... for about six inches.
Right-hand search.
Move along the perimeter keeping your right hand on the wall. Stay in visual, voice or touch contact with me at all times.
I can hear the fire.
And you could be almost on top of it before you see it. We'll deal with it then.
Couldn't we just wet down the whole room?
Sure. Except one gallon of water becomes 1,700 gallons of steam.
And a rescued victim becomes a scalded victim. Got it.
Plan B-- ?

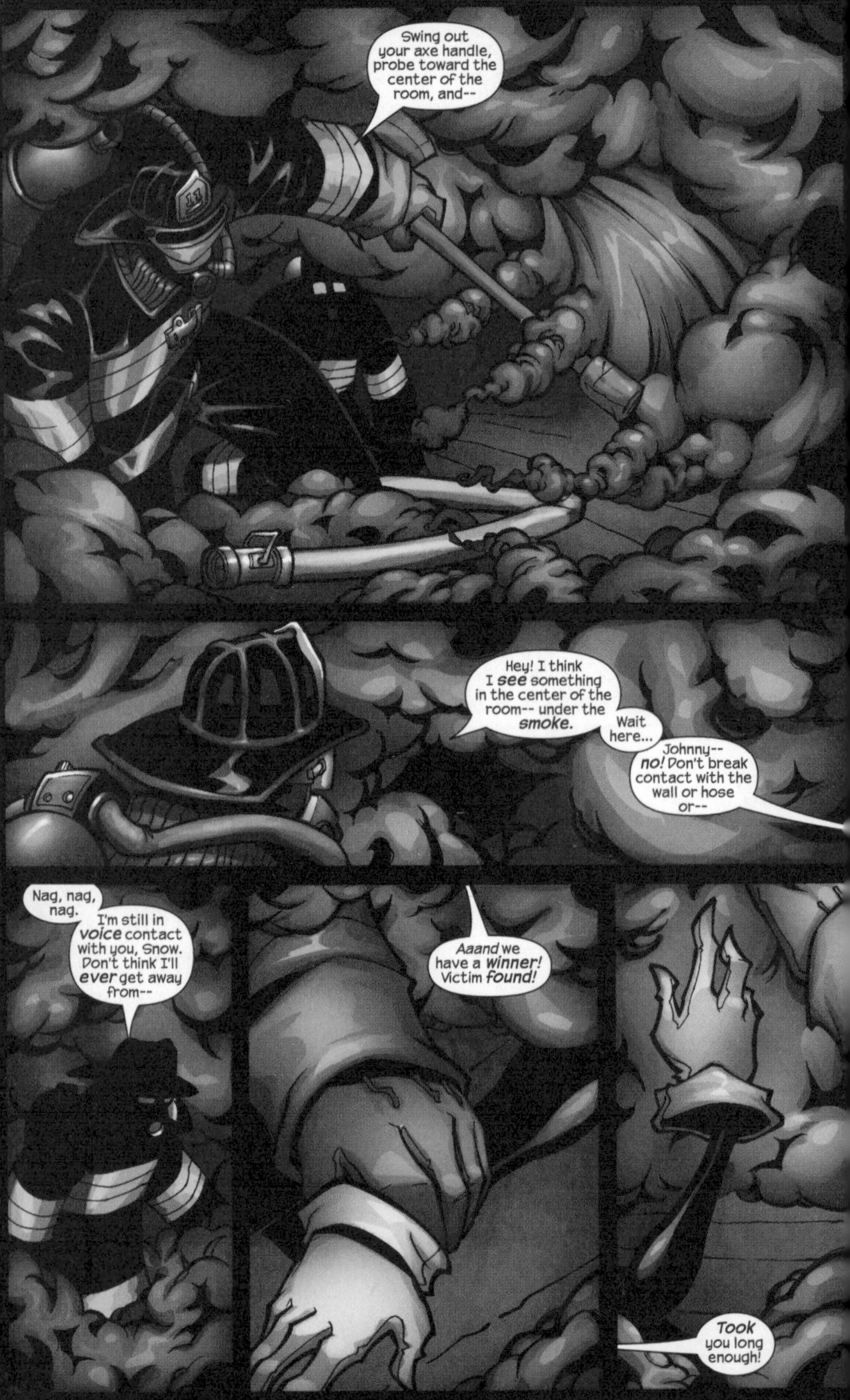
Swing out your axe handle, probe toward the center of the room, and--
Hey! I think I *see* something in the center of the room-- under the *smoke.*
Wait here...
Johnny-- *no!* Don't break contact with the wall or hose or--
Nag, nag, nag.
I'm still in *voice* contact with you, Snow. Don't think I'll *ever* get away from--
Aaand we have a *winner!* Victim *found!*
Took you long enough!

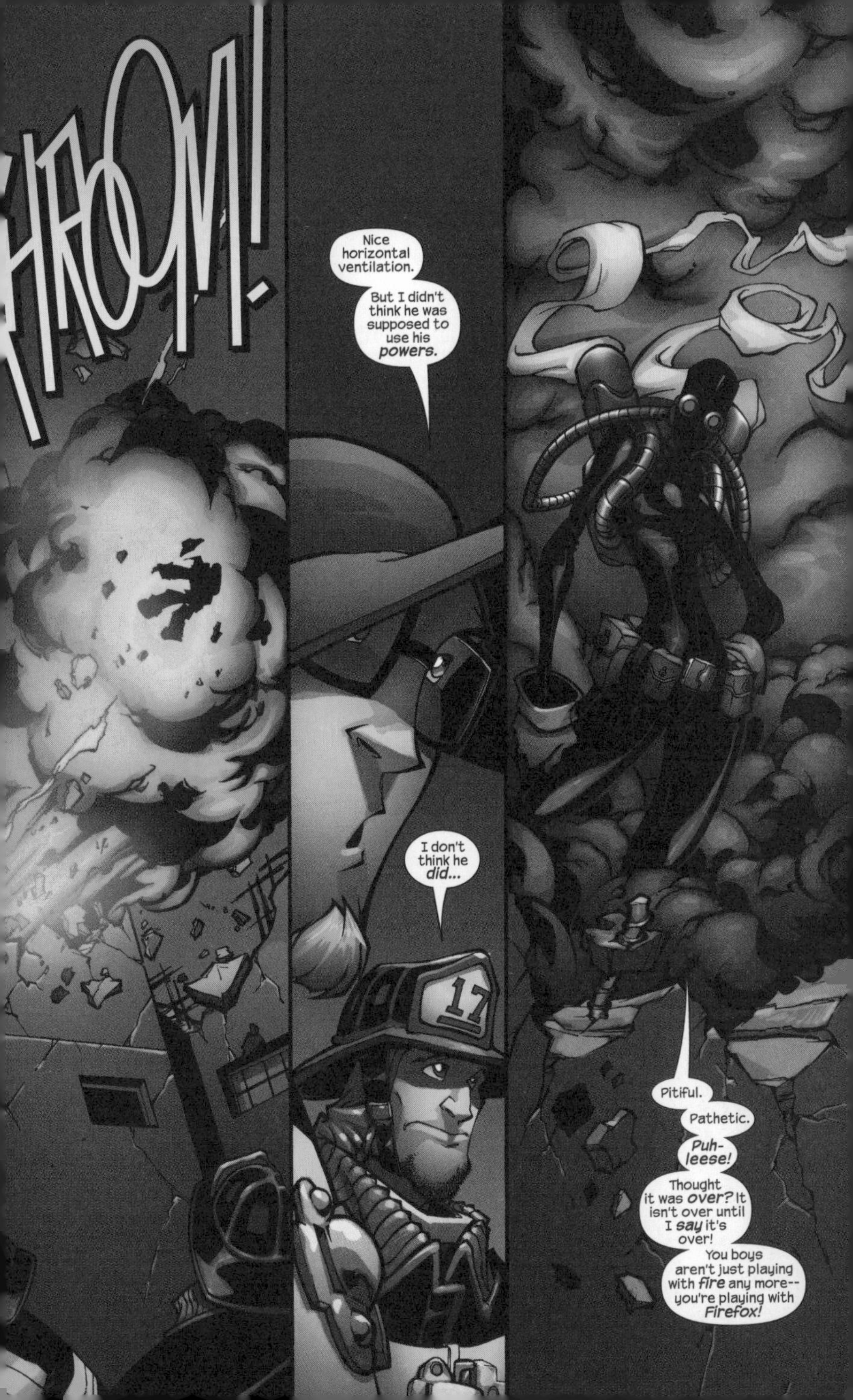
FHROOM!
Nice horizontal ventilation.
But I didn't think he was supposed to use his *powers.*
I don't think he *did...*
17
Pitiful.
Pathetic.
Puh-leese!
Thought it was *over?* It isn't over until I *say* it's over!
You boys aren't just playing with *fire* any more--you're playing with *Firefox!*

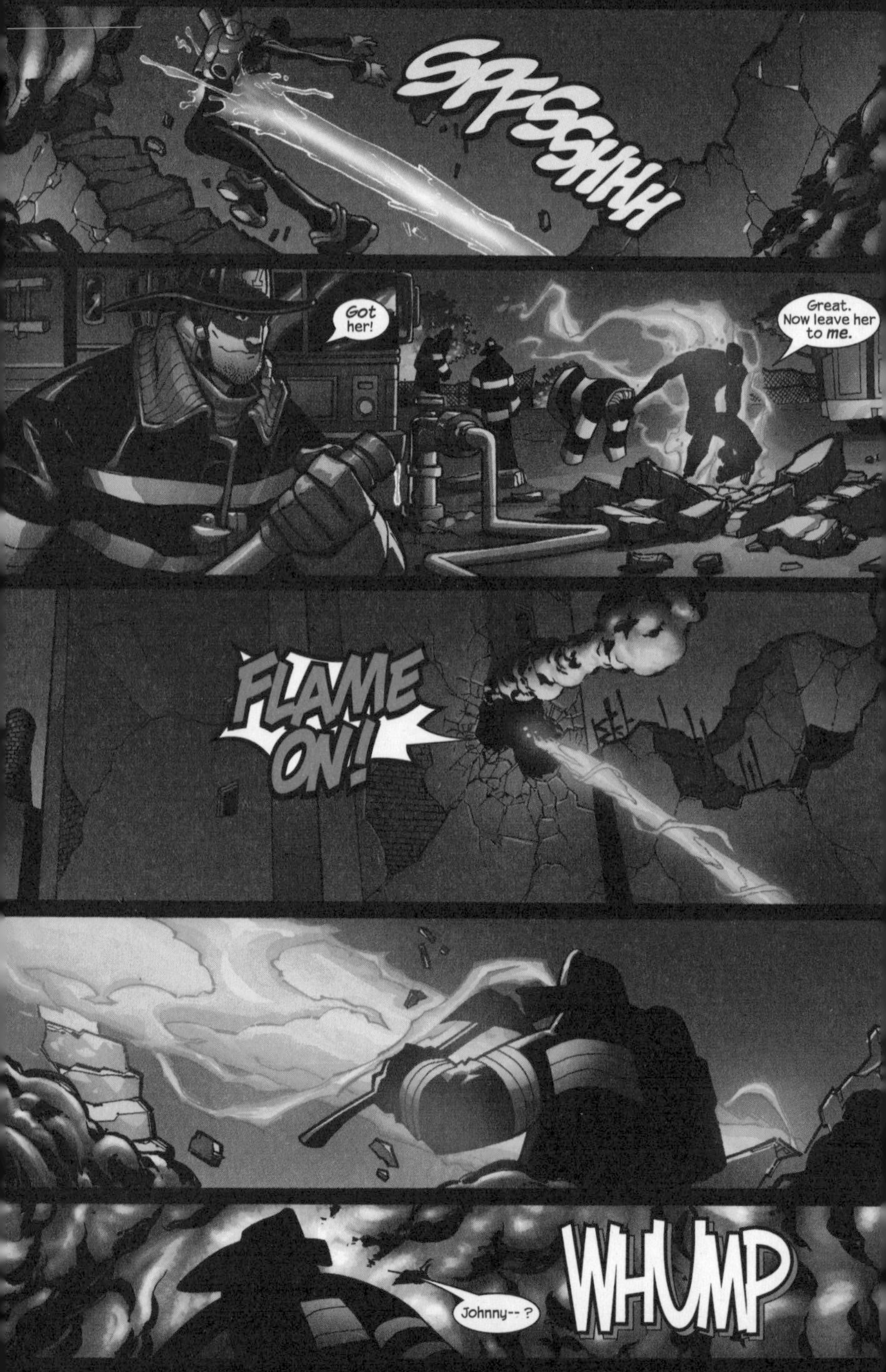
SPFSSHHHH
Got her!
Great. Now leave her to *me*.
FLAME ON!
Johnny-- ?
WHUMP

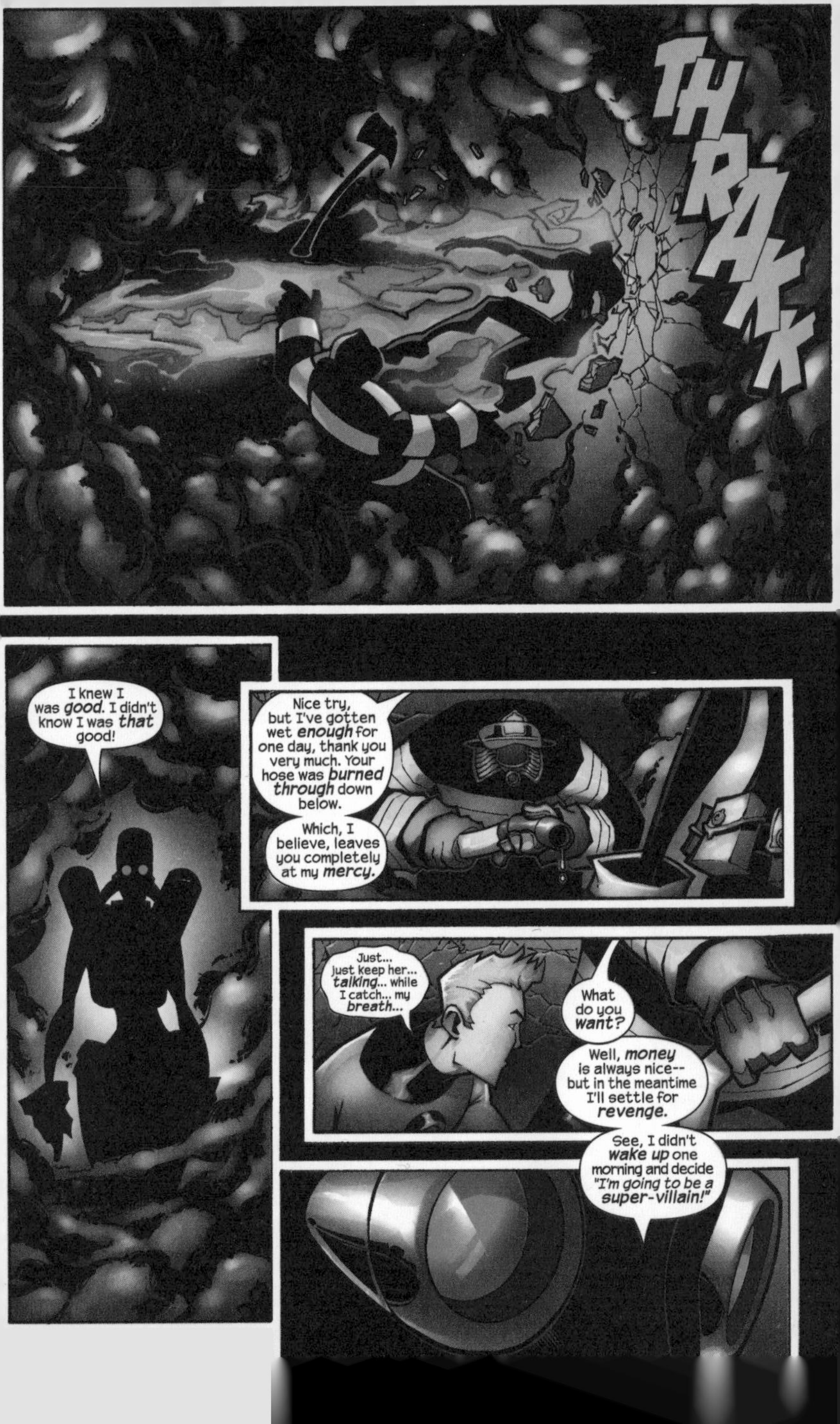
THRAKK
I knew I was good. I didn't know I was that good!
Nice try, but I've gotten wet enough for one day, thank you very much. Your hose was burned through down below.
Which, I believe, leaves you completely at my mercy.
Just... just keep her... talking... while I catch... my breath...
What do you want?
Well, money is always nice-- but in the meantime I'll settle for revenge.
See, I didn't wake up one morning and decide "I'm going to be a super-villain!"

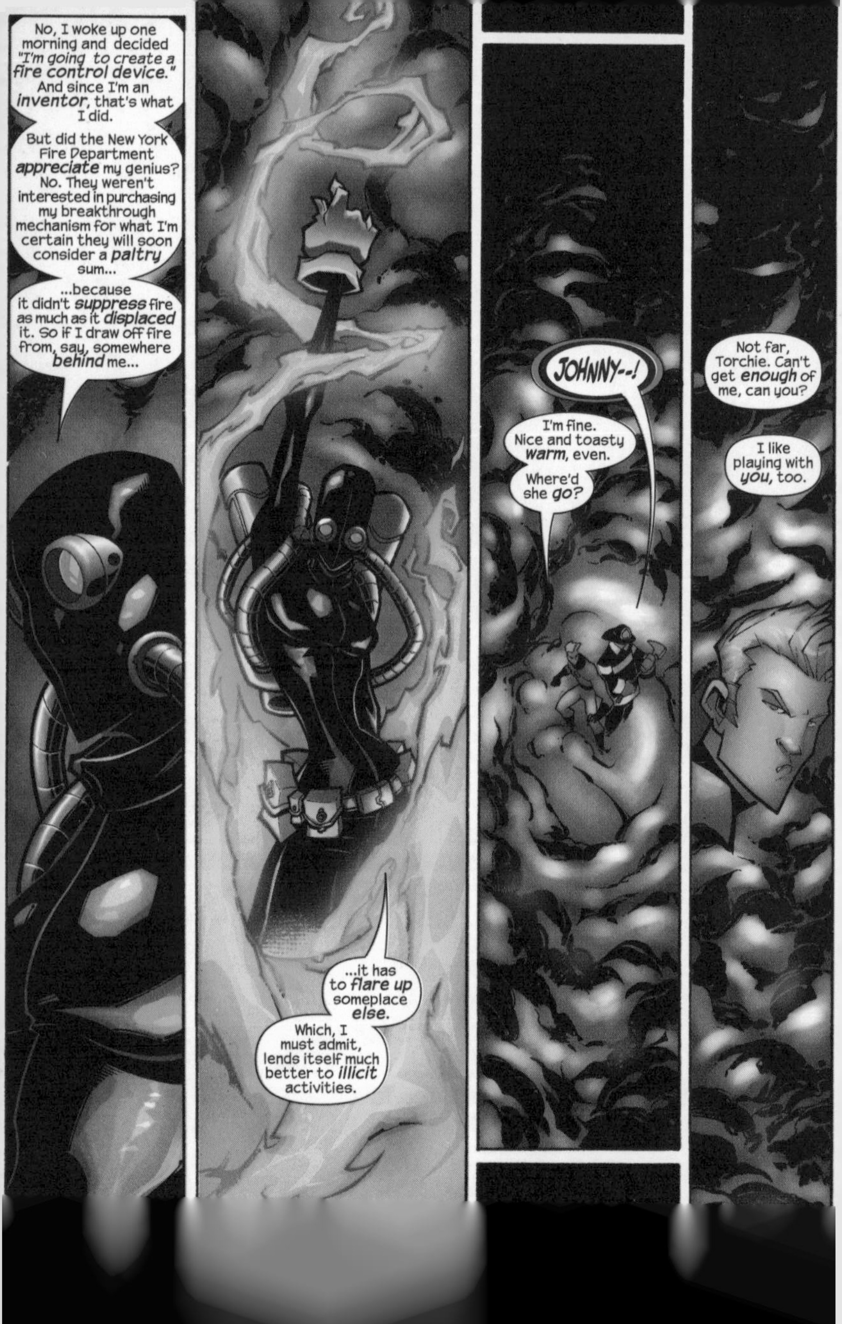
No, I woke up one morning and decided "I'm going to create a fire control device." And since I'm an inventor, that's what I did.
But did the New York Fire Department appreciate my genius? No. They weren't interested in purchasing my breakthrough mechanism for what I'm certain they will soon consider a paltry sum...
...because it didn't suppress fire as much as it displaced it. So if I draw off fire from, say, somewhere behind me...
...it has to flare up someplace else.
Which, I must admit, lends itself much better to illicit activities.
JOHNNY--!
I'm fine. Nice and toasty warm, even.
Where'd she go?
Not far, Torchie. Can't get enough of me, can you?
I like playing with you, too.

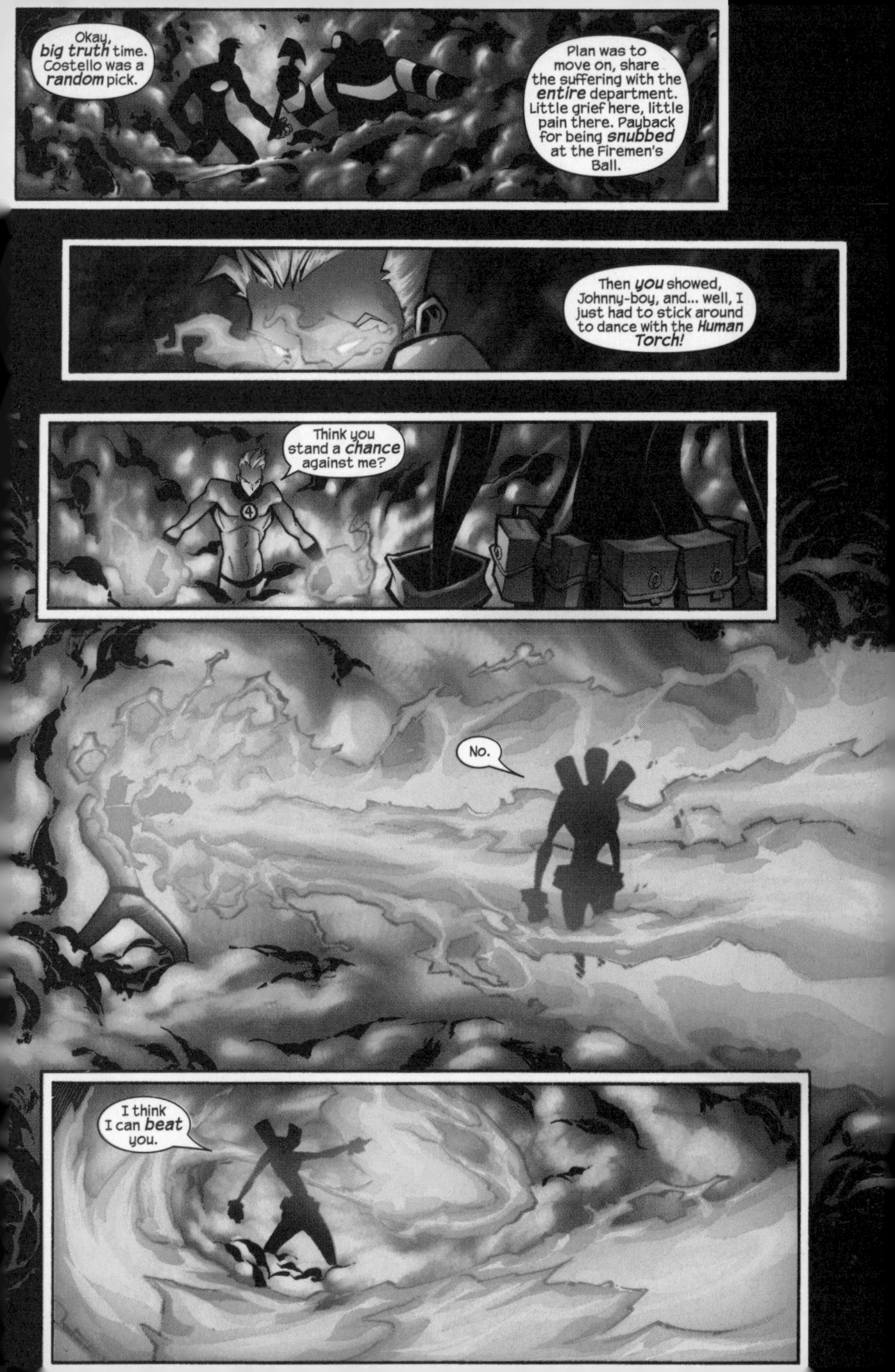
Okay, big truth time. Costello was a random pick.
Plan was to move on, share the suffering with the entire department. Little grief here, little pain there. Payback for being snubbed at the Firemen's Ball.
Then you showed, Johnny-boy, and... well, I just had to stick around to dance with the Human Torch!
Think you stand a chance against me?
No.
I think I can beat you.

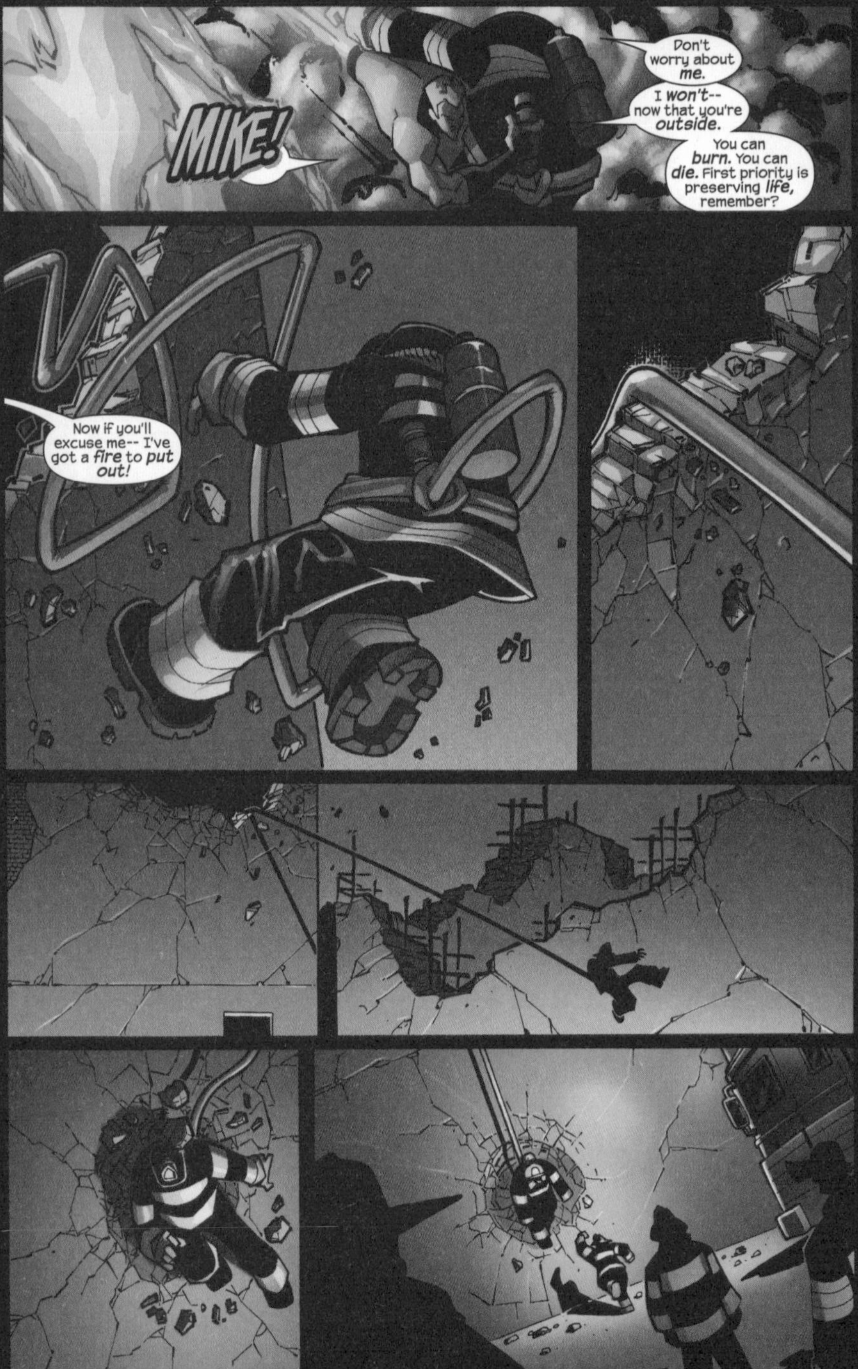
MIKE!
Don't worry about me.
I won't-- now that you're outside.
You can burn. You can die. First priority is preserving life, remember?
Now if you'll excuse me-- I've got a fire to put out!

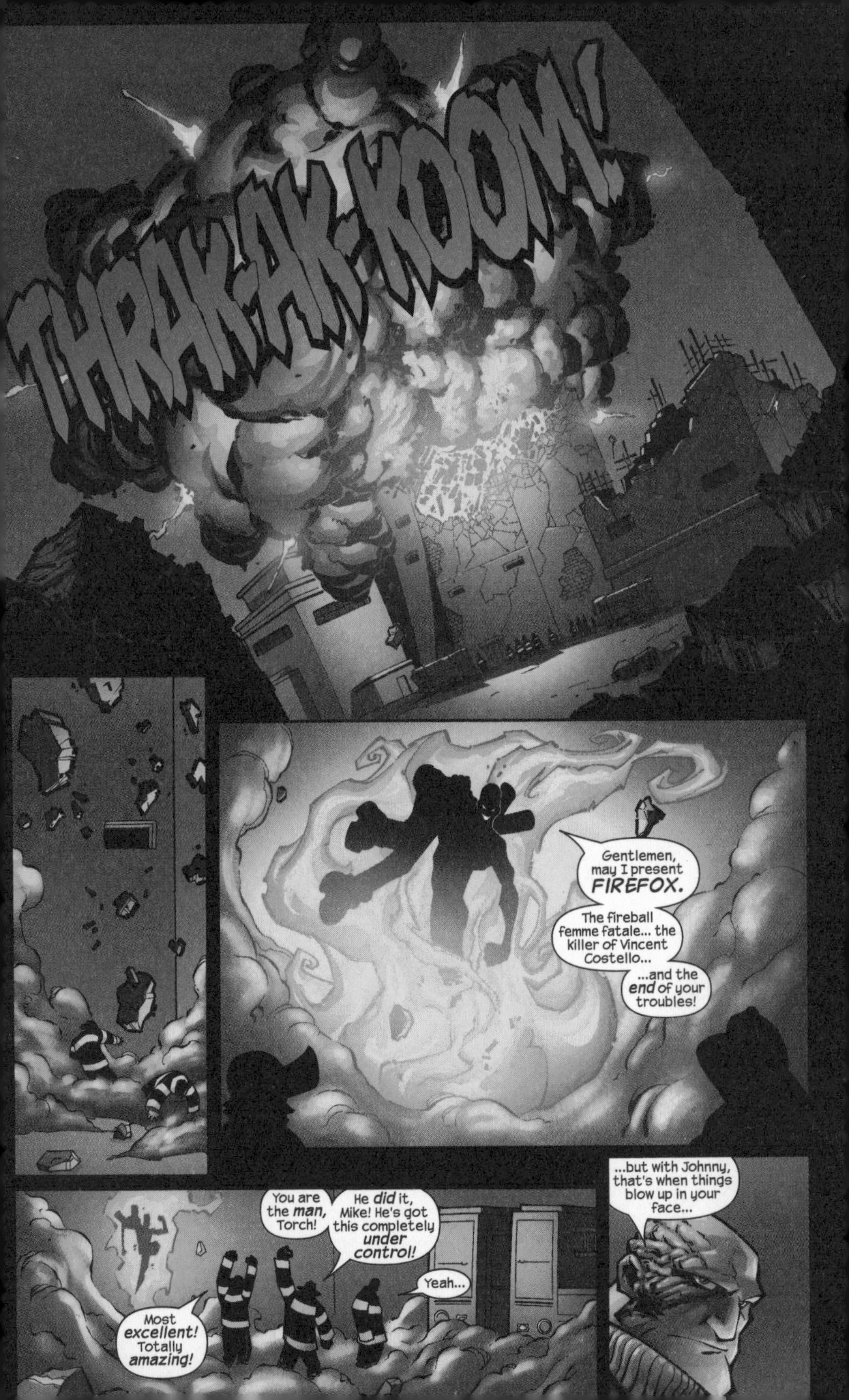
THRAK-AK-KOOM!
Gentlemen, may I present FIREFOX.
The fireball femme fatale... the killer of Vincent Costello...
...and the end of your troubles!
You are the man, Torch!
He did it, Mike! He's got this completely under control!
Yeah...
Most excellent! Totally amazing!
...but with Johnny, that's when things blow up in your face...

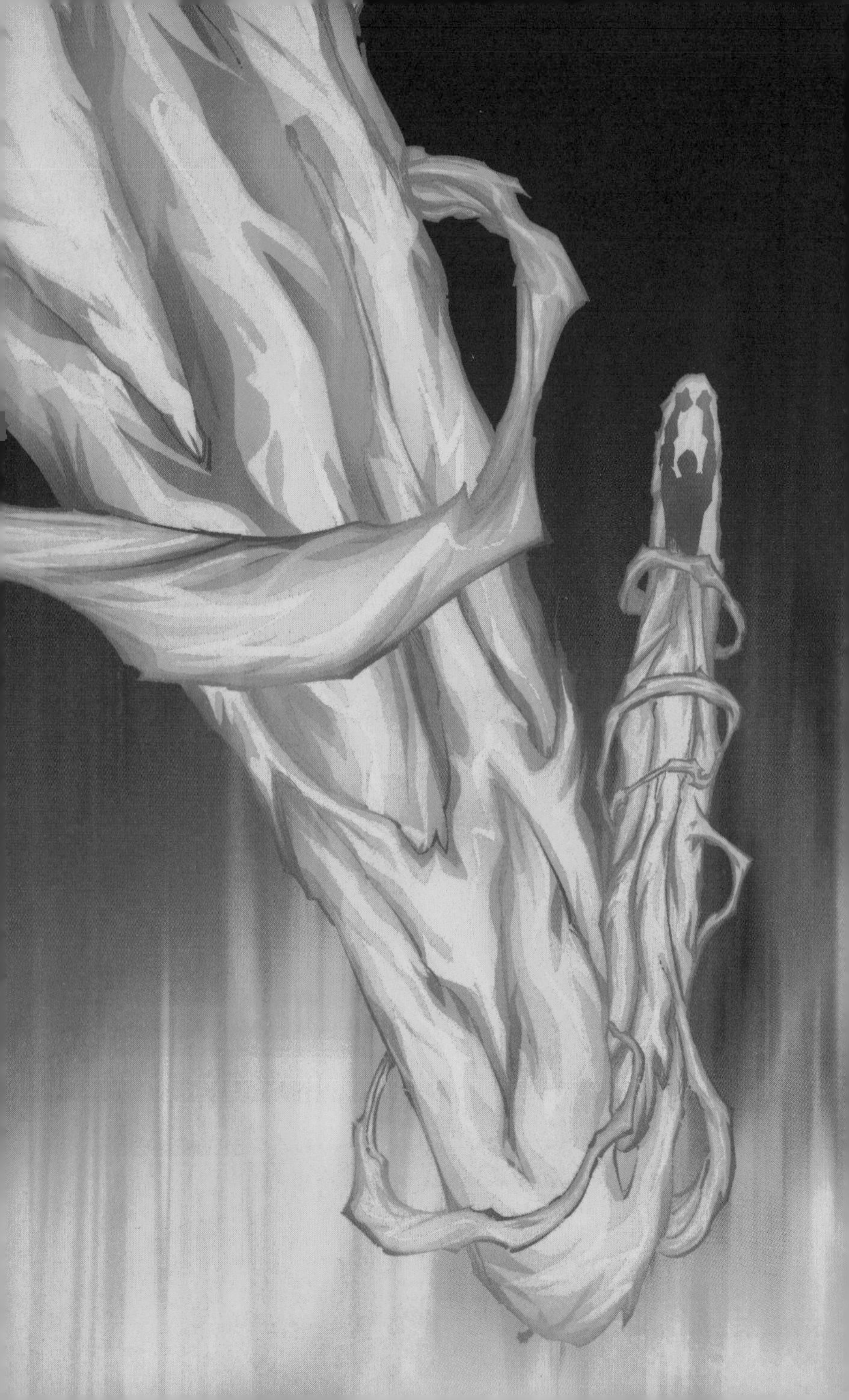

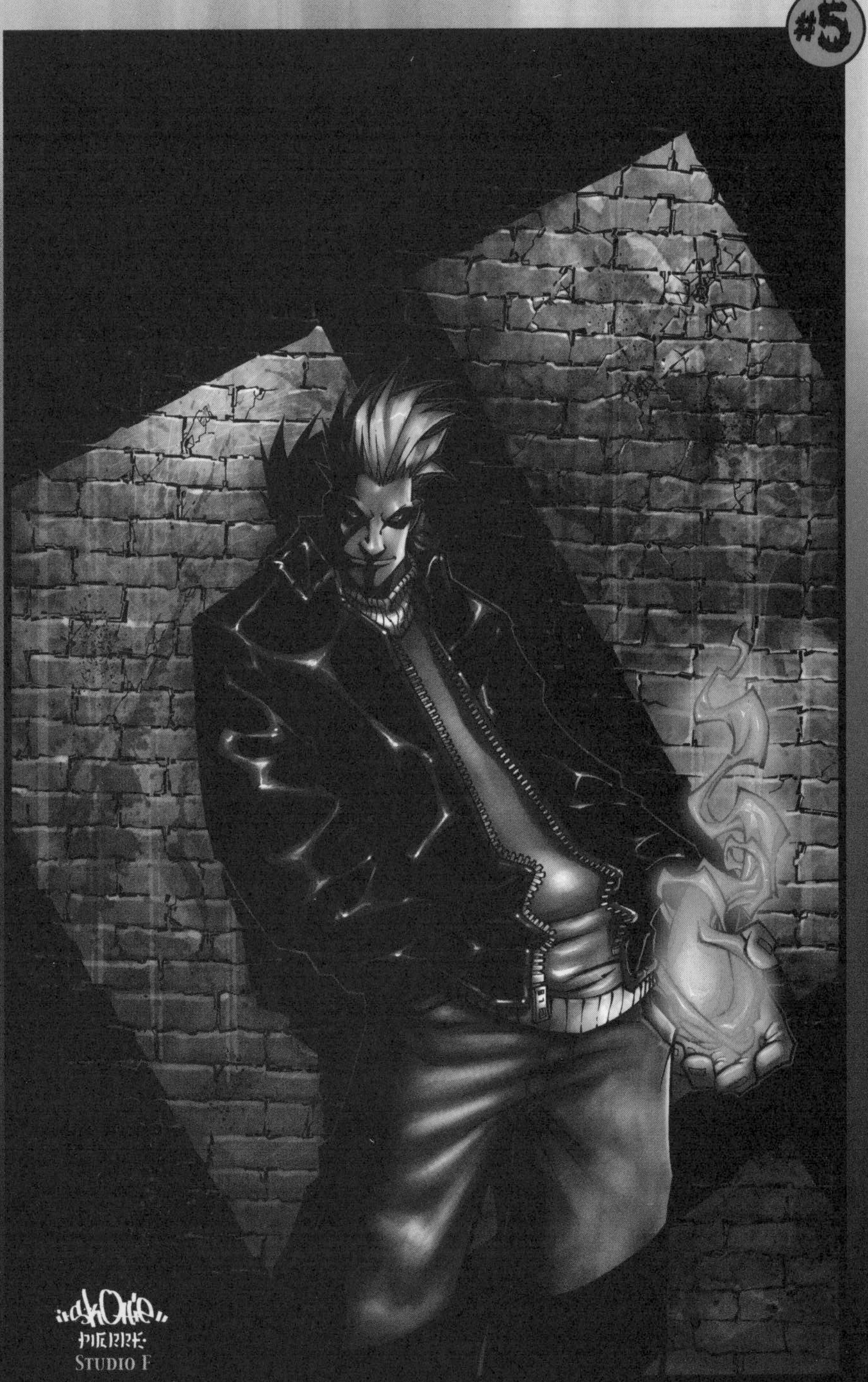
#5
Studio F

Take her mask off.

What?

I want to see her *face*. I want to see the face of the person who *killed* one of my men.

Firefox is just some *crazy* lady, Lieutenant. Mad scientist-type out to put a *hurt* on the fire department.

Ask *Snow*. He heard it *all*. There's no reason--

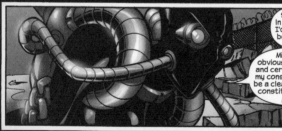

Sure there is, hero. In fact, there's nothing I'd like *better* than to be unmasked by these fine gentlemen.

Mind you, I'm obviously *restrained*, and certainly *not* giving my consent--so it would be a clear violation of my constitutional right to *privacy*.

Something I'm sure my *lawyer* would have a *field day* with...

Get her out of here.

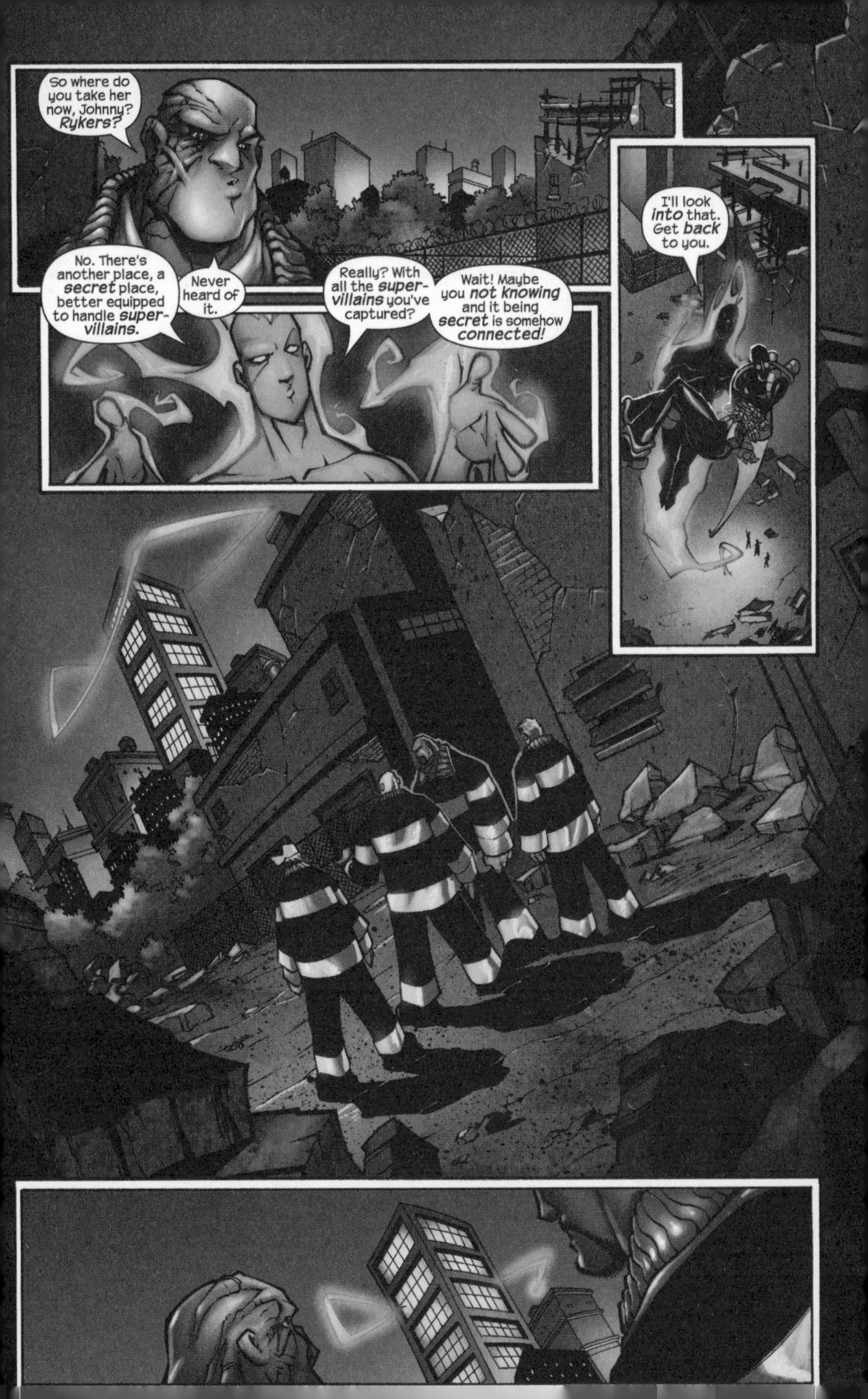

So where do you take her now, Johnny? Rykers?
I'll look into that. Get back to you.
No. There's another place, a secret place, better equipped to handle super-villains.
Never heard of it.
Really? With all the super-villains you've captured?
Wait! Maybe you not knowing and it being secret is somehow connected!

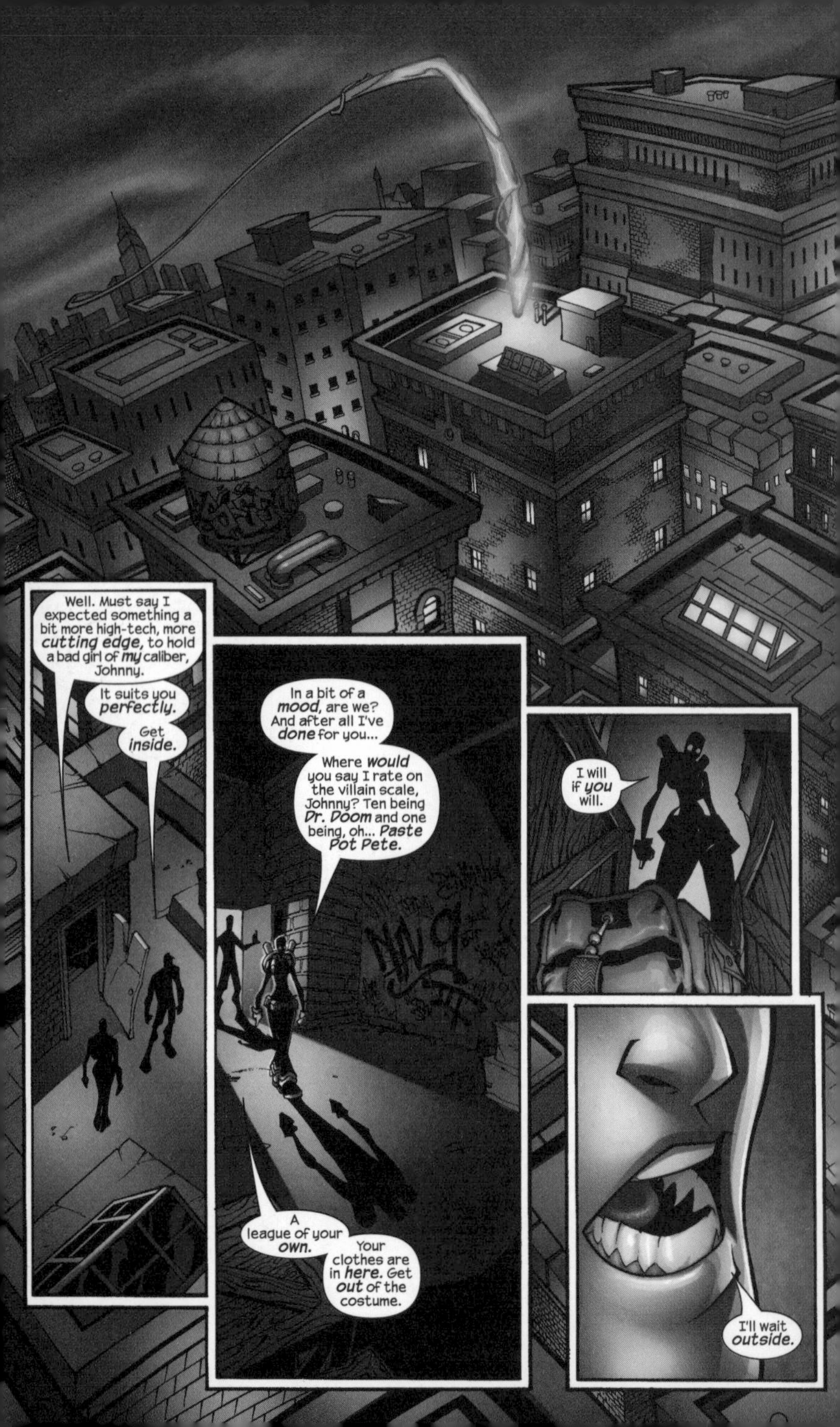
Well. Must say I expected something a bit more high-tech, more *cutting edge,* to hold a bad girl of *my* caliber, Johnny.
It suits you *perfectly.*
Get *inside.*
In a bit of a *mood,* are we? And after all I've *done* for you...
Where *would* you say I rate on the villain scale, Johnny? Ten being *Dr. Doom* and one being, oh... *Paste Pot Pete.*
A league of your *own.*
Your clothes are in *here.* Get *out* of the costume.
I will if *you* will.
I'll wait *outside.*

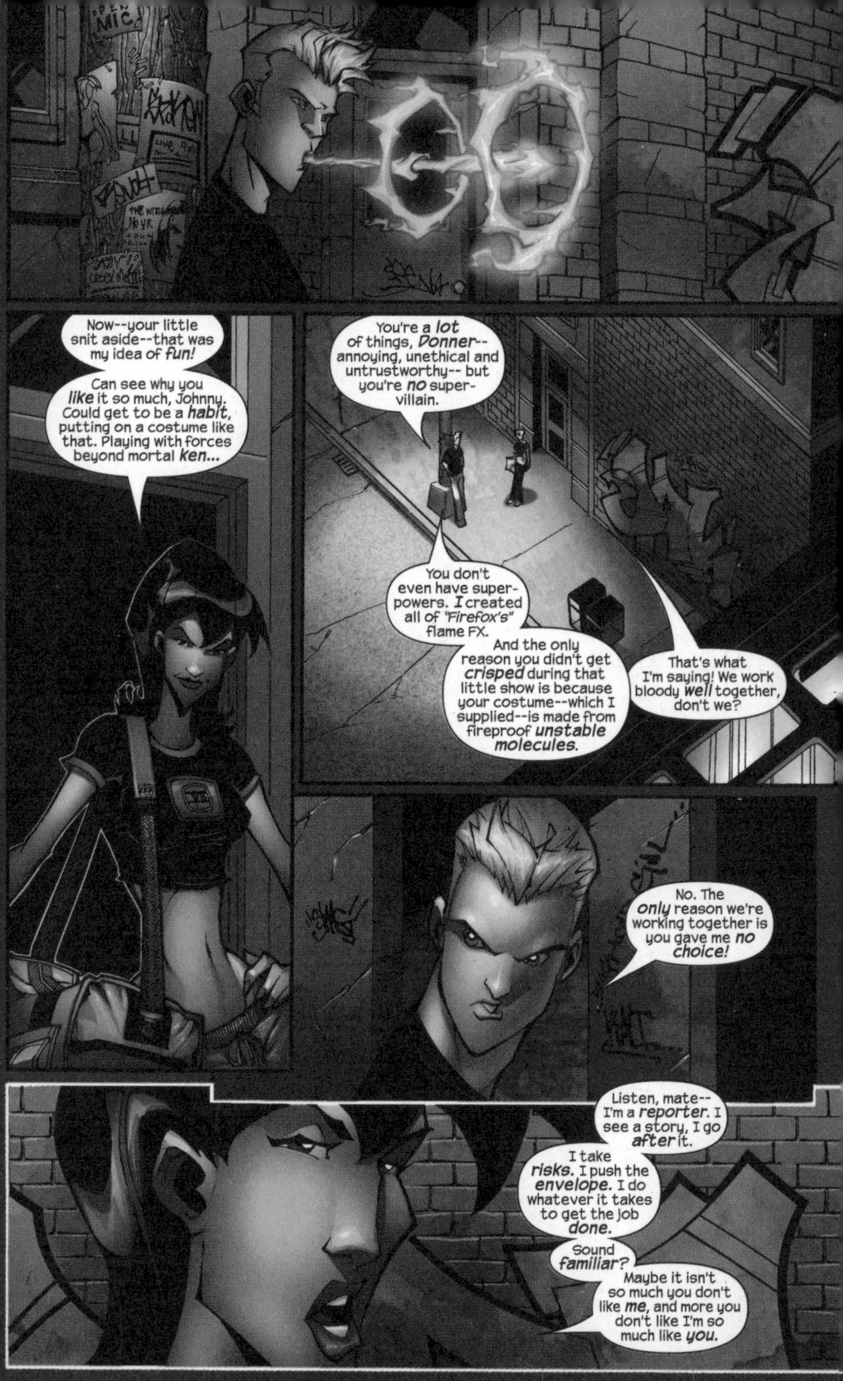
Now--your little snit aside--that was my idea of fun!
Can see why you like it so much, Johnny. Could get to be a habit, putting on a costume like that. Playing with forces beyond mortal ken...
You're a lot of things, Donner-- annoying, unethical and untrustworthy-- but you're no super-villain.
You don't even have super-powers. I created all of "Firefox's" flame FX.
And the only reason you didn't get crisped during that little show is because your costume--which I supplied--is made from fireproof unstable molecules.
That's what I'm saying! We work bloody well together, don't we?
No. The only reason we're working together is you gave me no choice!
Listen, mate-- I'm a reporter. I see a story, I go after it.
I take risks. I push the envelope. I do whatever it takes to get the job done.
Sound familiar?
Maybe it isn't so much you don't like me, and more you don't like I'm so much like you.

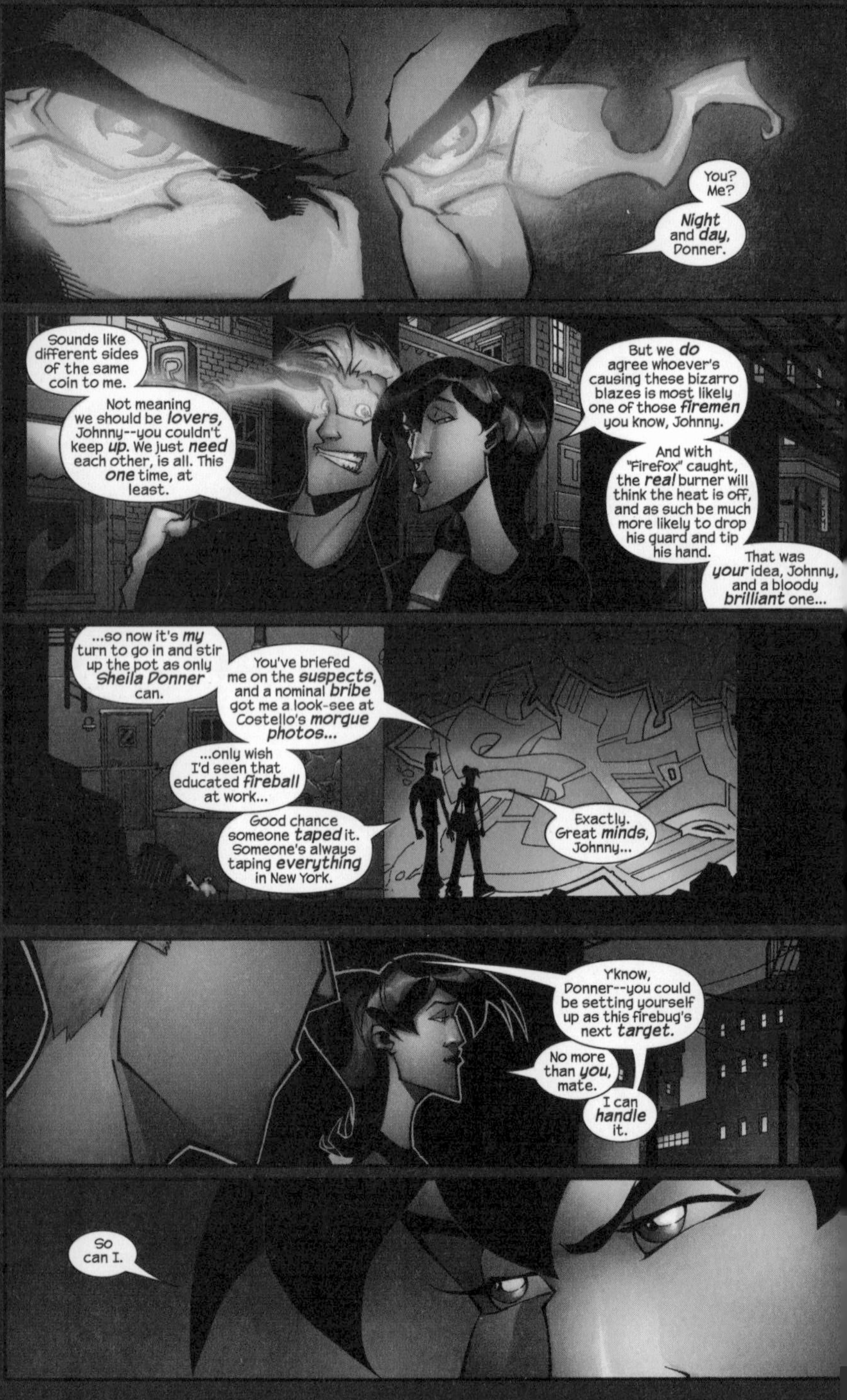
You? Me?
Night and day, Donner.
Sounds like different sides of the same coin to me.
Not meaning we should be lovers, Johnny--you couldn't keep up. We just need each other, is all. This one time, at least.
But we do agree whoever's causing these bizarro blazes is most likely one of those firemen you know, Johnny.
And with "Firefox" caught, the real burner will think the heat is off, and as such be much more likely to drop his guard and tip his hand.
That was your idea, Johnny, and a bloody brilliant one...
...so now it's my turn to go in and stir up the pot as only Sheila Donner can.
You've briefed me on the suspects, and a nominal bribe got me a look-see at Costello's morgue photos...
...only wish I'd seen that educated fireball at work...
Good chance someone taped it. Someone's always taping everything in New York.
Exactly. Great minds, Johnny...
Y'know, Donner--you could be setting yourself up as this firebug's next target.
No more than you, mate.
I can handle it.
So can I.

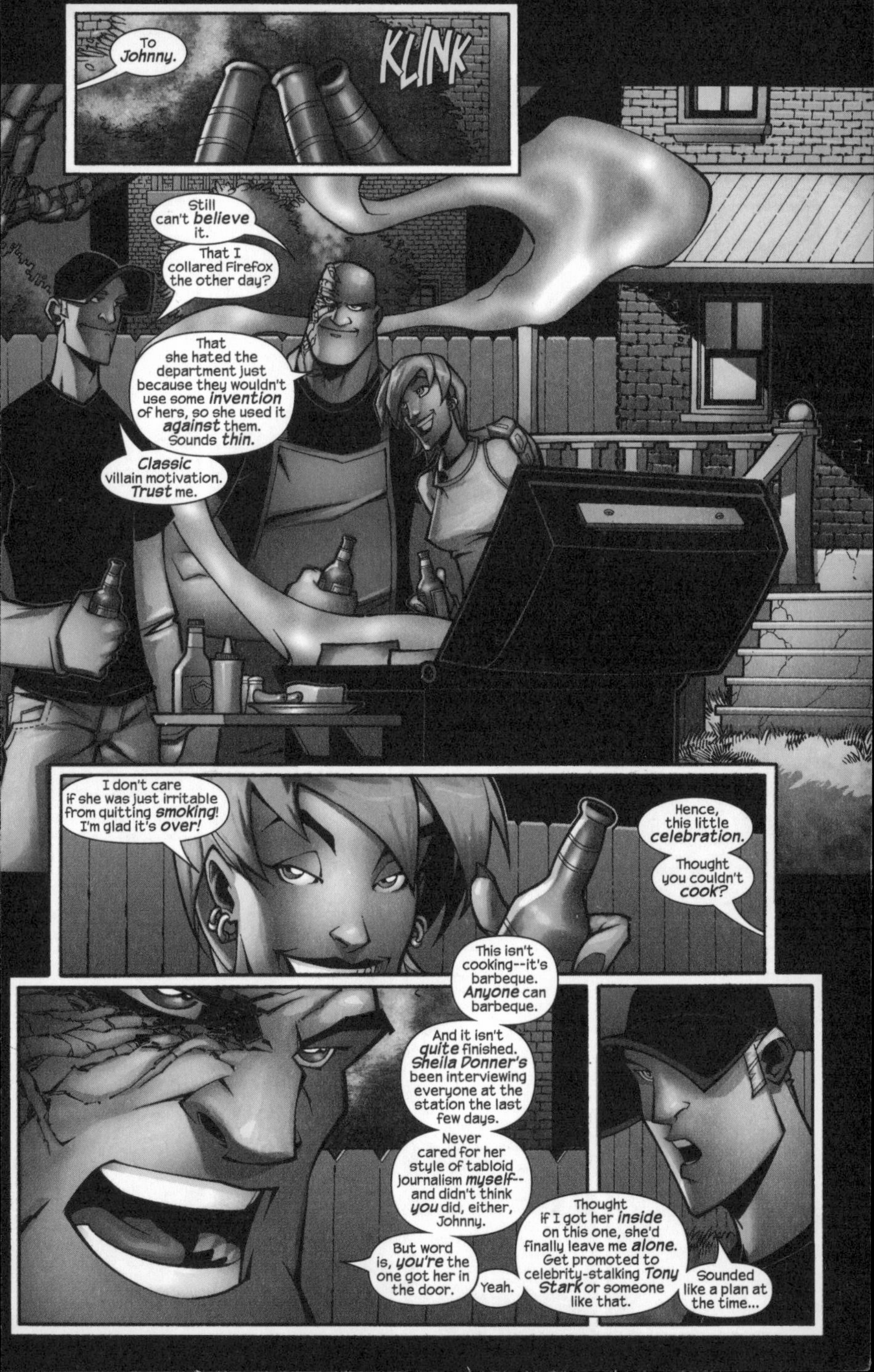
To Johnny.
KLINK
Still can't believe it.
That I collared Firefox the other day?
That she hated the department just because they wouldn't use some invention of hers, so she used it against them. Sounds thin.
Classic villain motivation. Trust me.
I don't care if she was just irritable from quitting smoking! I'm glad it's over!
Hence, this little celebration.
Thought you couldn't cook?
This isn't cooking--it's barbeque. Anyone can barbeque.
And it isn't quite finished. Sheila Donner's been interviewing everyone at the station the last few days.
Never cared for her style of tabloid journalism myself--and didn't think you did, either, Johnny.
But word is, you're the one got her in the door.
Yeah.
Thought if I got her inside on this one, she'd finally leave me alone. Get promoted to celebrity-stalking Tony Stark or someone like that.
Sounded like a plan at the time...

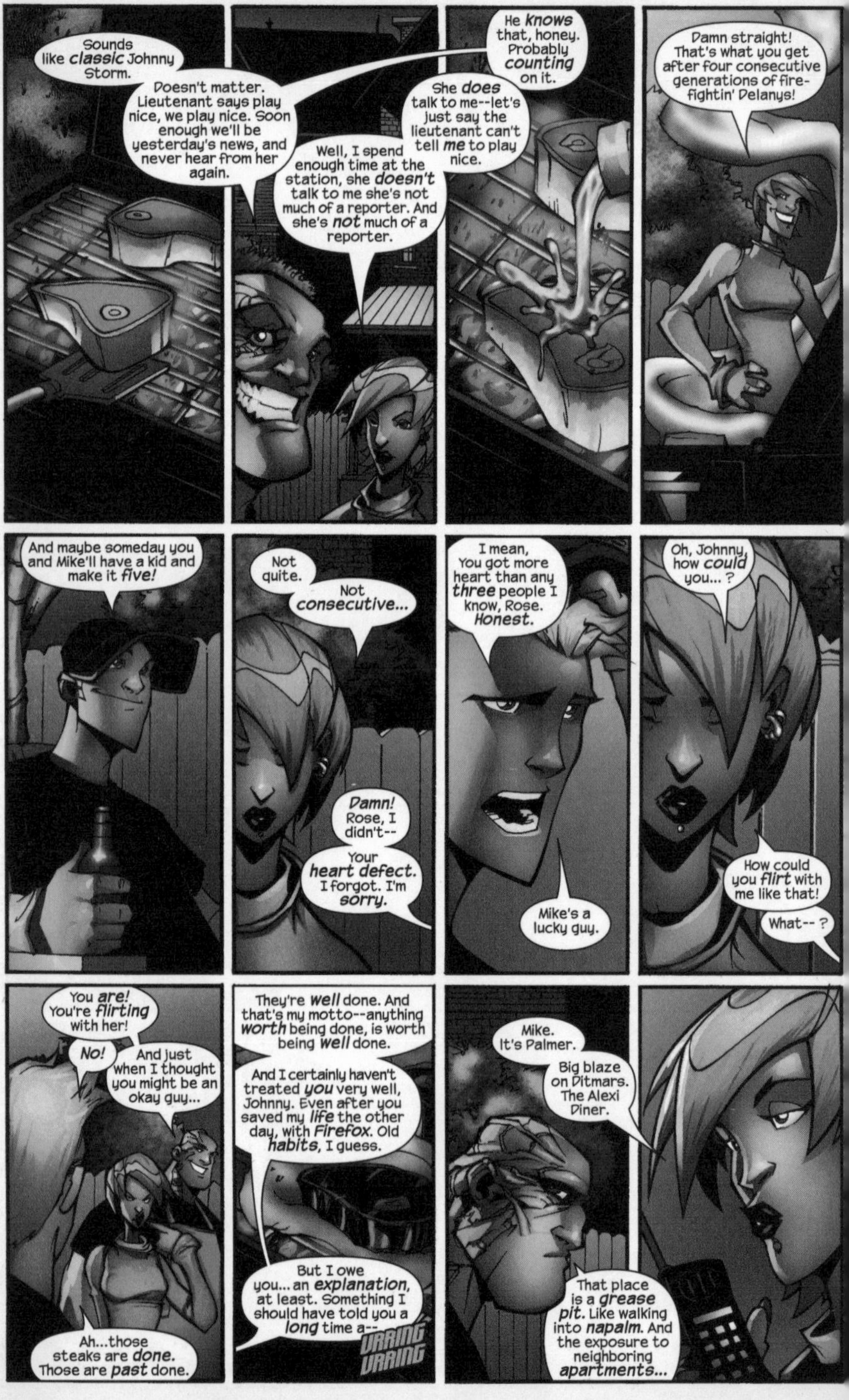
Sounds like classic Johnny Storm.
Doesn't matter. Lieutenant says play nice, we play nice. Soon enough we'll be yesterday's news, and never hear from her again.
Well, I spend enough time at the station, she doesn't talk to me she's not much of a reporter. And she's not much of a reporter.
He knows that, honey. Probably counting on it.
She does talk to me--let's just say the lieutenant can't tell me to play nice.
Damn straight! That's what you get after four consecutive generations of fire-fightin' Delanys!
And maybe someday you and Mike'll have a kid and make it five!
Not quite.
Not consecutive...
Damn! Rose, I didn't--
Your heart defect. I forgot. I'm sorry.
I mean, You got more heart than any three people I know, Rose. Honest.
Mike's a lucky guy.
Oh, Johnny, how could you...?
How could you flirt with me like that!
What--?
You are! You're flirting with her!
No!
And just when I thought you might be an okay guy...
Ah...those steaks are done. Those are past done.
They're well done. And that's my motto--anything worth being done, is worth being well done.
And I certainly haven't treated you very well, Johnny. Even after you saved my life the other day, with Firefox. Old habits, I guess.
But I owe you... an explanation, at least. Something I should have told you a long time a--
URRING URRING
Mike. It's Palmer.
Big blaze on Ditmars. The Alexi Diner.
That place is a grease pit. Like walking into napalm. And the exposure to neighboring apartments...

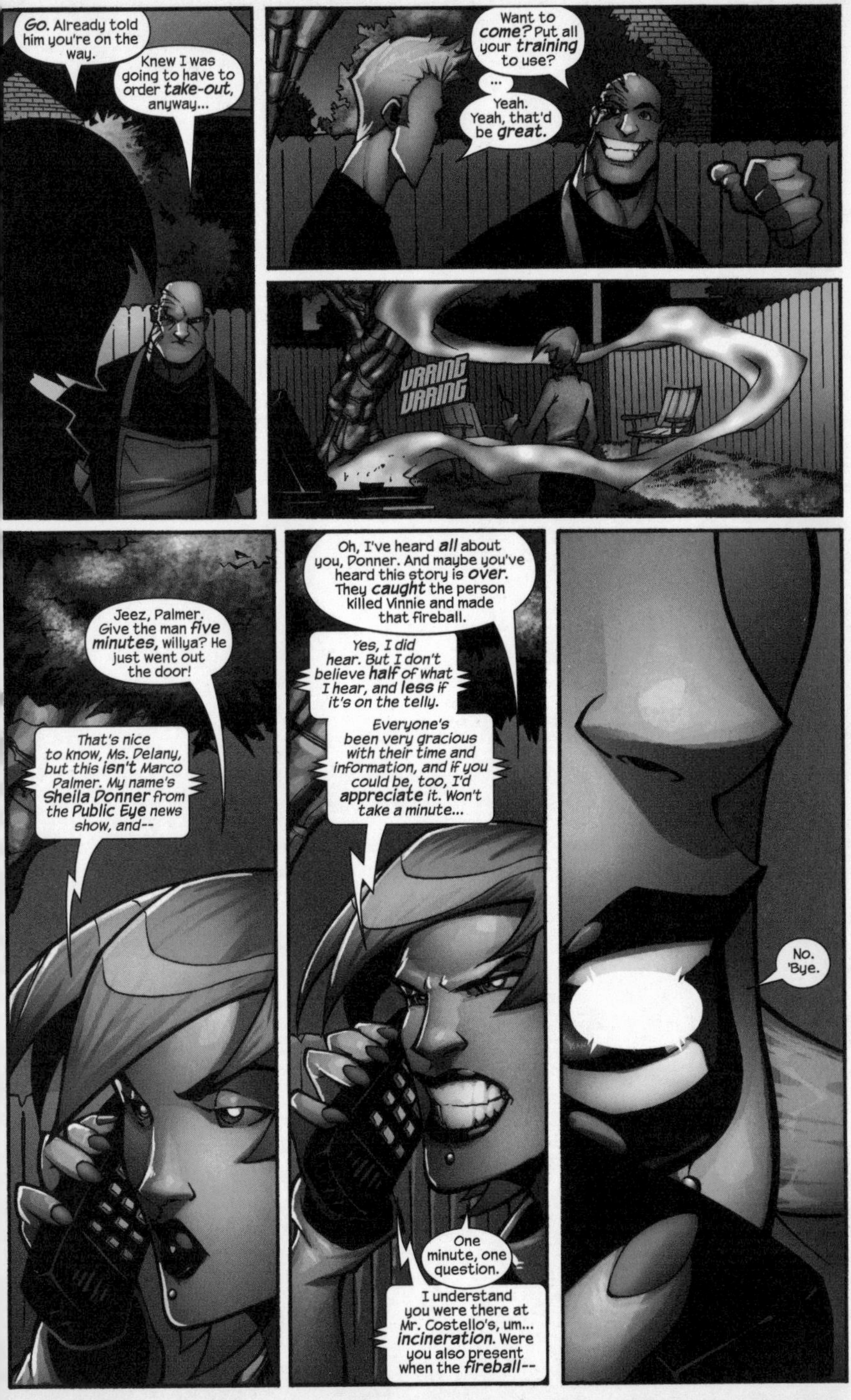

Go. Already told him you're on the way.
Knew I was going to have to order take-out, anyway...
Want to come? Put all your training to use?
...
Yeah. Yeah, that'd be great.
VRRING VRRING
Jeez, Palmer. Give the man five minutes, willya? He just went out the door!
That's nice to know, Ms. Delany, but this isn't Marco Palmer. My name's Sheila Donner from the Public Eye news show, and--
Oh, I've heard all about you, Donner. And maybe you've heard this story is over. They caught the person killed Vinnie and made that fireball.
Yes, I did hear. But I don't believe half of what I hear, and less if it's on the telly.
Everyone's been very gracious with their time and information, and if you could be, too, I'd appreciate it. Won't take a minute...
One minute, one question.
I understand you were there at Mr. Costello's, um... incineration. Were you also present when the fireball--
No. 'Bye.

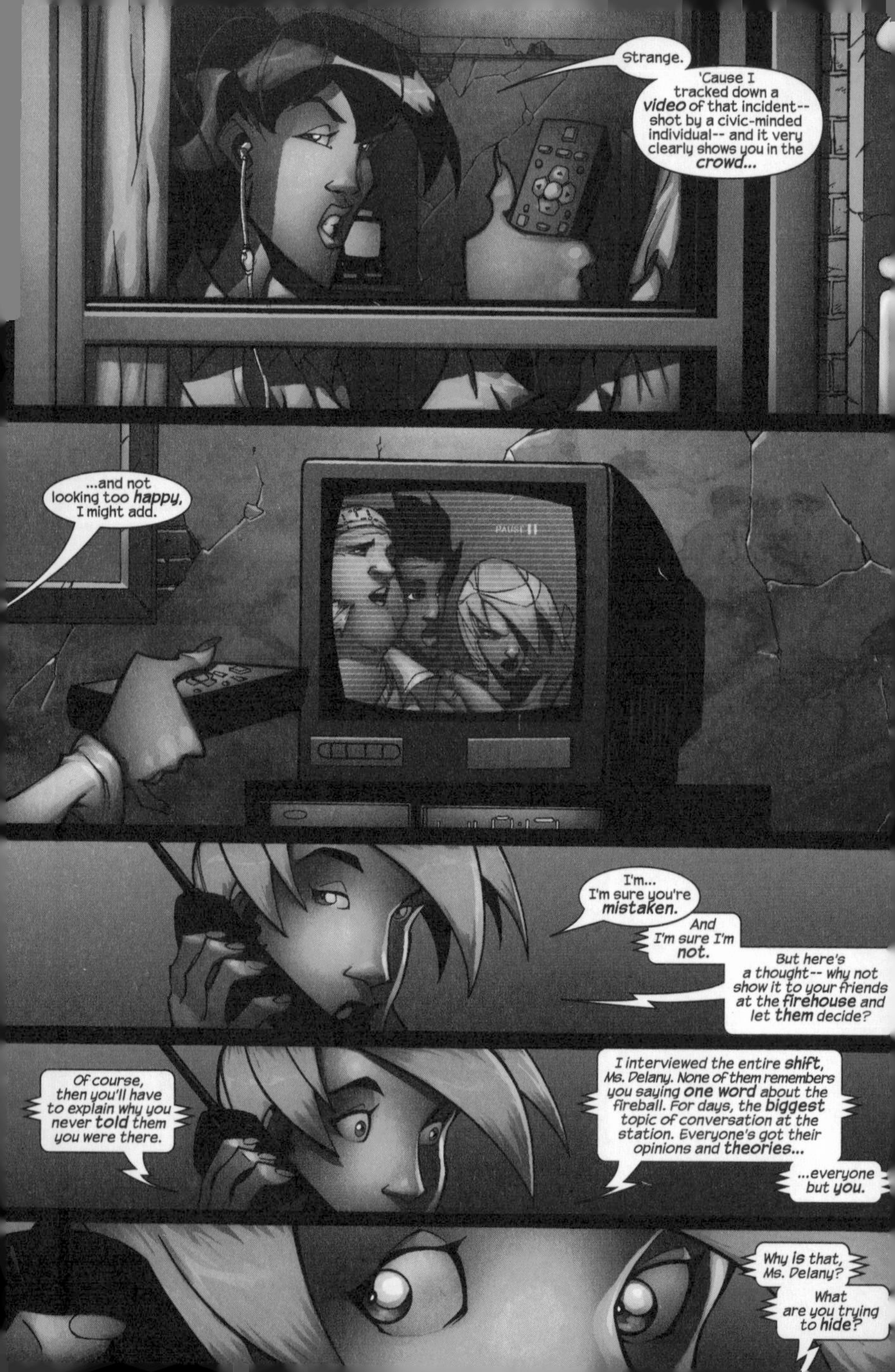
Strange.
'Cause I tracked down a *video* of that incident-- shot by a civic-minded individual-- and it very clearly shows you in the *crowd*...
...and not looking too *happy*, I might add.
PAUSE
I'm... I'm sure you're **mistaken**.
And I'm sure I'm **not**.
But here's a thought-- why not show it to your friends at the **firehouse** and let **them** decide?
Of course, then you'll have to explain why you never **told** them you were there.
I interviewed the entire **shift**, Ms. Delany. None of them remembers you saying **one word** about the fireball. For days, the **biggest** topic of conversation at the station. Everyone's got their opinions and **theories**...
...everyone but **you**.
Why **is** that, Ms. Delany?
What are you trying to **hide**?

ALEXI'S
Get more *foam* on her-- she's still heating up!
And make sure that apartment building's *evacuated!*
Clarke, Hahn-- you *read* me? You in *position?*
Say the *word,* Lieutenant.
C'mon, Clarke, everyone knows *grease* is the wor--
THWOOOM
Clarke, Hahn-- *report!* You *okay?*
Better than when I *ate* at that place!
Yeah, and there was some hurlage *that* night, too!
Got some *hot spots* here, Lieutenant. Time to work our...

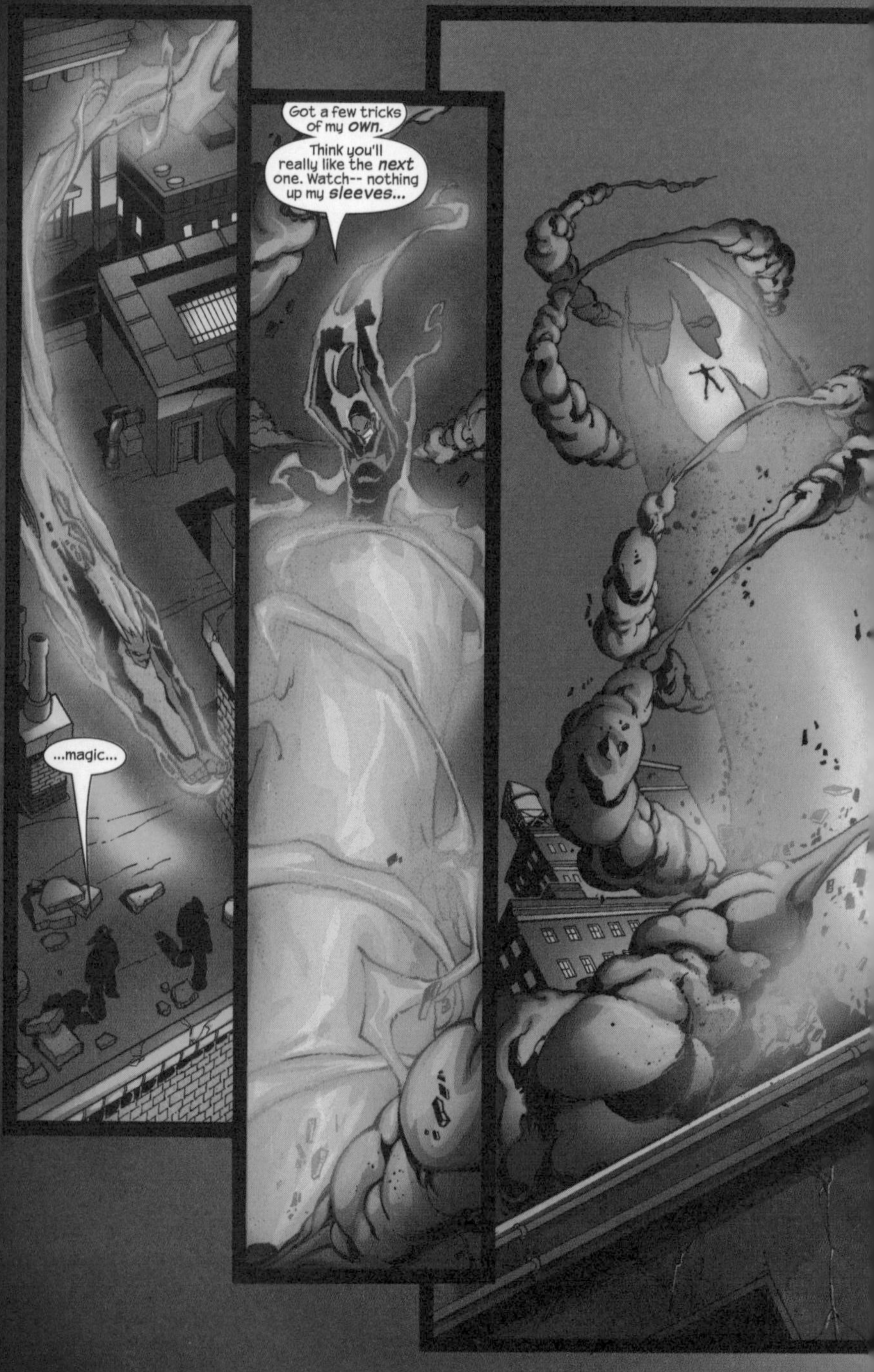
...magic...
Got a few tricks of my *own*.
Think you'll really like the *next* one. Watch-- nothing up my *sleeves*...

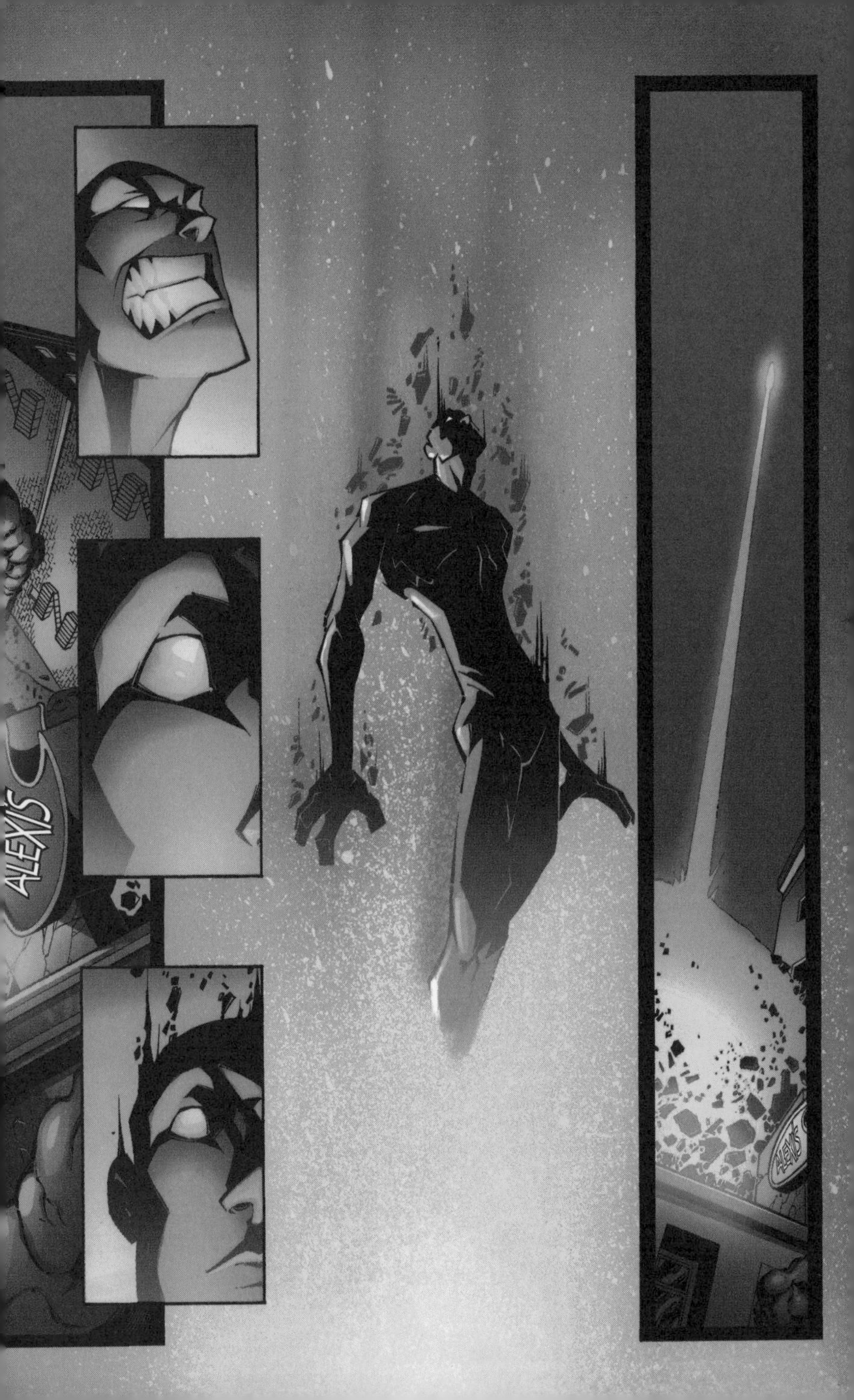
ALEXIS

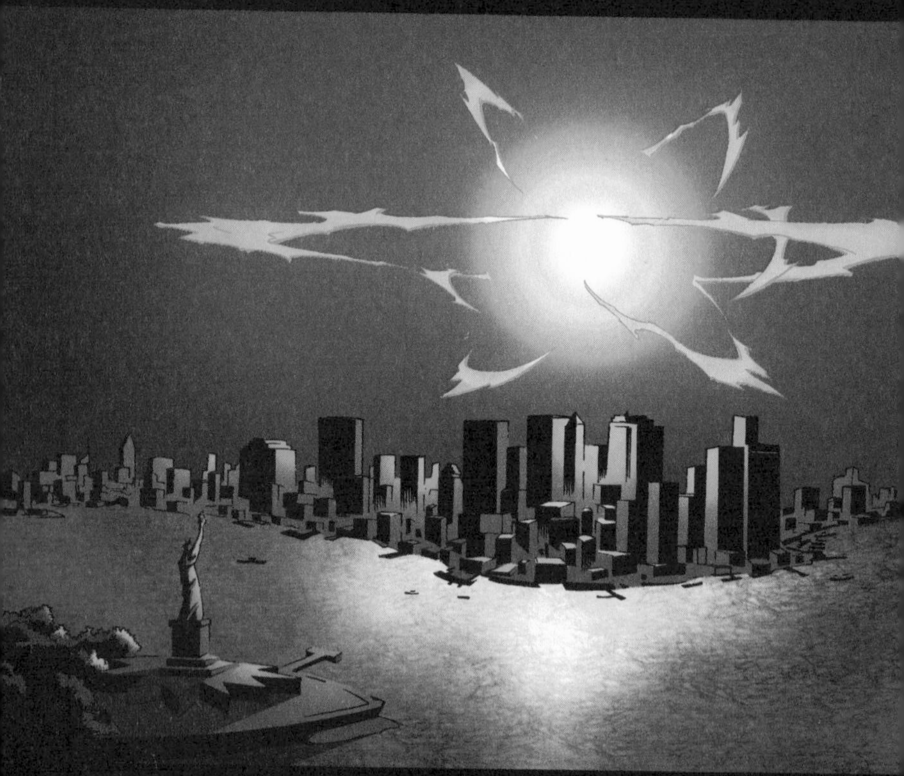

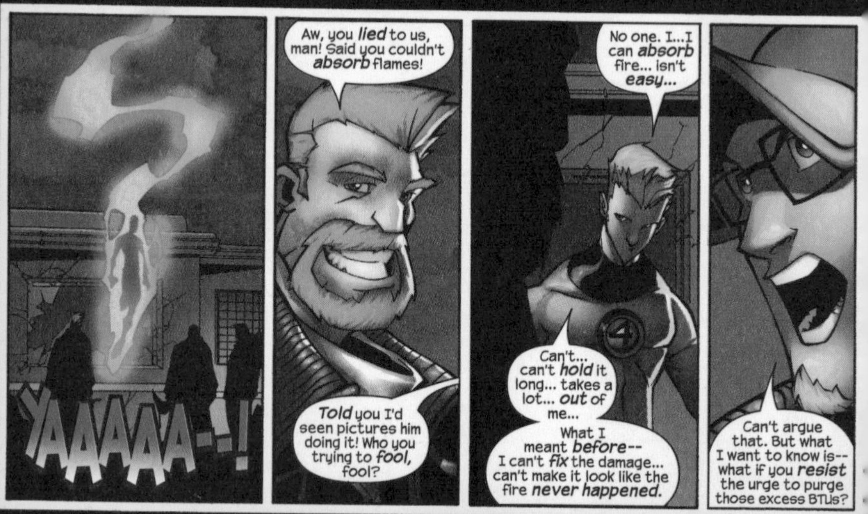
YAAAAA--!
Aw, you lied to us, man! Said you couldn't absorb flames!
Told you I'd seen pictures him doing it! Who you trying to fool, fool?
No one. I...I can absorb fire... isn't easy...
Can't... can't hold it long... takes a lot... out of me...
What I meant before-- I can't fix the damage... can't make it look like the fire never happened.
Can't argue that. But what I want to know is-- what if you resist the urge to purge those excess BTUs?

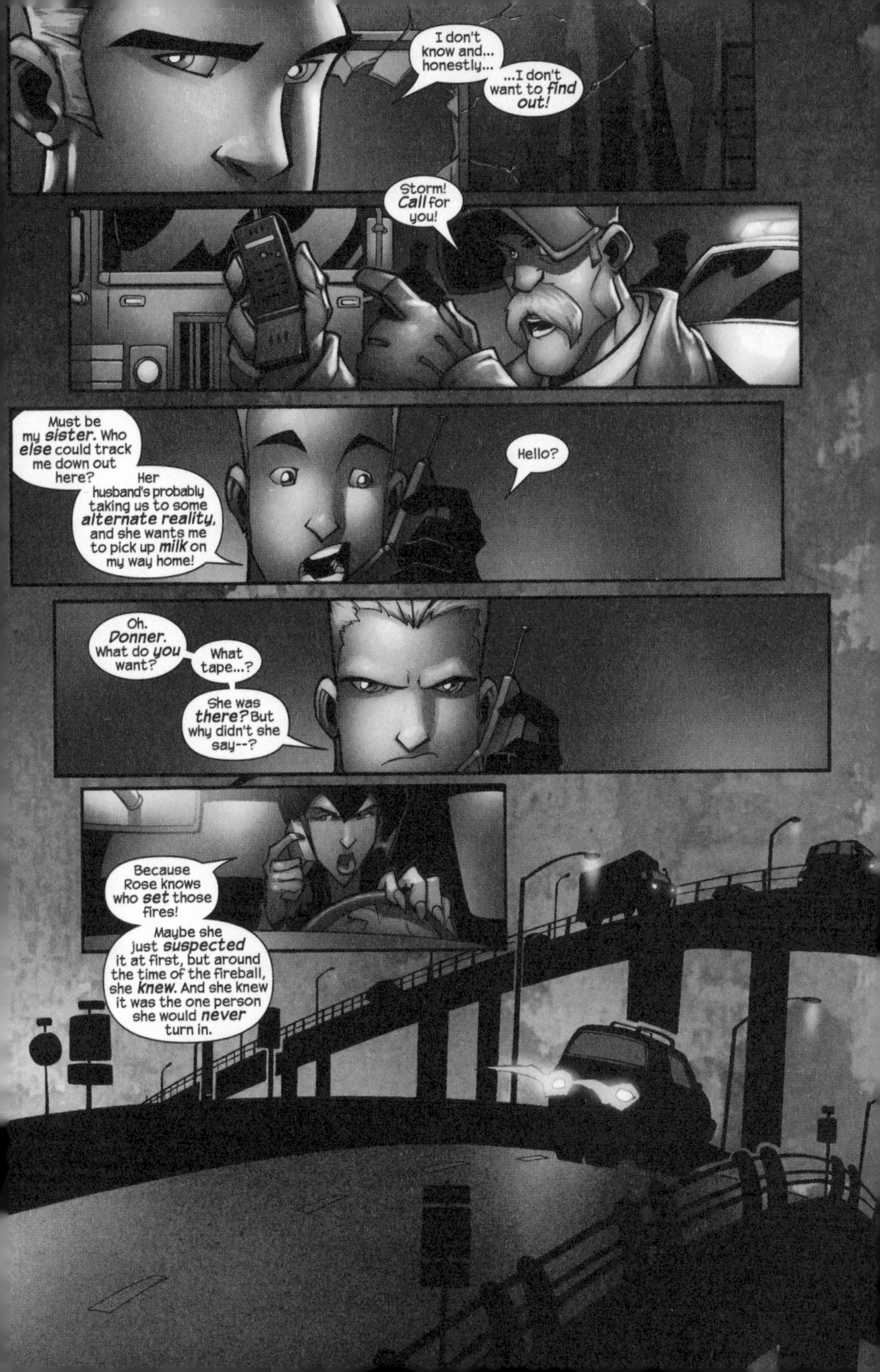
I don't know and... honestly...
...I don't want to *find out!*
Storm! *Call* for you!
Must be my *sister*. Who *else* could track me down out here?
Her husband's probably taking us to some *alternate reality*, and she wants me to pick up *milk* on my way home!
Hello?
Oh. *Donner*. What do *you* want?
What tape...?
She was *there?* But why didn't she say--?
Because Rose knows who *set* those fires!
Maybe she just *suspected* it at first, but around the time of the fireball, she *knew*. And she knew it was the one person she would *never* turn in.

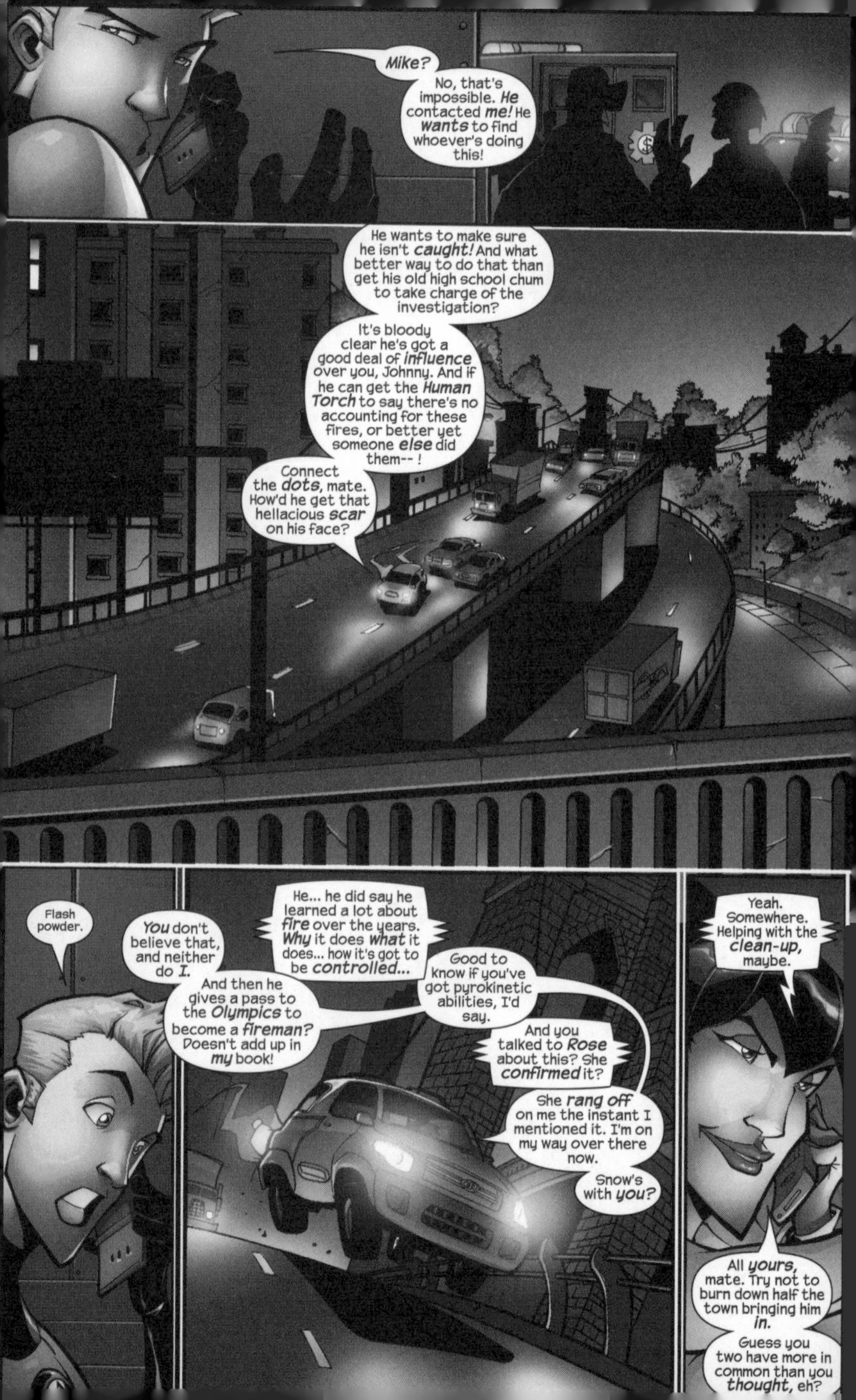
Mike?
No, that's impossible. He contacted me! He wants to find whoever's doing this!
He wants to make sure he isn't caught! And what better way to do that than get his old high school chum to take charge of the investigation?
It's bloody clear he's got a good deal of influence over you, Johnny. And if he can get the Human Torch to say there's no accounting for these fires, or better yet someone else did them-- !
Connect the dots, mate. How'd he get that hellacious scar on his face?
Flash powder.
You don't believe that, and neither do I.
And then he gives a pass to the Olympics to become a fireman? Doesn't add up in my book!
He... he did say he learned a lot about fire over the years. Why it does what it does... how it's got to be controlled...
Good to know if you've got pyrokinetic abilities, I'd say.
And you talked to Rose about this? She confirmed it?
She rang off on me the instant I mentioned it. I'm on my way over there now.
Snow's with you?
Yeah. Somewhere. Helping with the clean-up, maybe.
All yours, mate. Try not to burn down half the town bringing him in.
Guess you two have more in common than you thought, eh?

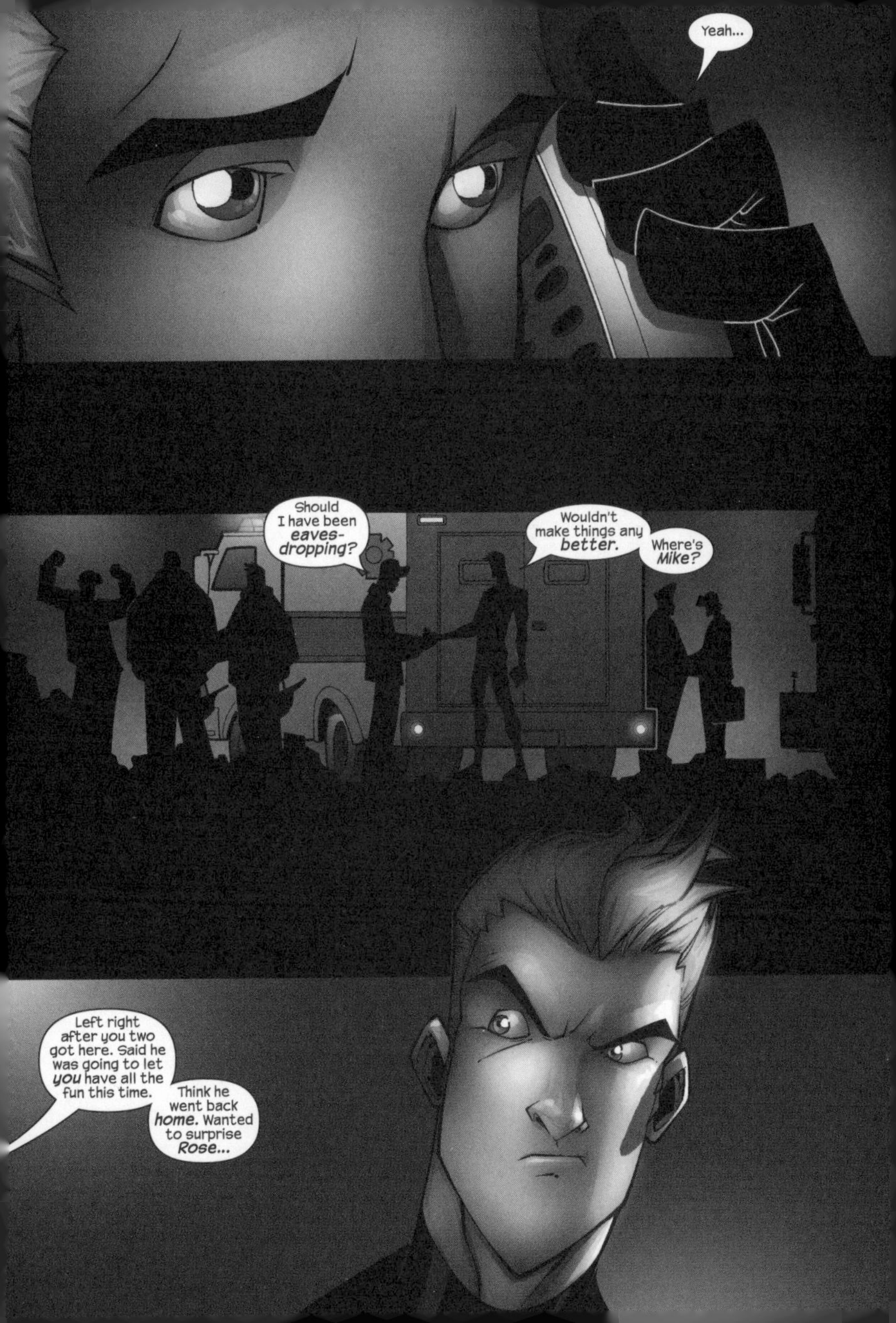

Yeah...
Should I have been eaves-dropping?
Wouldn't make things any better.
Where's Mike?
Left right after you two got here. Said he was going to let you have all the fun this time.
Think he went back home. Wanted to surprise Rose...

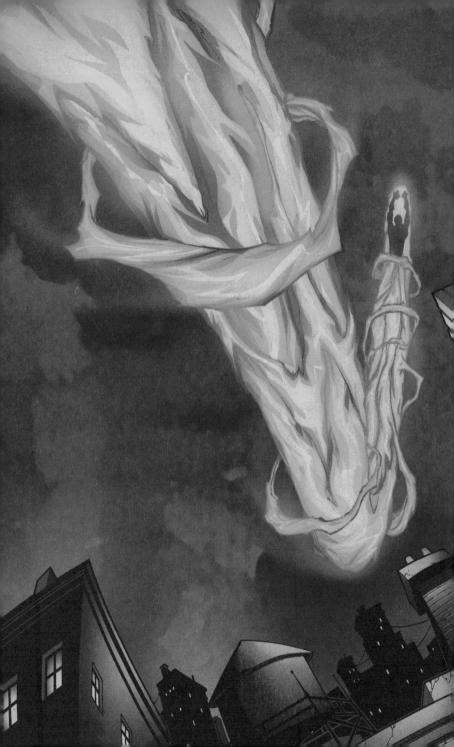

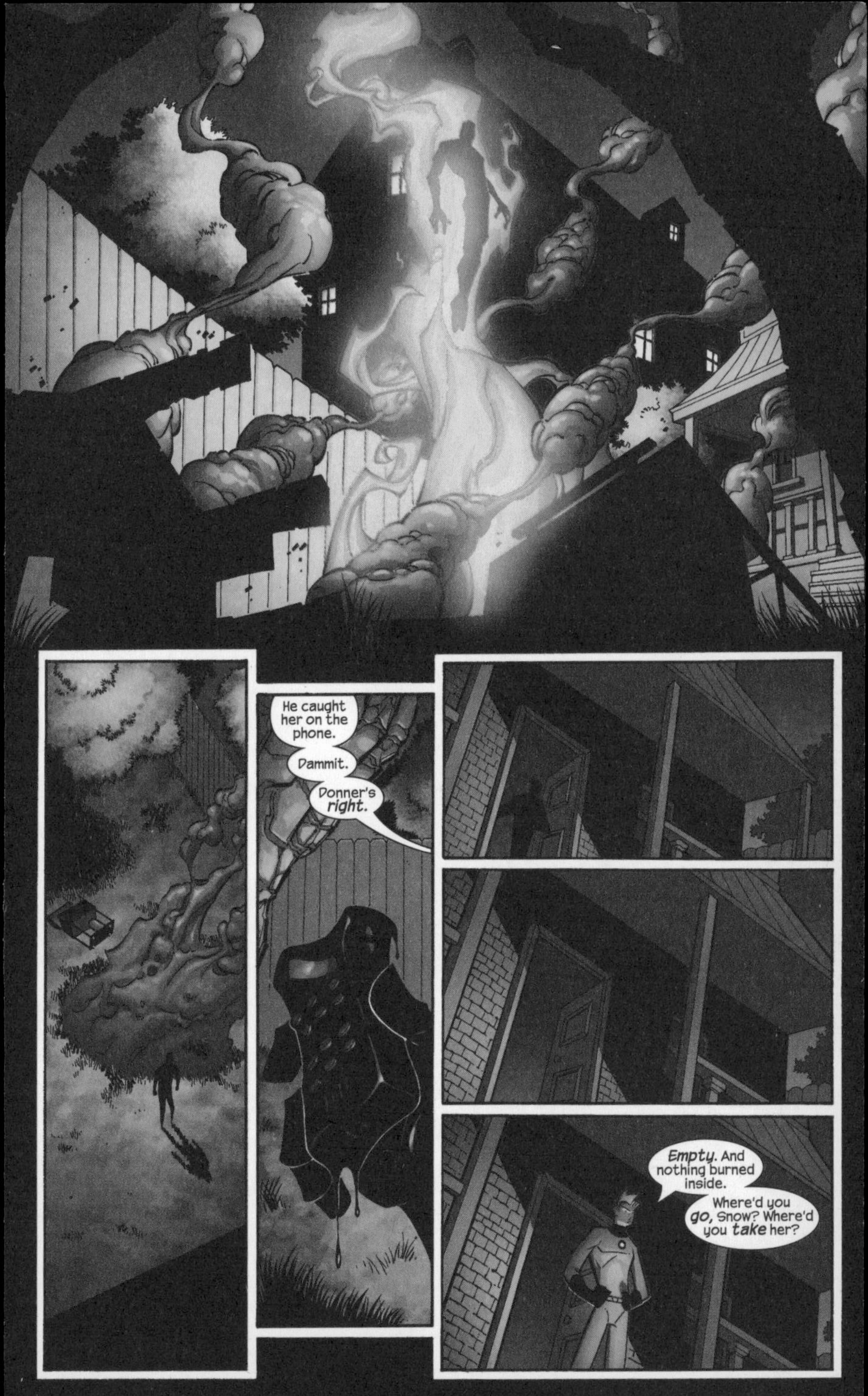
He caught her on the phone.
Dammit.
Donner's *right*.
Empty. And nothing burned inside.
Where'd you *go*, Snow? Where'd you *take* her?

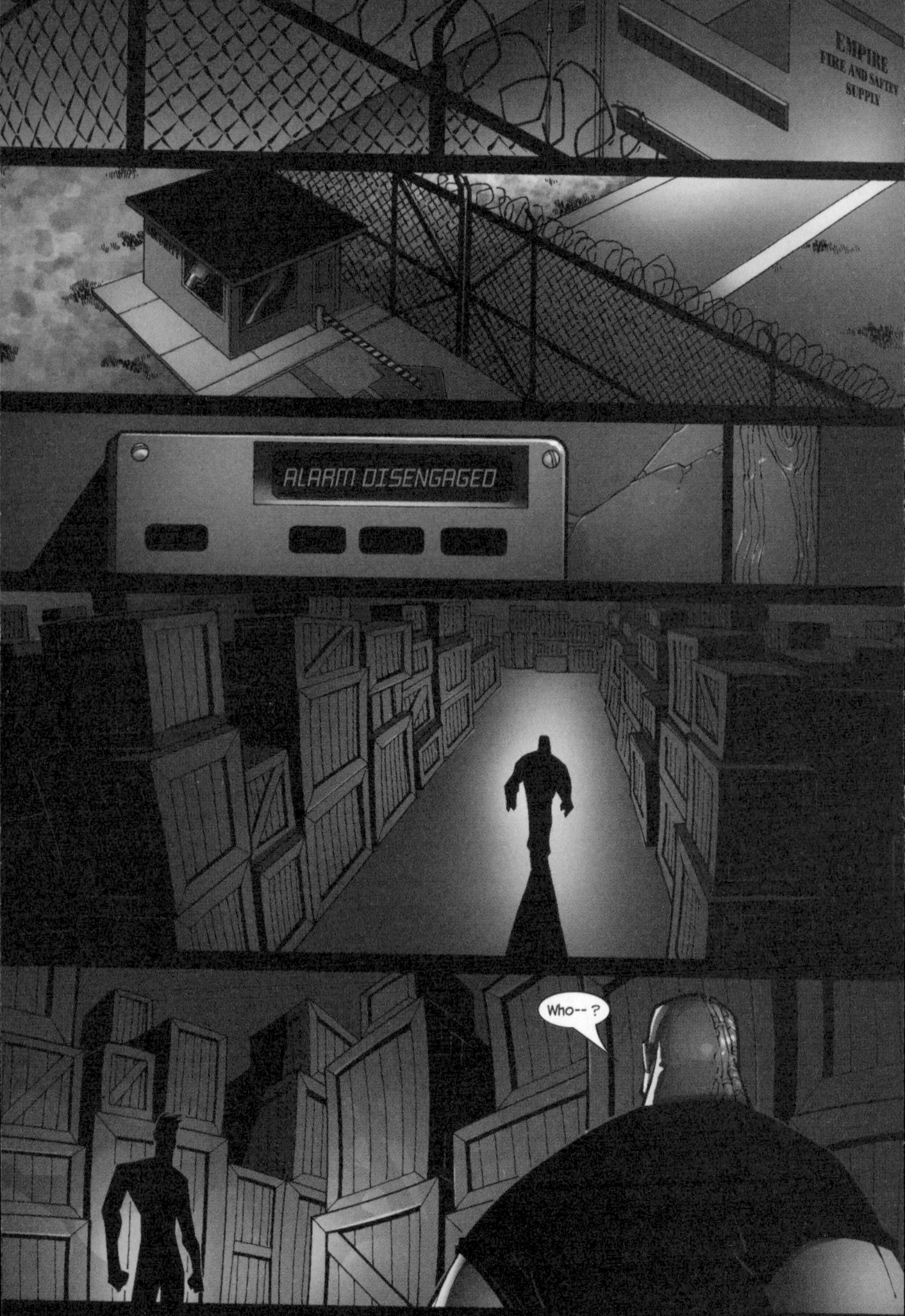
EMPIRE
FIRE AND SAFETY
SUPPLY
ALARM DISENGAGED
Who-- ?

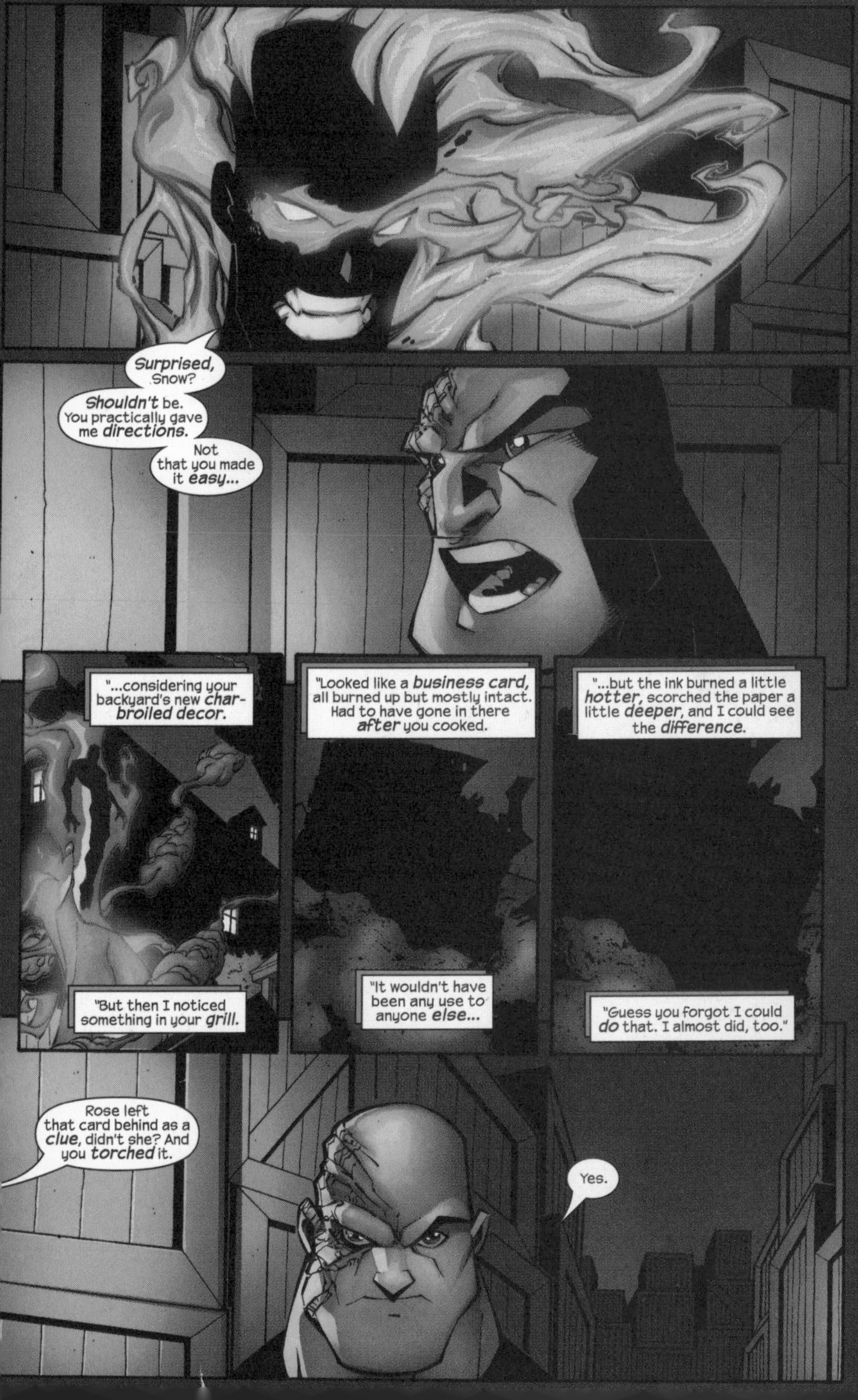
Surprised, Snow?
Shouldn't be. You practically gave me directions.
Not that you made it easy...
"...considering your backyard's new char-broiled decor.
"But then I noticed something in your grill.
"Looked like a business card, all burned up but mostly intact. Had to have gone in there after you cooked.
"It wouldn't have been any use to anyone else...
"...but the ink burned a little hotter, scorched the paper a little deeper, and I could see the difference.
"Guess you forgot I could do that. I almost did, too."
Rose left that card behind as a clue, didn't she? And you torched it.
Yes.

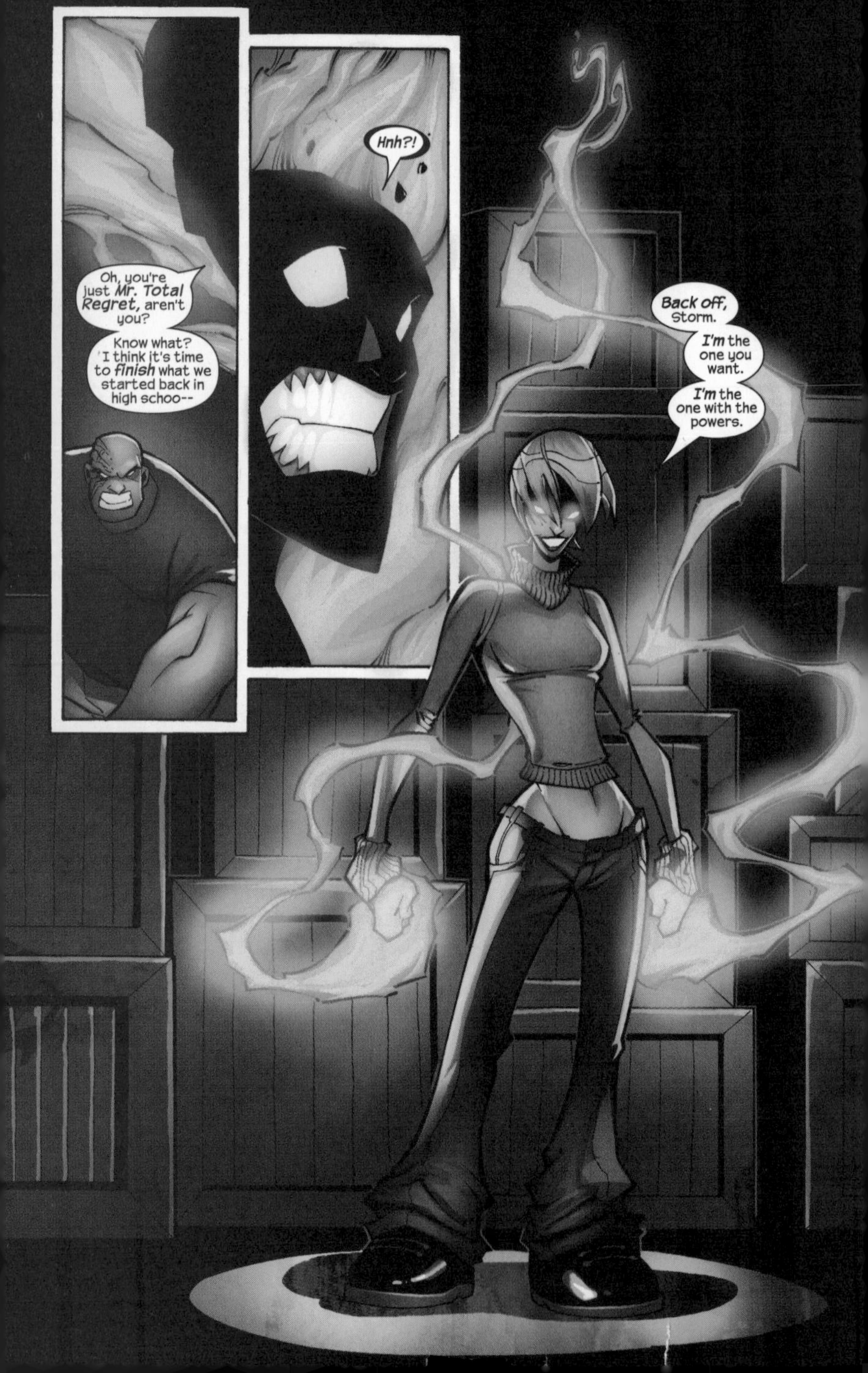
Oh, you're just *Mr. Total Regret*, aren't you?
Know what? I think it's time to *finish* what we started back in high schoo--
Hnh?!
Back off, Storm.
I'm the one you want.
I'm the one with the powers.

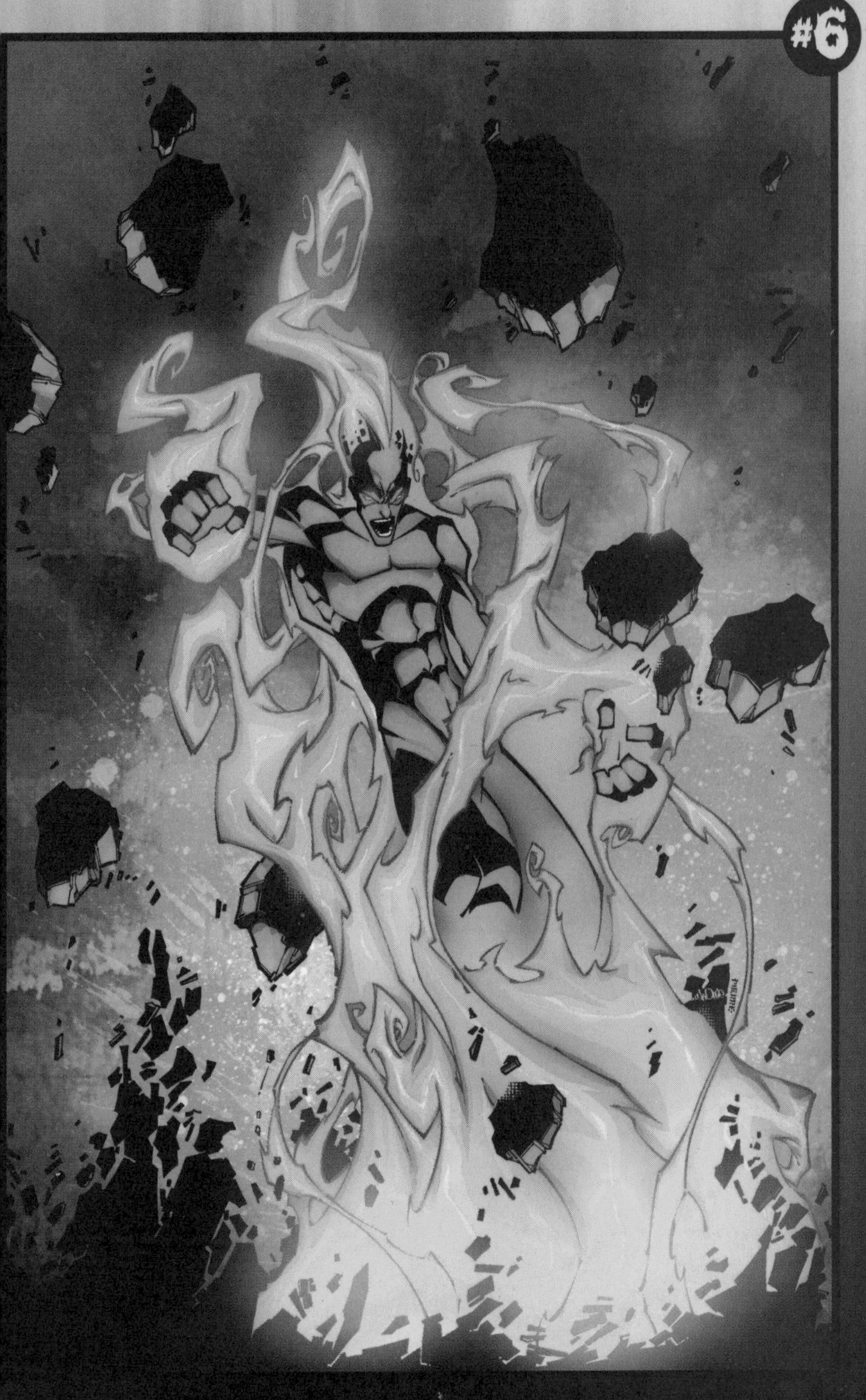
#6

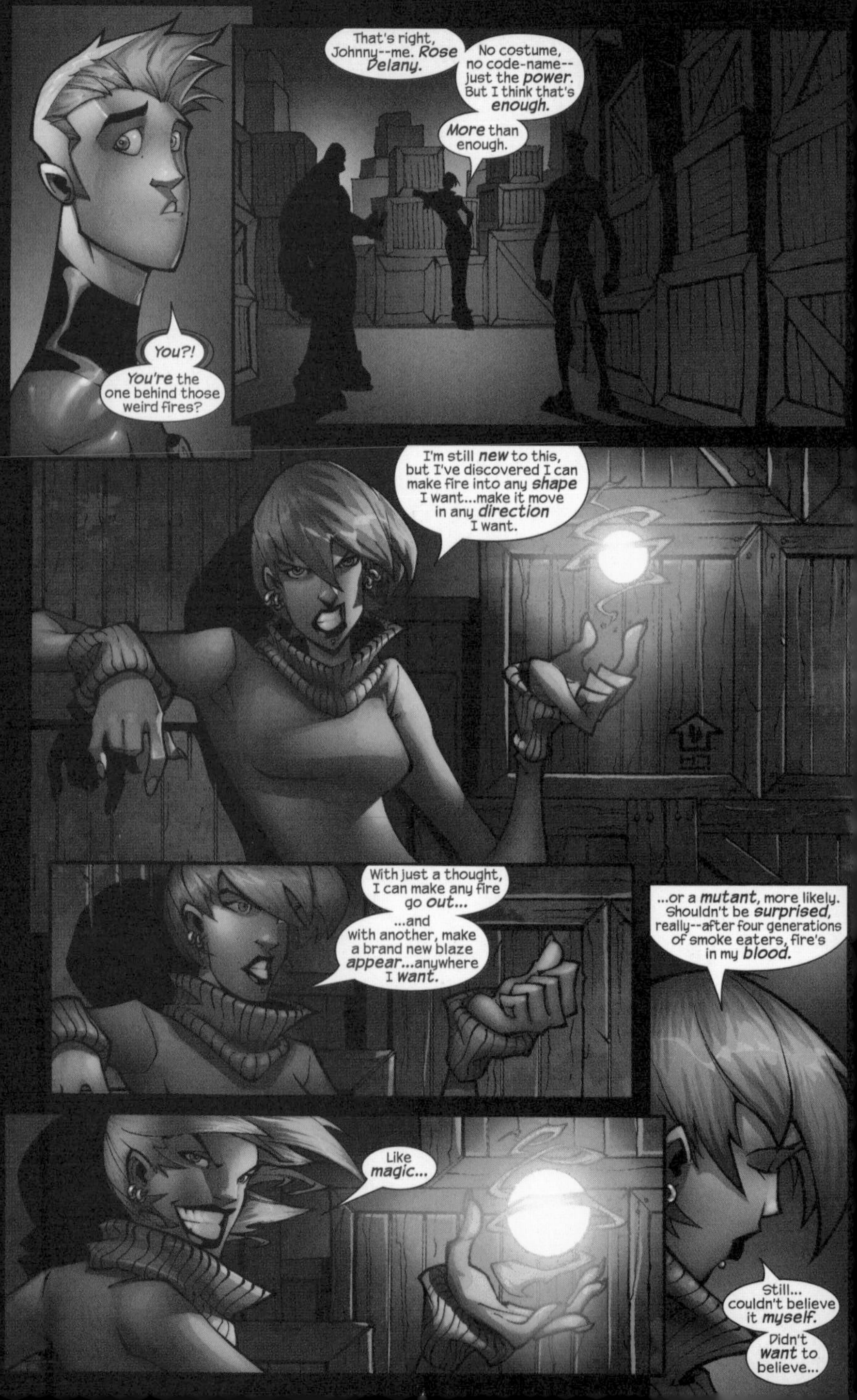
That's right, Johnny--me. Rose Delany.
No costume, no code-name--just the power. But I think that's enough.
More than enough.
You?!
You're the one behind those weird fires?
I'm still new to this, but I've discovered I can make fire into any shape I want...make it move in any direction I want.
With just a thought, I can make any fire go out...
...and with another, make a brand new blaze appear...anywhere I want.
Like magic...
...or a mutant, more likely. Shouldn't be surprised, really--after four generations of smoke eaters, fire's in my blood.
Still... couldn't believe it myself.
Didn't want to believe...

"...especially that *first* time.

"Vinnie was no worse than *usual* that day. It wasn't just he rode the probies too hard, it's more he enjoyed it too *much*-- and I'd finally *had* it.

"I felt this anger, this...*heat* build in me, and just as I was going to tell Vinnie to go to Hell...

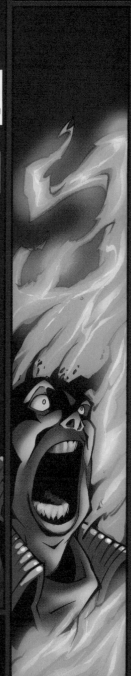

"I thought it was a *coincidence*, is all. A *terrible* coincidence.

"That's what it *had* to be, right?

"But then there was the brownstone fire-- Brandon Crowe's house.

"I remember hoping the fire would *get* that smug, drug-dealing scumbag, and the same feeling of *heat* growing inside me...

"...then out of nowhere, that *fireball*.

"I was...transfixed. Amazed. Shocked. Horrified.

Thrilled.

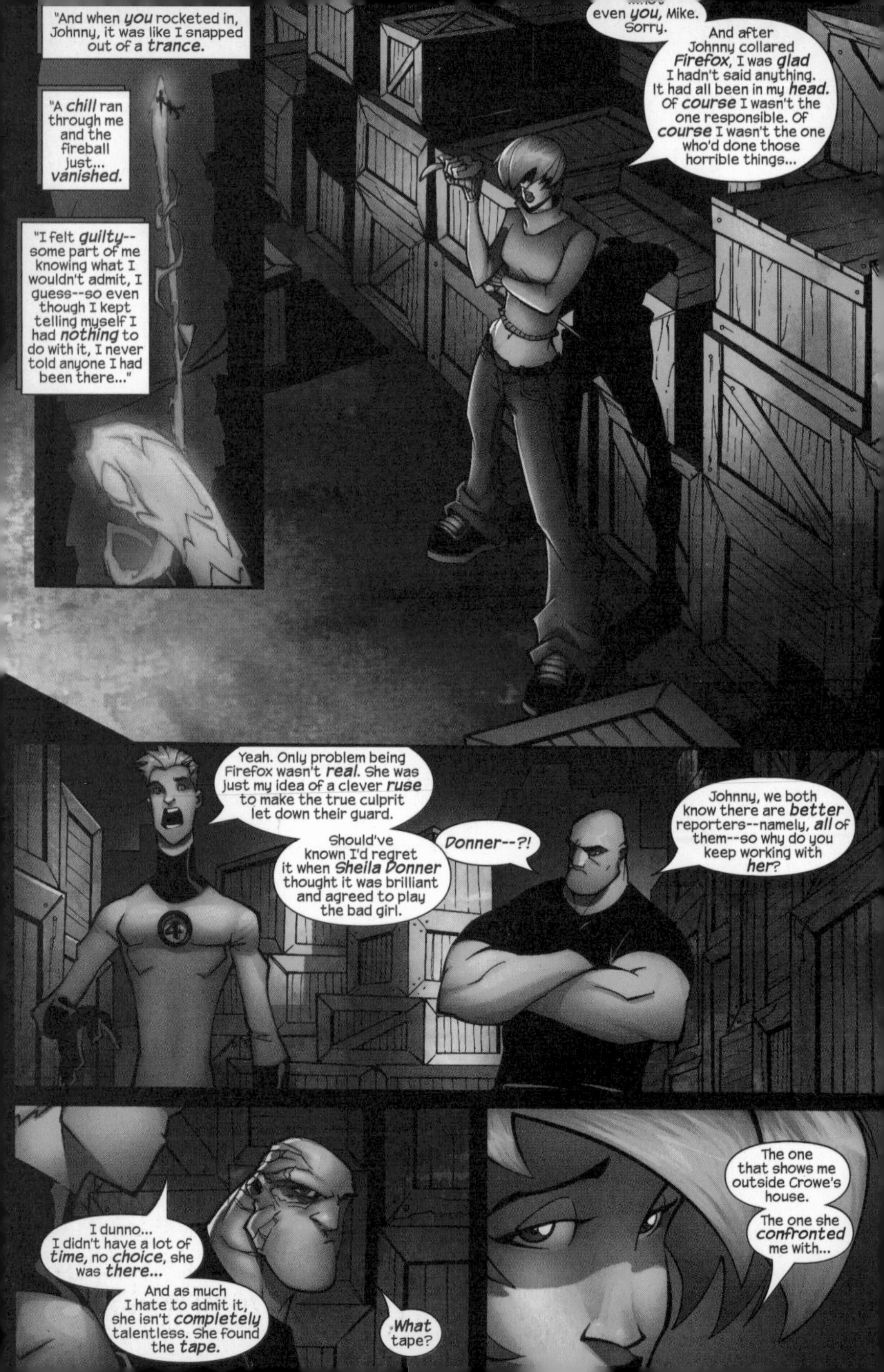
"And when you rocketed in, Johnny, it was like I snapped out of a trance.
"A chill ran through me and the fireball just... vanished.
"I felt guilty--some part of me knowing what I wouldn't admit, I guess--so even though I kept telling myself I had nothing to do with it, I never told anyone I had been there..."
even you, Mike. Sorry.
And after Johnny collared Firefox, I was glad I hadn't said anything. It had all been in my head. Of course I wasn't the one responsible. Of course I wasn't the one who'd done those horrible things...
Yeah. Only problem being Firefox wasn't real. She was just my idea of a clever ruse to make the true culprit let down their guard.
Should've known I'd regret it when Sheila Donner thought it was brilliant and agreed to play the bad girl.
Donner--?!
Johnny, we both know there are better reporters--namely, all of them--so why do you keep working with her?
I dunno... I didn't have a lot of time, no choice, she was there...
And as much I hate to admit it, she isn't completely talentless. She found the tape.
What tape?
The one that shows me outside Crowe's house.
The one she confronted me with...

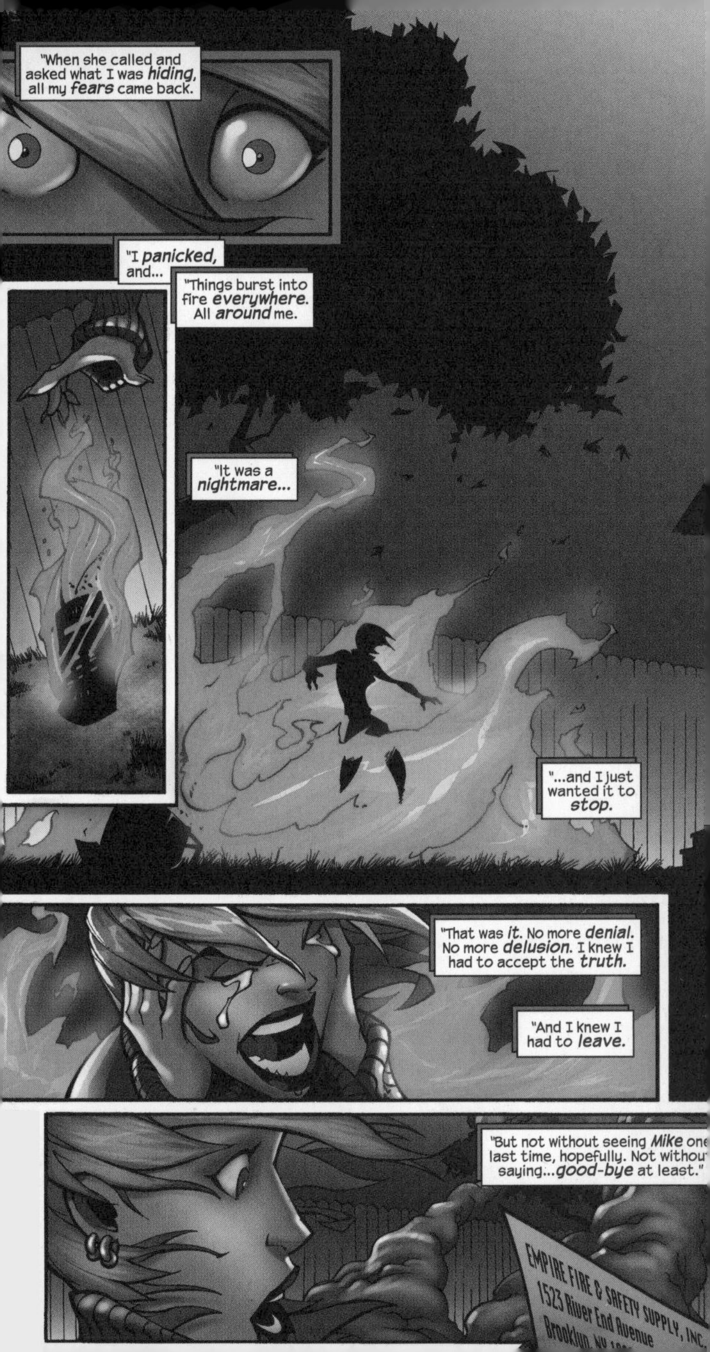
"When she called and asked what I was *hiding*, all my *fears* came back.
"I *panicked*, and...
"Things burst into fire *everywhere*. All *around* me.
"It was a *nightmare*...
"...and I just wanted it to *stop*.
"That was *it*. No more *denial*. No more *delusion*. I knew I had to accept the *truth*.
"And I knew I had to *leave*.
"But not without seeing *Mike* one last time, hopefully. Not without saying...*good-bye* at least."
EMPIRE FIRE & SAFETY SUPPLY, INC.
1523 River End Avenue
Brooklyn, NY

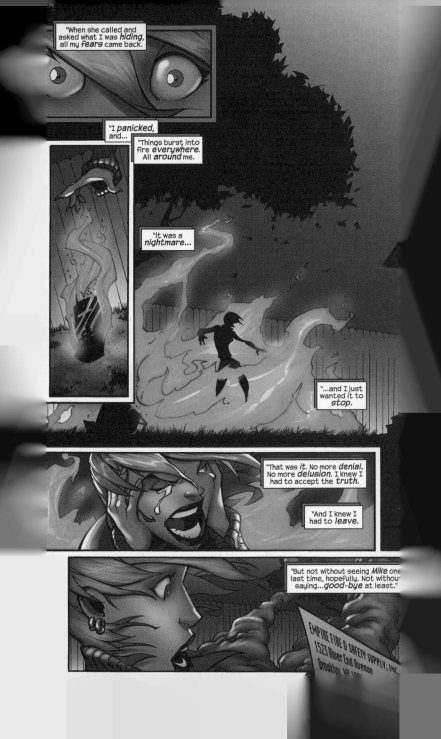

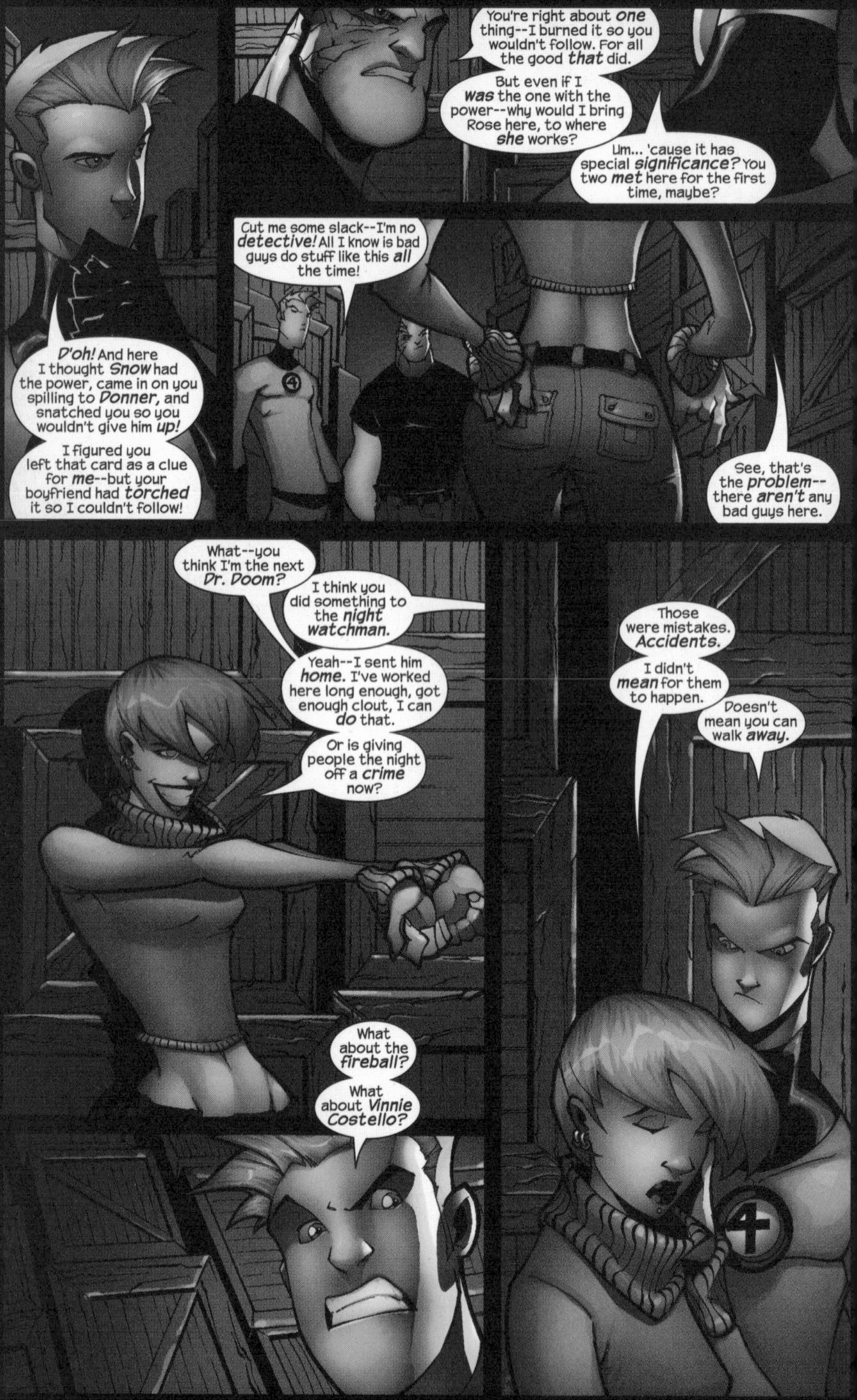
You're right about one thing--I burned it so you wouldn't follow. For all the good that did.
But even if I was the one with the power--why would I bring Rose here, to where she works?
Um... 'cause it has special significance? You two met here for the first time, maybe?
D'oh! And here I thought Snow had the power, came in on you spilling to Donner, and snatched you so you wouldn't give him up!
I figured you left that card as a clue for me--but your boyfriend had torched it so I couldn't follow!
Cut me some slack--I'm no detective! All I know is bad guys do stuff like this all the time!
See, that's the problem--there aren't any bad guys here.
What--you think I'm the next Dr. Doom?
I think you did something to the night watchman.
Yeah--I sent him home. I've worked here long enough, got enough clout, I can do that.
Or is giving people the night off a crime now?
What about the fireball?
What about Vinnie Costello?
Those were mistakes. Accidents.
I didn't mean for them to happen.
Doesn't mean you can walk away.

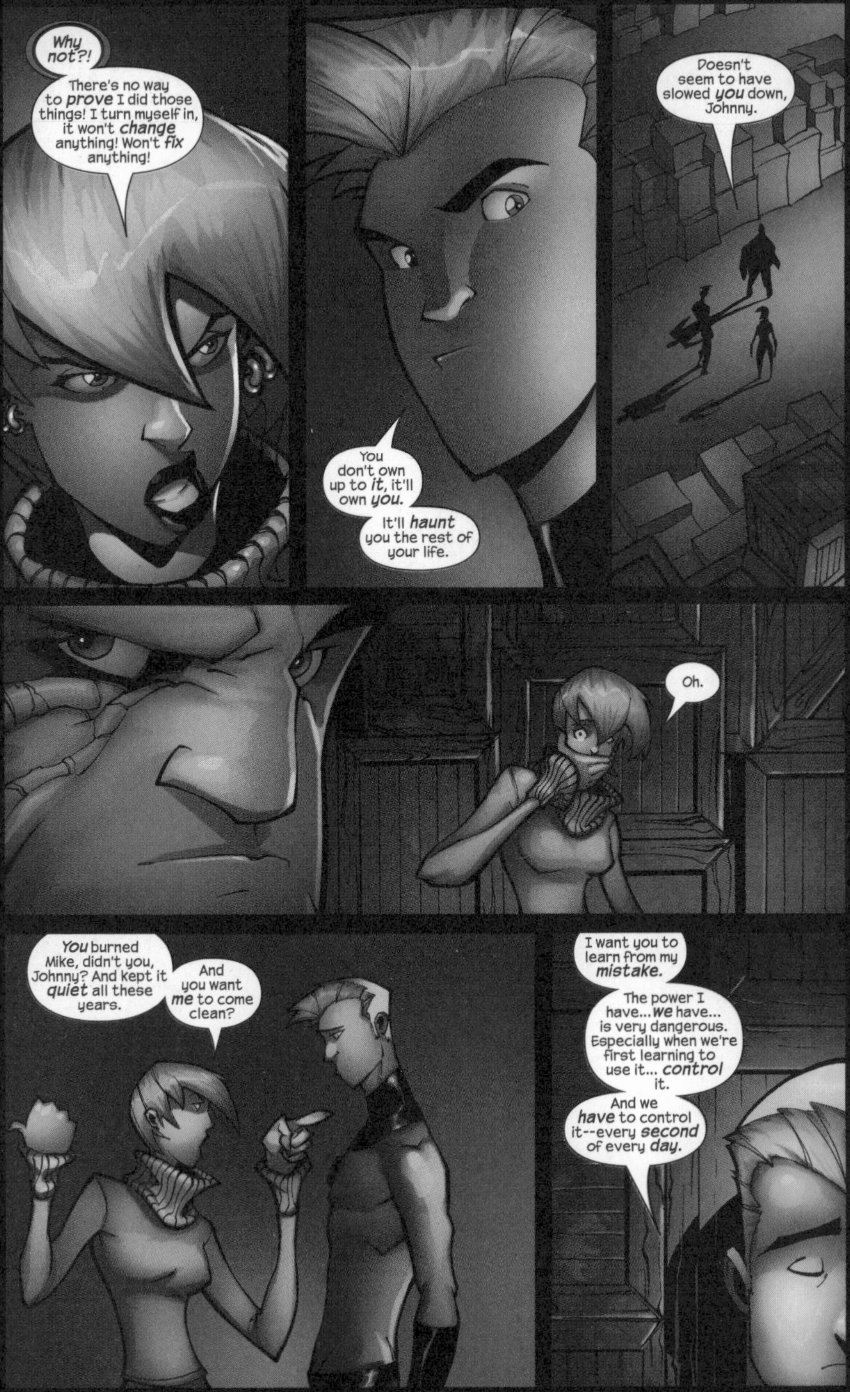
Why not?!
There's no way to prove I did those things! I turn myself in, it won't change anything! Won't fix anything!
You don't own up to it, it'll own you.
It'll haunt you the rest of your life.
Doesn't seem to have slowed you down, Johnny.
Oh.
You burned Mike, didn't you, Johnny? And kept it quiet all these years.
And you want me to come clean?
I want you to learn from my mistake.
The power I have... we have... is very dangerous. Especially when we're first learning to use it... control it.
And we have to control it--every second of every day.

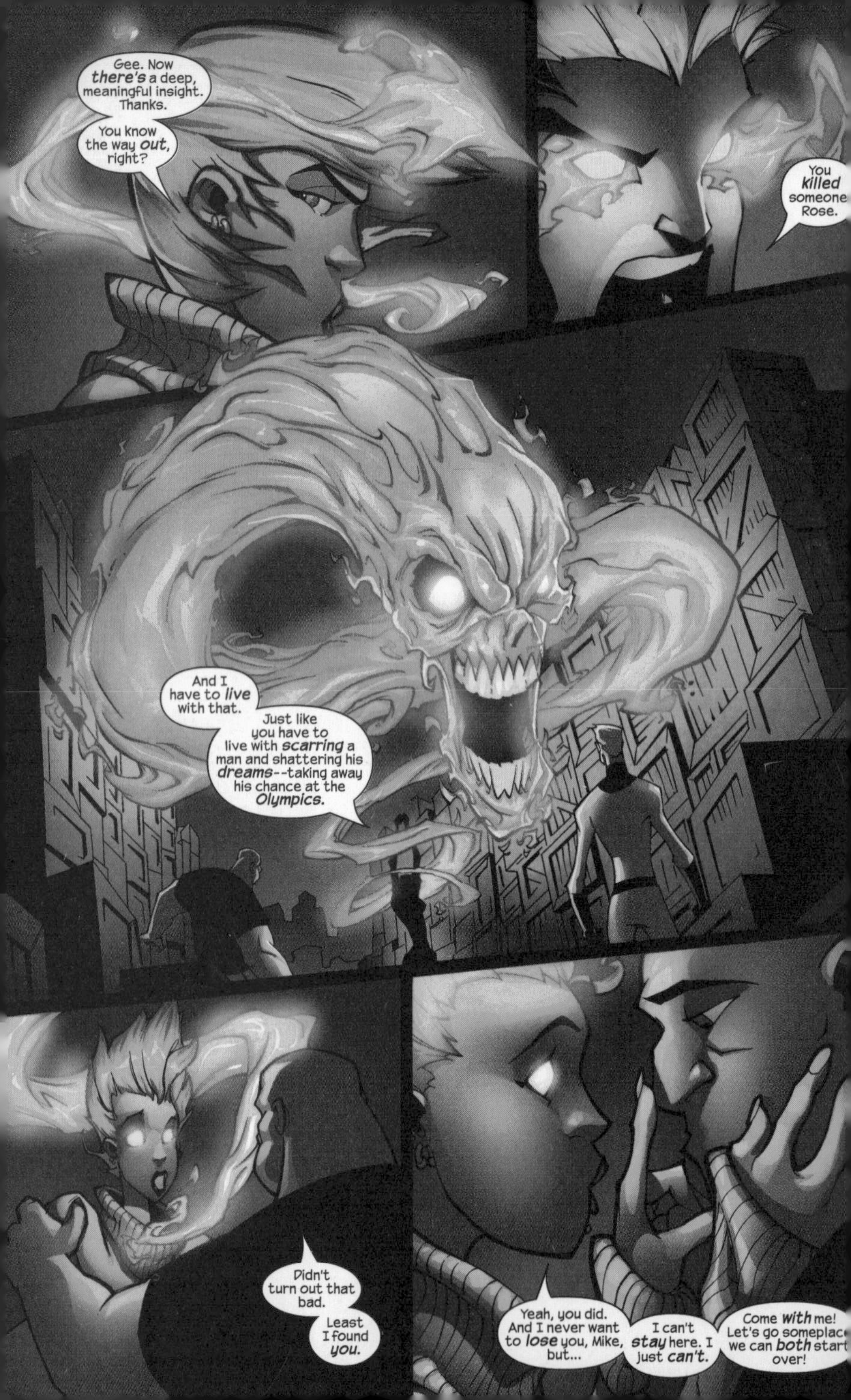
Gee. Now there's a deep, meaningful insight. Thanks.
You know the way out, right?
You killed someone Rose.
And I have to live with that.
Just like you have to live with scarring a man and shattering his dreams--taking away his chance at the Olympics.
Didn't turn out that bad.
Least I found you.
Yeah, you did. And I never want to lose you, Mike, but...
I can't stay here. I just can't.
Come with me! Let's go someplac we can both start over!

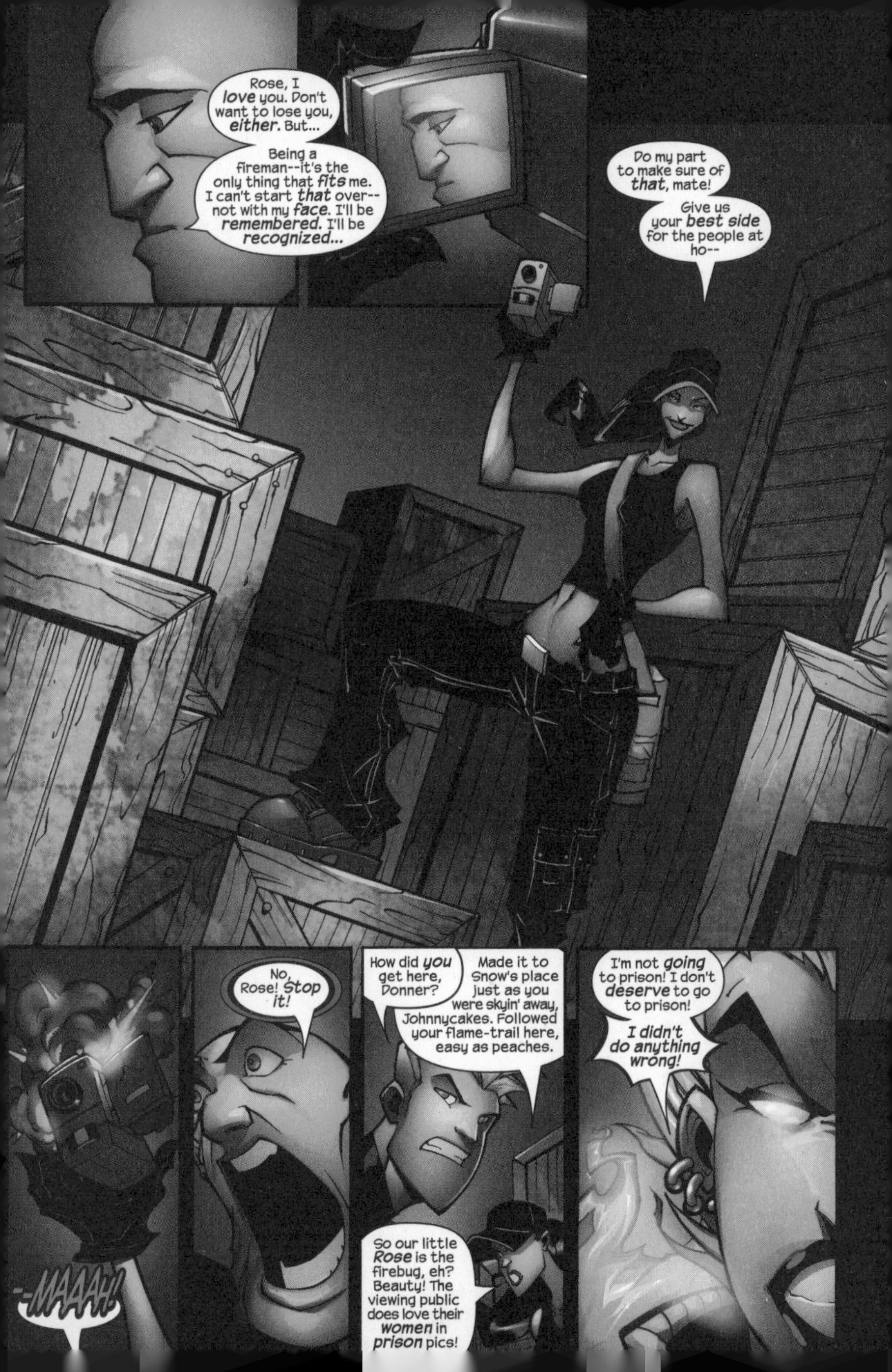

Rose, I love you. Don't want to lose you, either. But...
Being a fireman--it's the only thing that fits me. I can't start that over--not with my face. I'll be remembered. I'll be recognized...
Do my part to make sure of that, mate!
Give us your best side for the people at ho--
-MAAAH!
No, Rose! Stop it!
How did you get here, Donner?
Made it to Snow's place just as you were skyin' away, Johnnycakes. Followed your flame-trail here, easy as peaches.
So our little Rose is the firebug, eh? Beauty! The viewing public does love their women in prison pics!
I'm not going to prison! I don't deserve to go to prison!
I didn't do anything wrong!

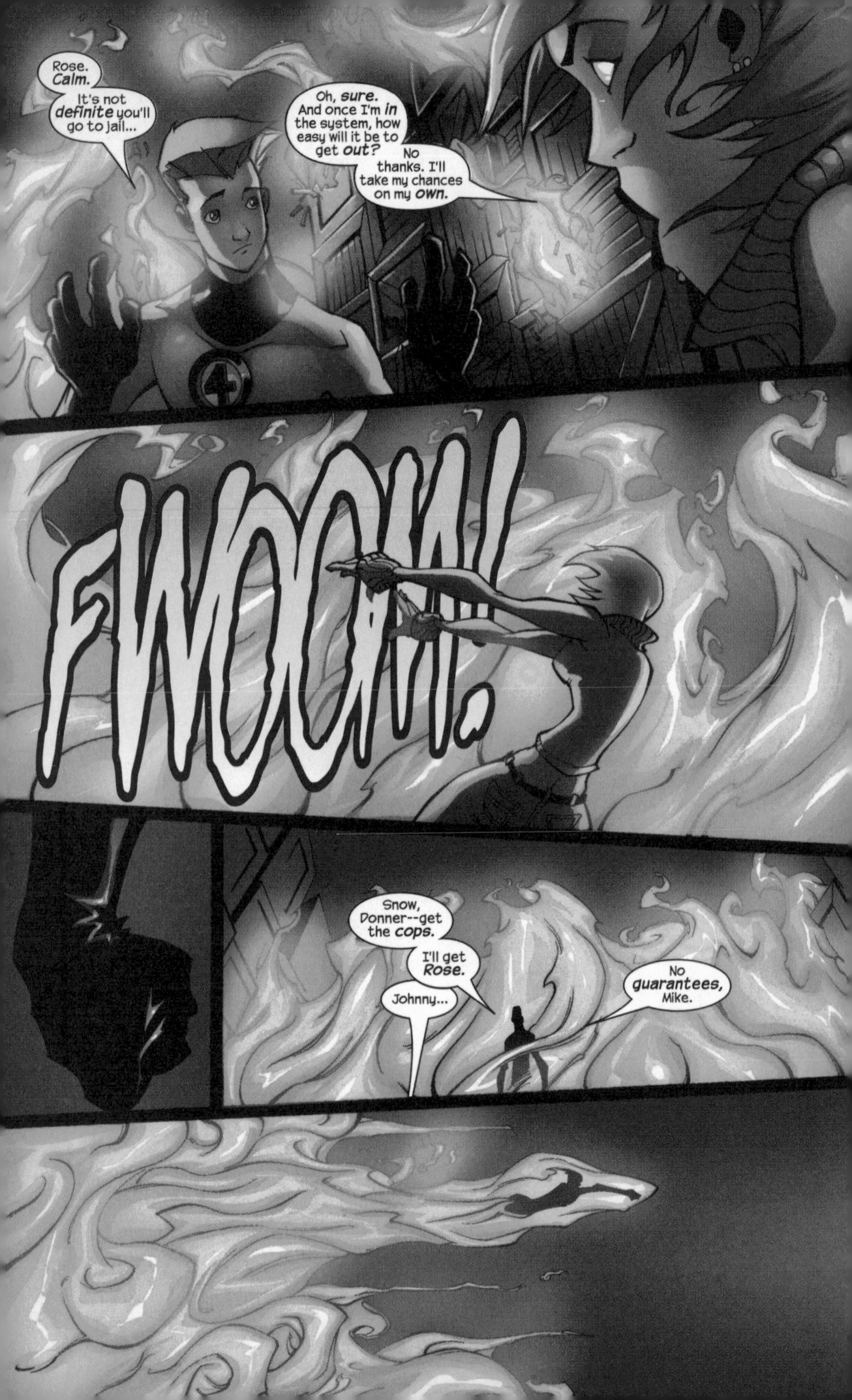
Rose. Calm.
It's not definite you'll go to jail...
Oh, sure. And once I'm in the system, how easy will it be to get out?
No thanks. I'll take my chances on my own.
FWOOM!
Snow, Donner--get the cops.
I'll get Rose.
Johnny...
No guarantees, Mike.

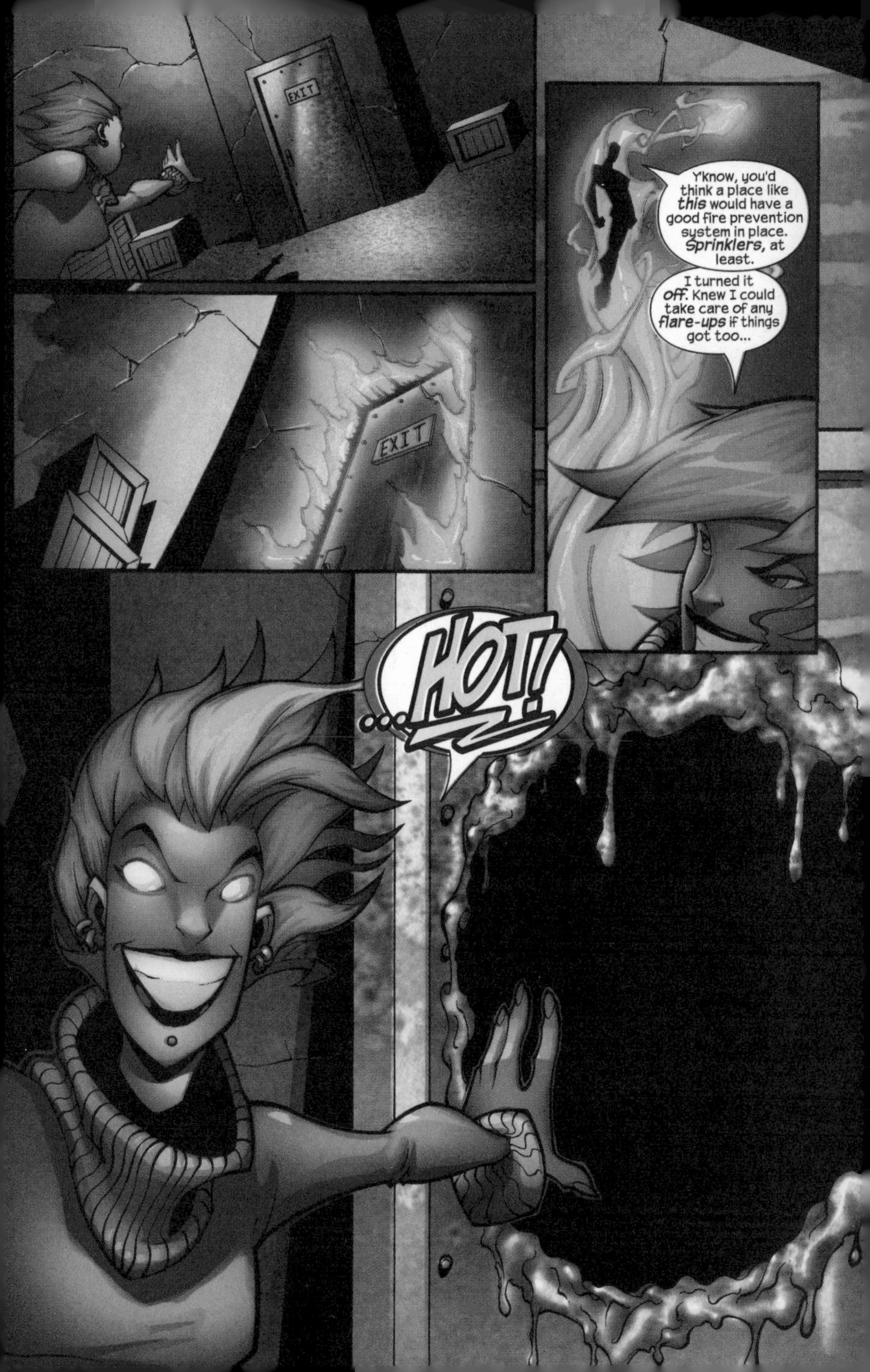

EXIT
EXIT
Y'know, you'd think a place like this would have a good fire prevention system in place. Sprinklers, at least.
I turned it off. Knew I could take care of any flare-ups if things got too...
...HOT!

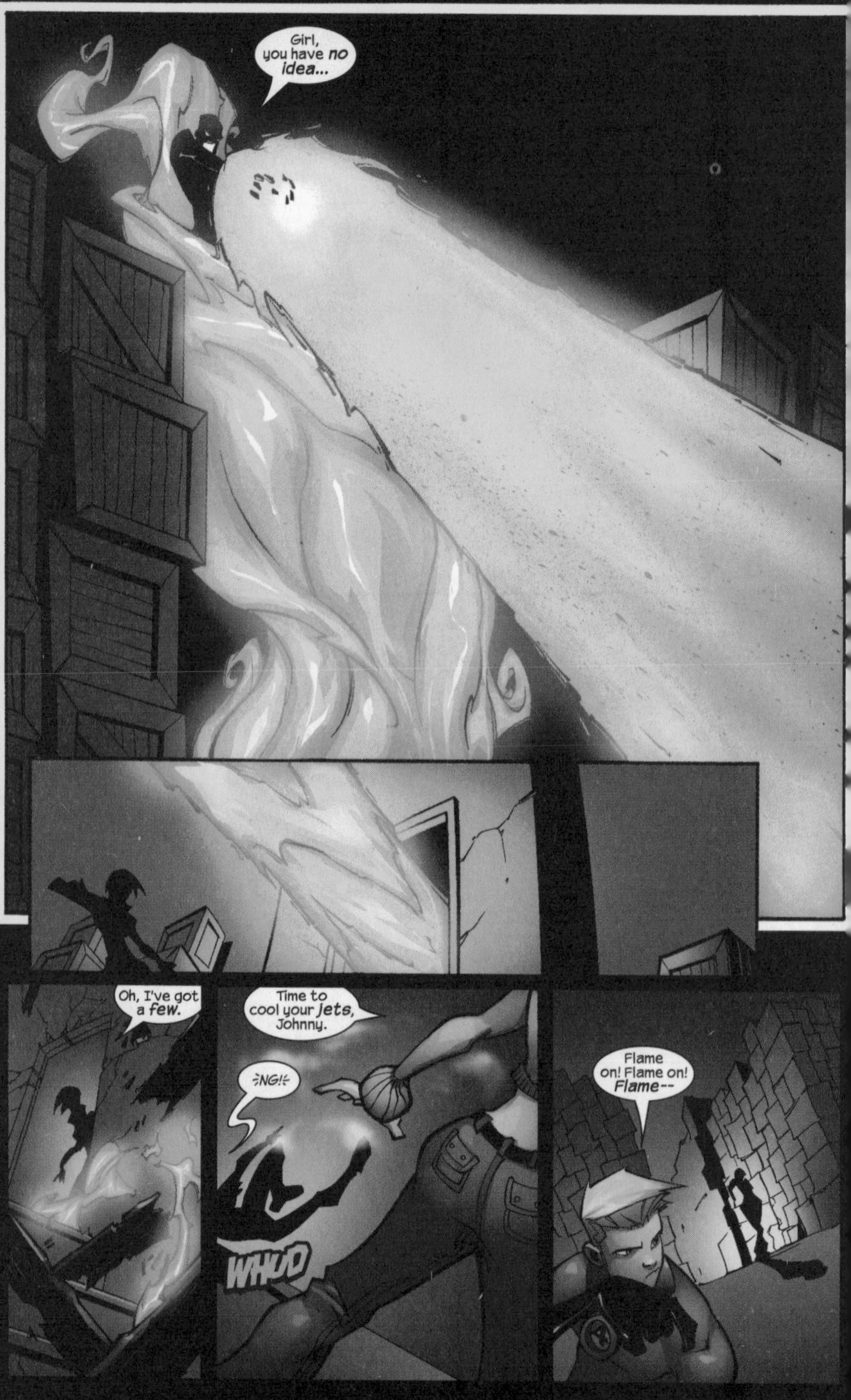

Girl, you have no idea...
Oh, I've got a few.
Time to cool your jets, Johnny.
NG!
WHUD
Flame on! Flame on! Flame--

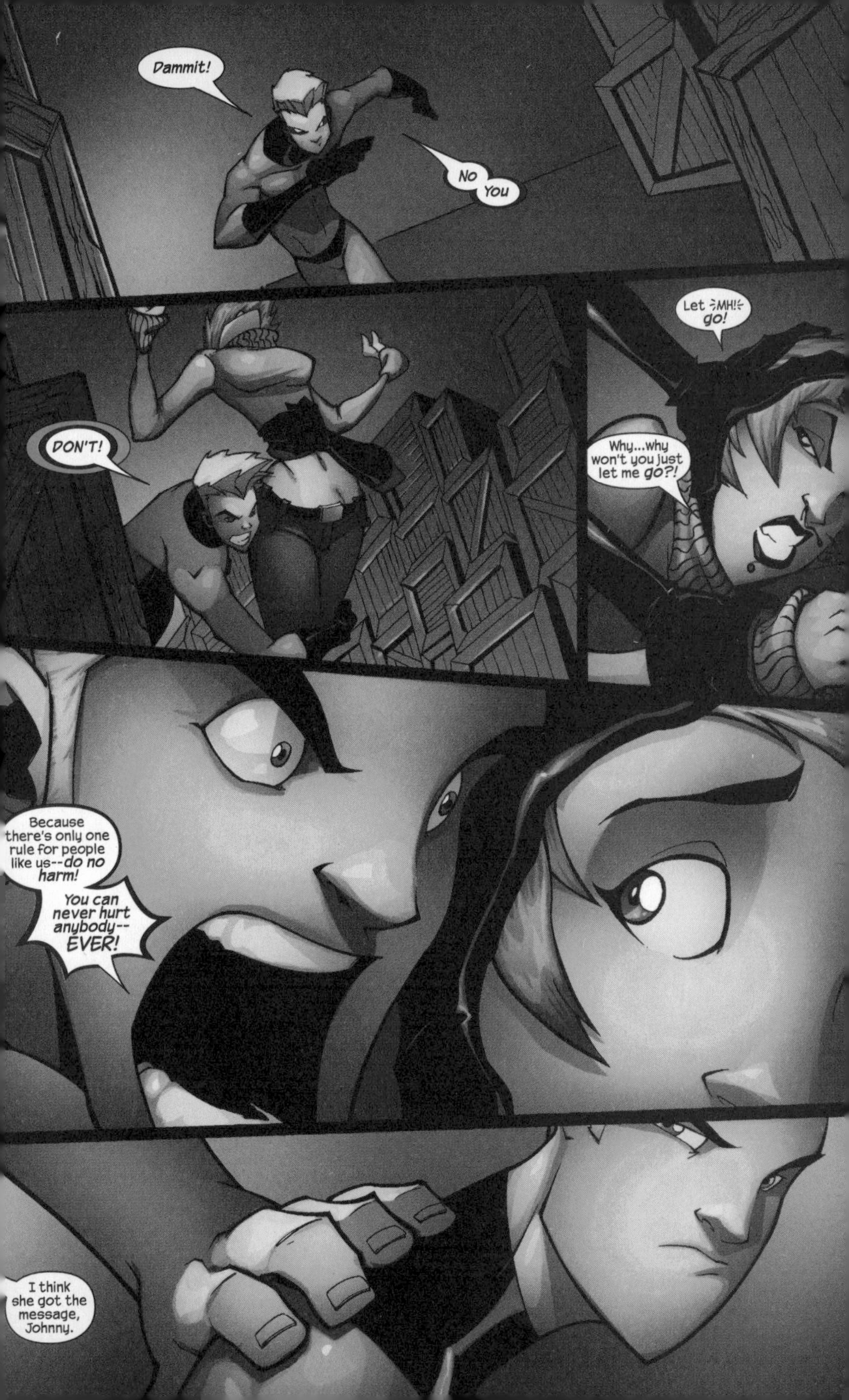

Dammit!
No You
DON'T!
Let ≈MH!≈ go!
Why...why won't you just let me go?!
Because there's only one rule for people like us--do no harm!
You can never hurt anybody--EVER!
I think she got the message, Johnny.

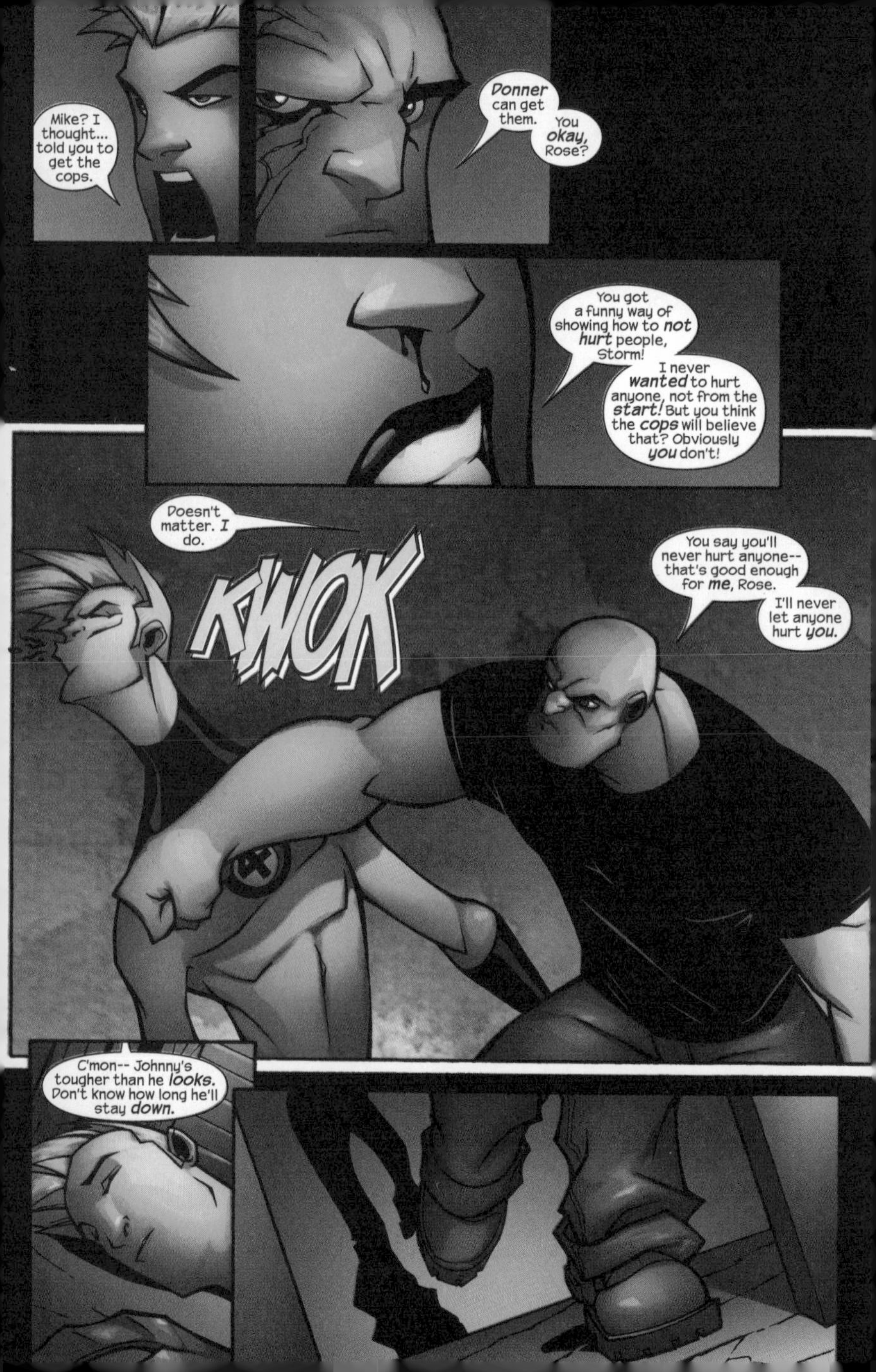

Mike? I thought... told you to get the cops.
Donner can get them.
You okay, Rose?
You got a funny way of showing how to not hurt people, Storm!
I never wanted to hurt anyone, not from the start! But you think the cops will believe that? Obviously you don't!
Doesn't matter. I do.
KWOK
You say you'll never hurt anyone-- that's good enough for me, Rose.
I'll never let anyone hurt you.
C'mon-- Johnny's tougher than he looks. Don't know how long he'll stay down.

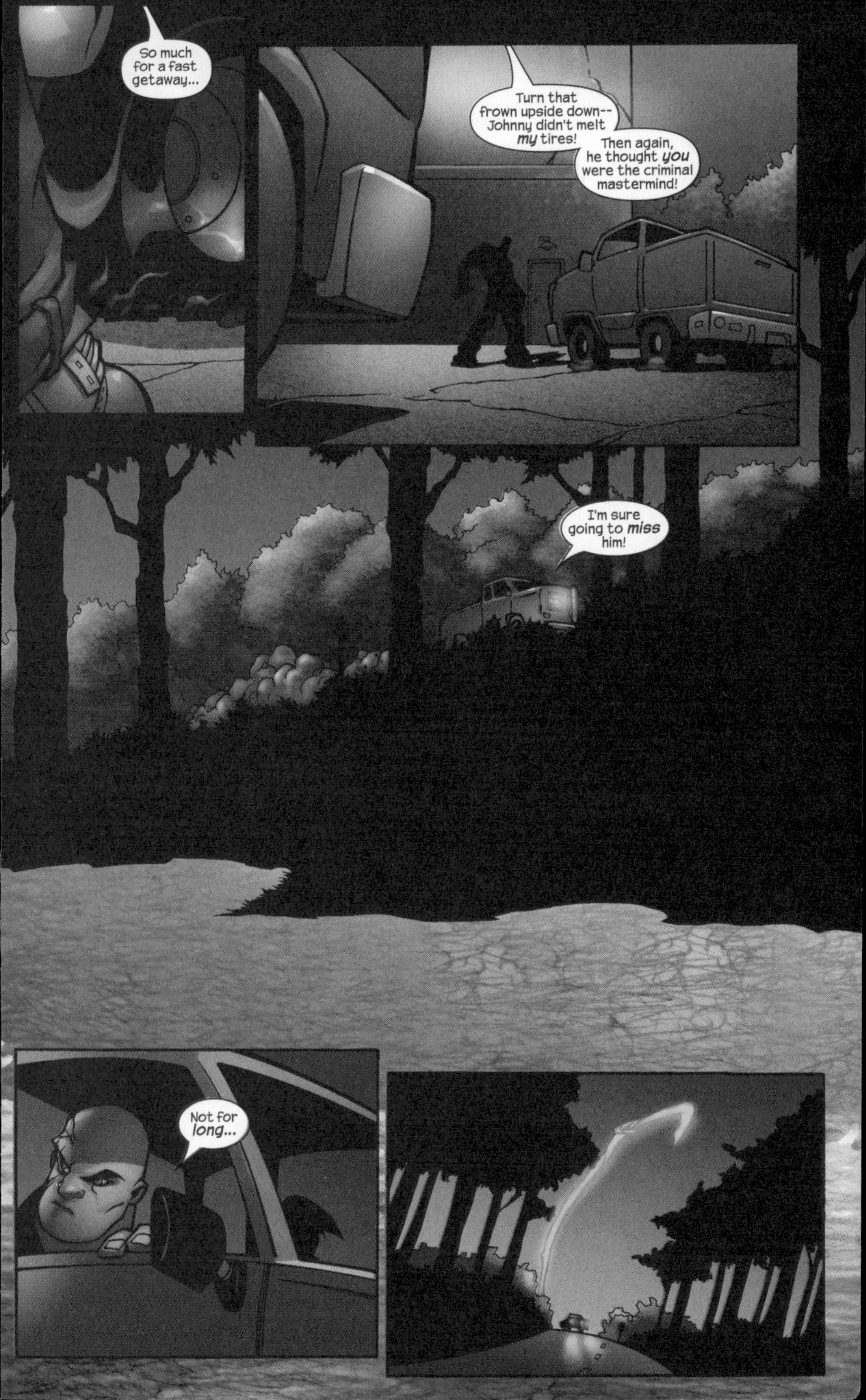
So much for a fast getaway...
Turn that frown upside down-- Johnny didn't melt *my* tires!
Then again, he thought *you* were the criminal mastermind!
I'm sure going to *miss* him!
Not for *long*...

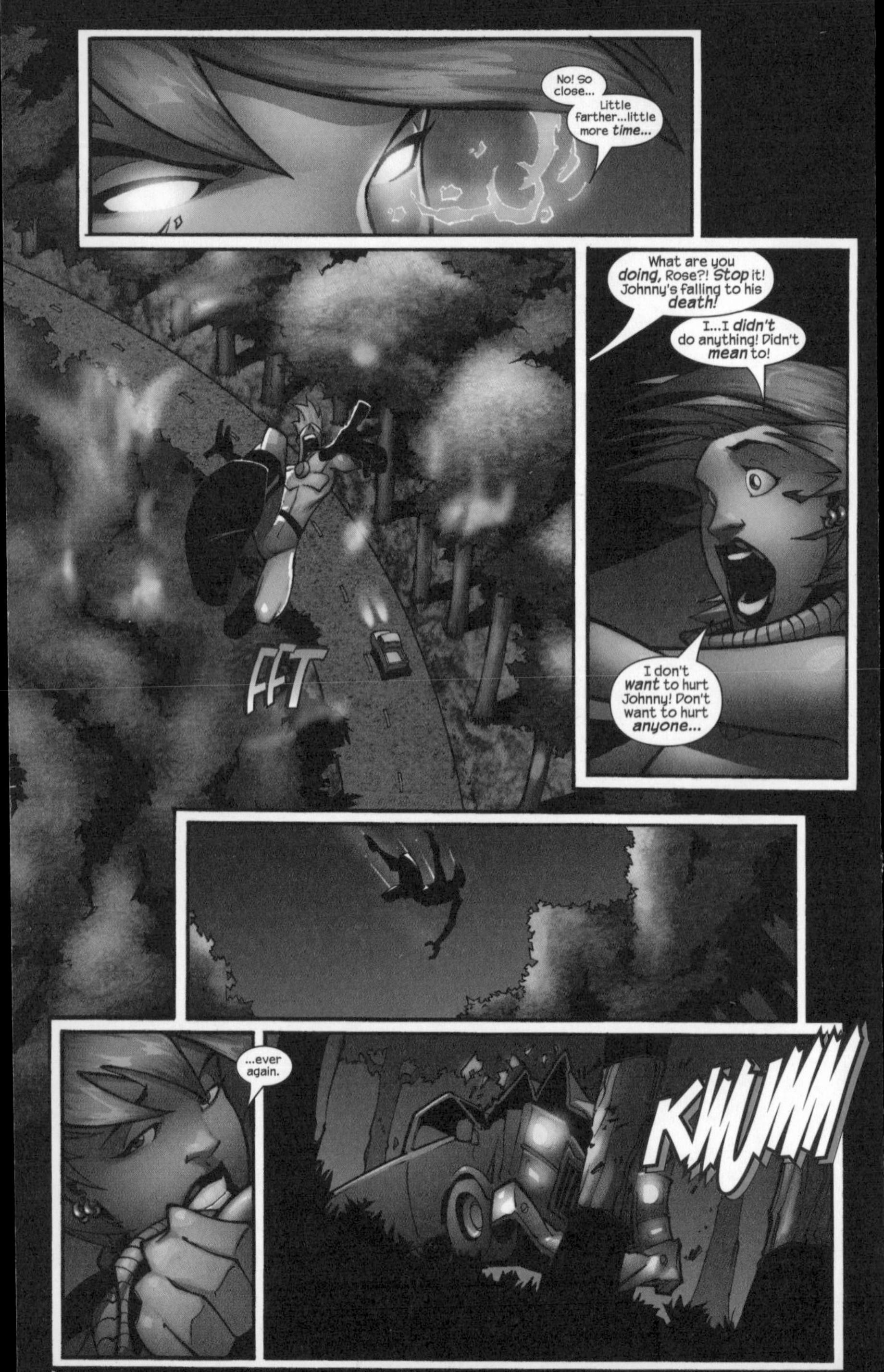
No! So close...
Little farther...little more time...
What are you doing, Rose?! Stop it! Johnny's falling to his death!
I...I didn't do anything! Didn't mean to!
FFT
I don't want to hurt Johnny! Don't want to hurt anyone...
...ever again.
KHUMM

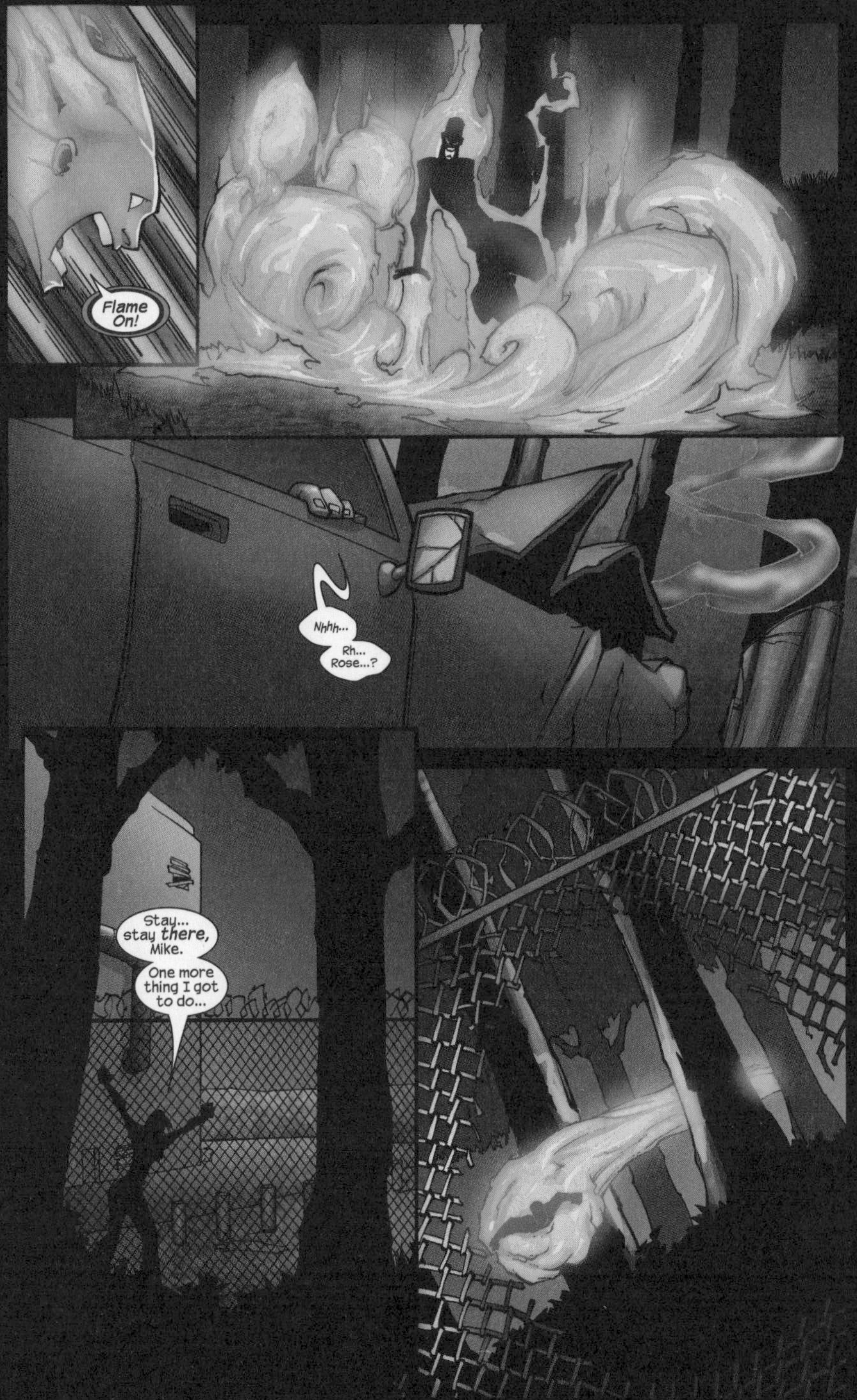
Flame On!
Nhhh...
Rh... Rose...?
Stay... stay *there*, Mike.
One more thing I got to do...

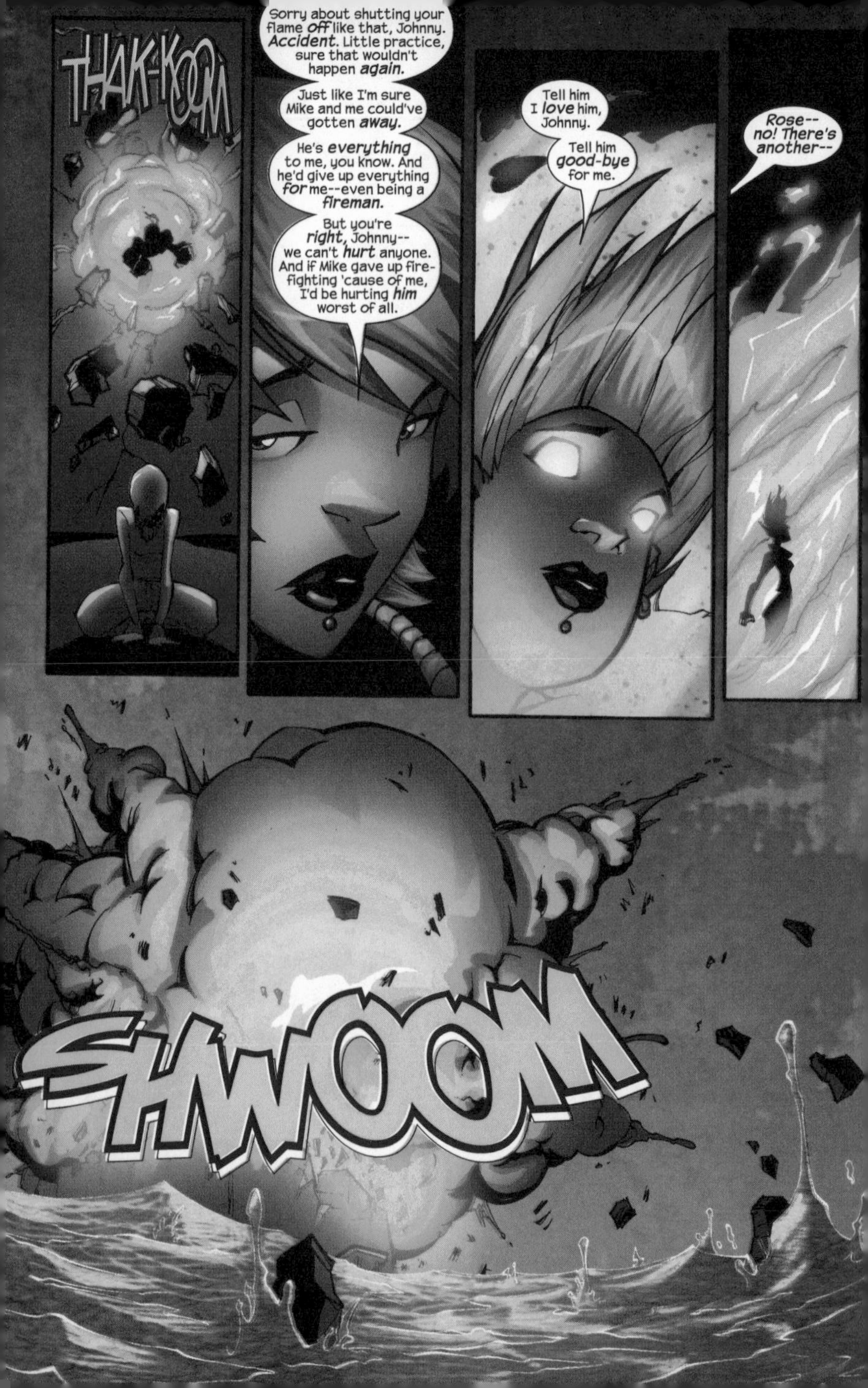

THAK-KOOM
Sorry about shutting your flame off like that, Johnny. Accident. Little practice, sure that wouldn't happen again.
Just like I'm sure Mike and me could've gotten away.
He's everything to me, you know. And he'd give up everything for me--even being a fireman.
But you're right, Johnny-- we can't hurt anyone. And if Mike gave up fire-fighting 'cause of me, I'd be hurting him worst of all.
Tell him I love him, Johnny.
Tell him good-bye for me.
Rose-- no! There's another--
SHWOOM

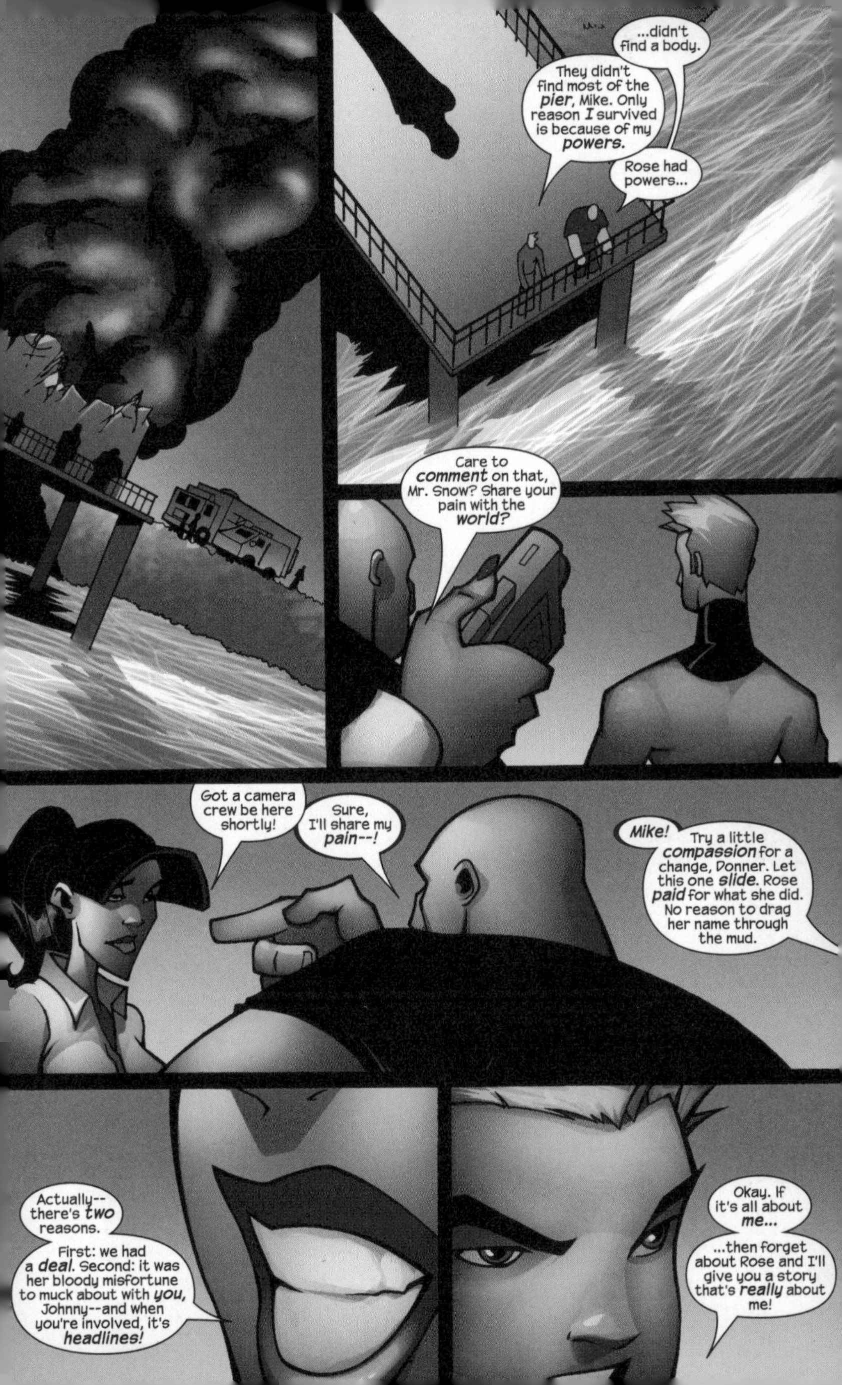
They didn't find most of the pier, Mike. Only reason I survived is because of my powers.
...didn't find a body.
Rose had powers...
Care to comment on that, Mr. Snow? Share your pain with the world?
Got a camera crew be here shortly!
Sure, I'll share my pain--!
Mike!
Try a little compassion for a change, Donner. Let this one slide. Rose paid for what she did. No reason to drag her name through the mud.
Actually-- there's two reasons.
First: we had a deal. Second: it was her bloody misfortune to muck about with you, Johnny--and when you're involved, it's headlines!
Okay. If it's all about me...
...then forget about Rose and I'll give you a story that's really about me!

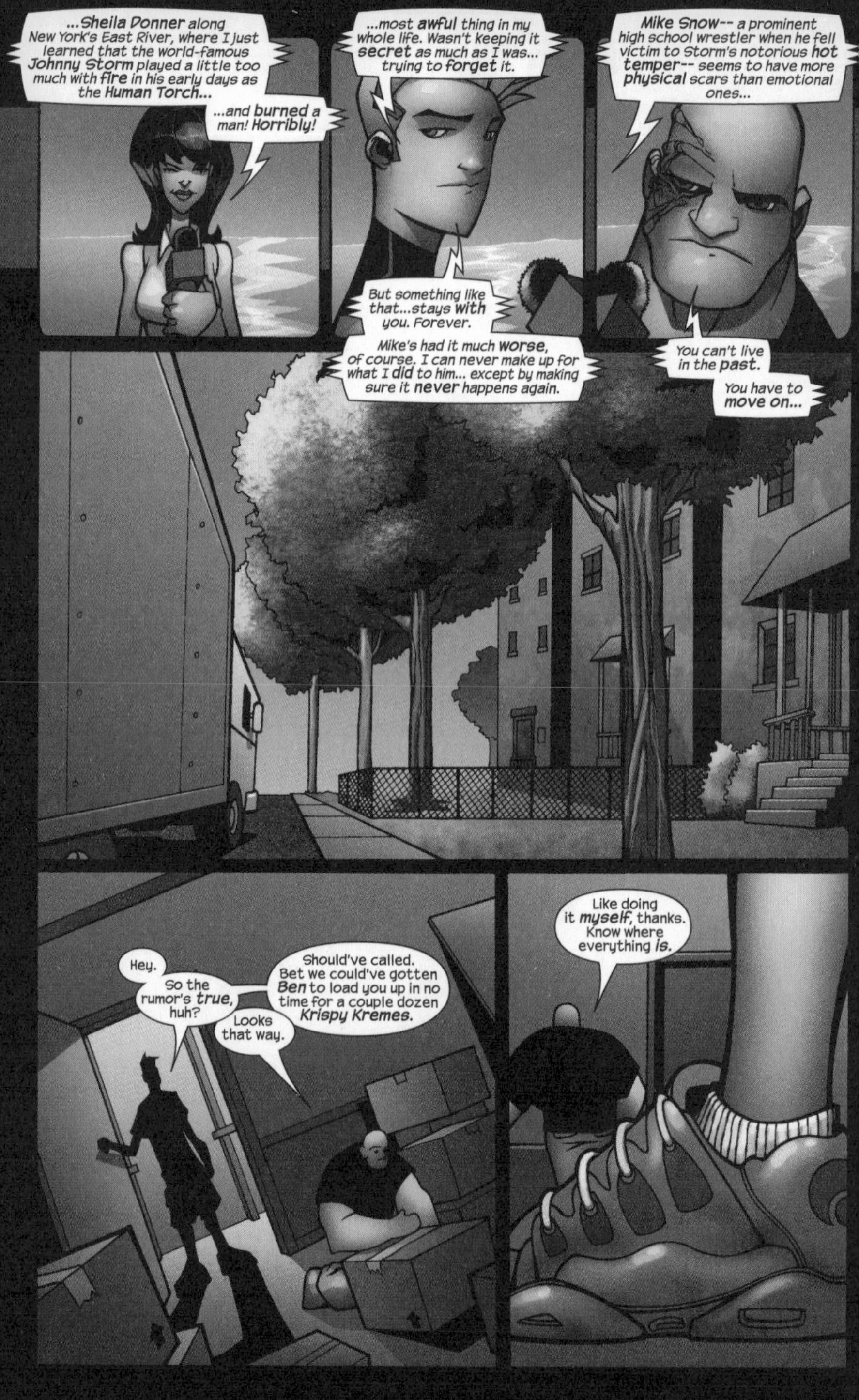
...Sheila Donner along New York's East River, where I just learned that the world-famous Johnny Storm played a little too much with fire in his early days as the Human Torch...
...and burned a man! Horribly!
...most awful thing in my whole life. Wasn't keeping it secret as much as I was... trying to forget it.
Mike Snow-- a prominent high school wrestler when he fell victim to Storm's notorious hot temper-- seems to have more physical scars than emotional ones...
But something like that...stays with you. Forever.
Mike's had it much worse, of course. I can never make up for what I did to him... except by making sure it never happens again.
You can't live in the past.
You have to move on...
Hey.
So the rumor's true, huh?
Looks that way.
Should've called. Bet we could've gotten Ben to load you up in no time for a couple dozen Krispy Kremes.
Like doing it myself, thanks. Know where everything is.

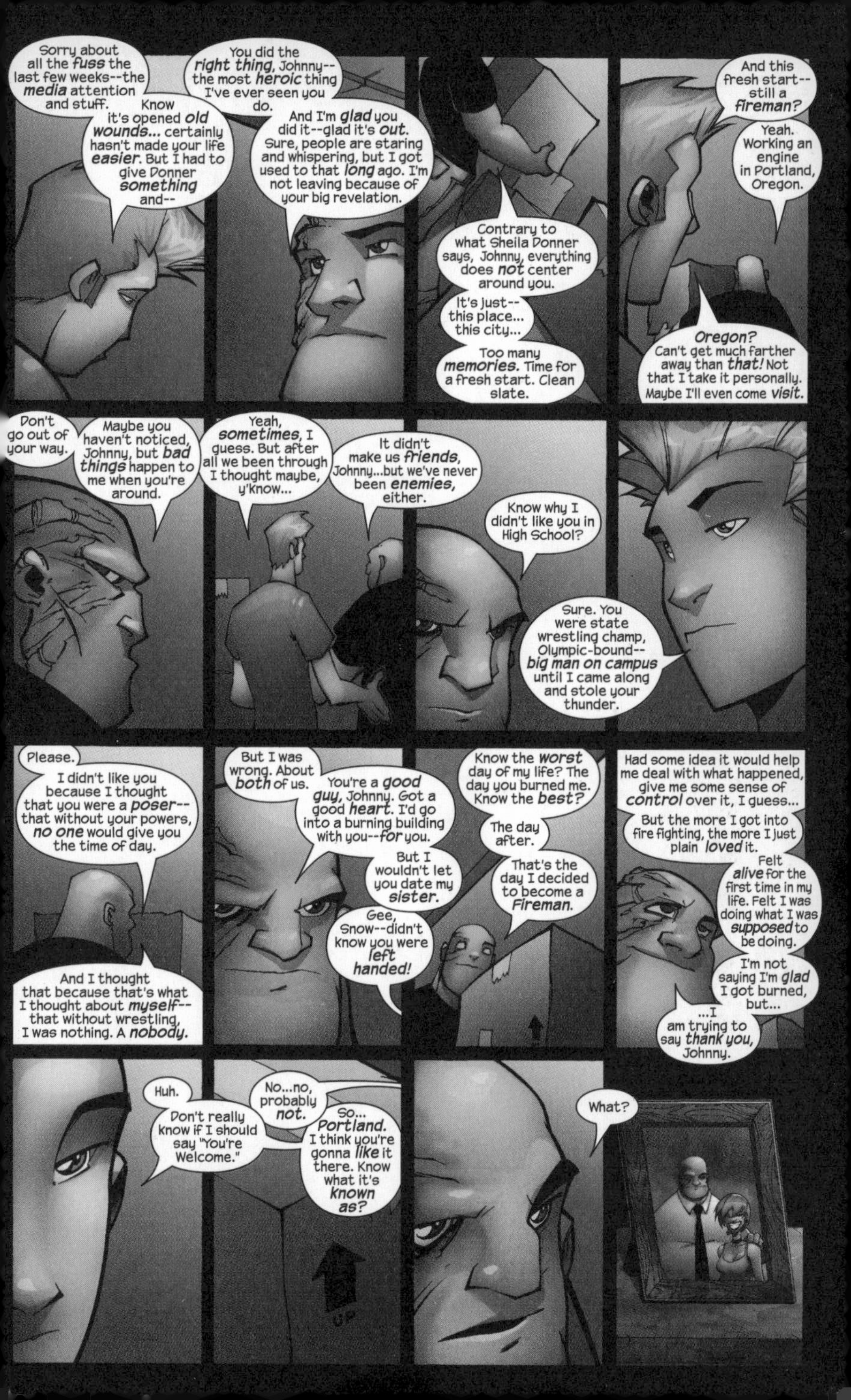
Sorry about all the fuss the last few weeks--the media attention and stuff.
Know it's opened old wounds... certainly hasn't made your life easier. But I had to give Donner something and--
You did the right thing, Johnny--the most heroic thing I've ever seen you do.
And I'm glad you did it--glad it's out. Sure, people are staring and whispering, but I got used to that long ago. I'm not leaving because of your big revelation.
Contrary to what Sheila Donner says, Johnny, everything does not center around you.
It's just--this place... this city...
Too many memories. Time for a fresh start. Clean slate.
And this fresh start--still a fireman?
Yeah. Working an engine in Portland, Oregon.
Oregon? Can't get much farther away than that! Not that I take it personally. Maybe I'll even come visit.
Don't go out of your way.
Maybe you haven't noticed, Johnny, but bad things happen to me when you're around.
Yeah, sometimes, I guess. But after all we been through I thought maybe, y'know...
It didn't make us friends, Johnny...but we've never been enemies, either.
Know why I didn't like you in High School?
Sure. You were state wrestling champ, Olympic-bound--big man on campus until I came along and stole your thunder.
Please.
I didn't like you because I thought that you were a poser--that without your powers, no one would give you the time of day.
And I thought that because that's what I thought about myself--that without wrestling, I was nothing. A nobody.
But I was wrong. About both of us.
You're a good guy, Johnny. Got a good heart. I'd go into a burning building with you--for you.
But I wouldn't let you date my sister.
Gee, Snow--didn't know you were left handed!
Know the worst day of my life? The day you burned me. Know the best?
The day after.
That's the day I decided to become a Fireman.
Had some idea it would help me deal with what happened, give me some sense of control over it, I guess...
But the more I got into fire fighting, the more I just plain loved it.
Felt alive for the first time in my life. Felt I was doing what I was supposed to be doing.
I'm not saying I'm glad I got burned, but...
...I am trying to say thank you, Johnny.
Huh.
Don't really know if I should say "You're Welcome."
No...no, probably not.
So... Portland. I think you're gonna like it there. Know what it's known as?
UP
What?

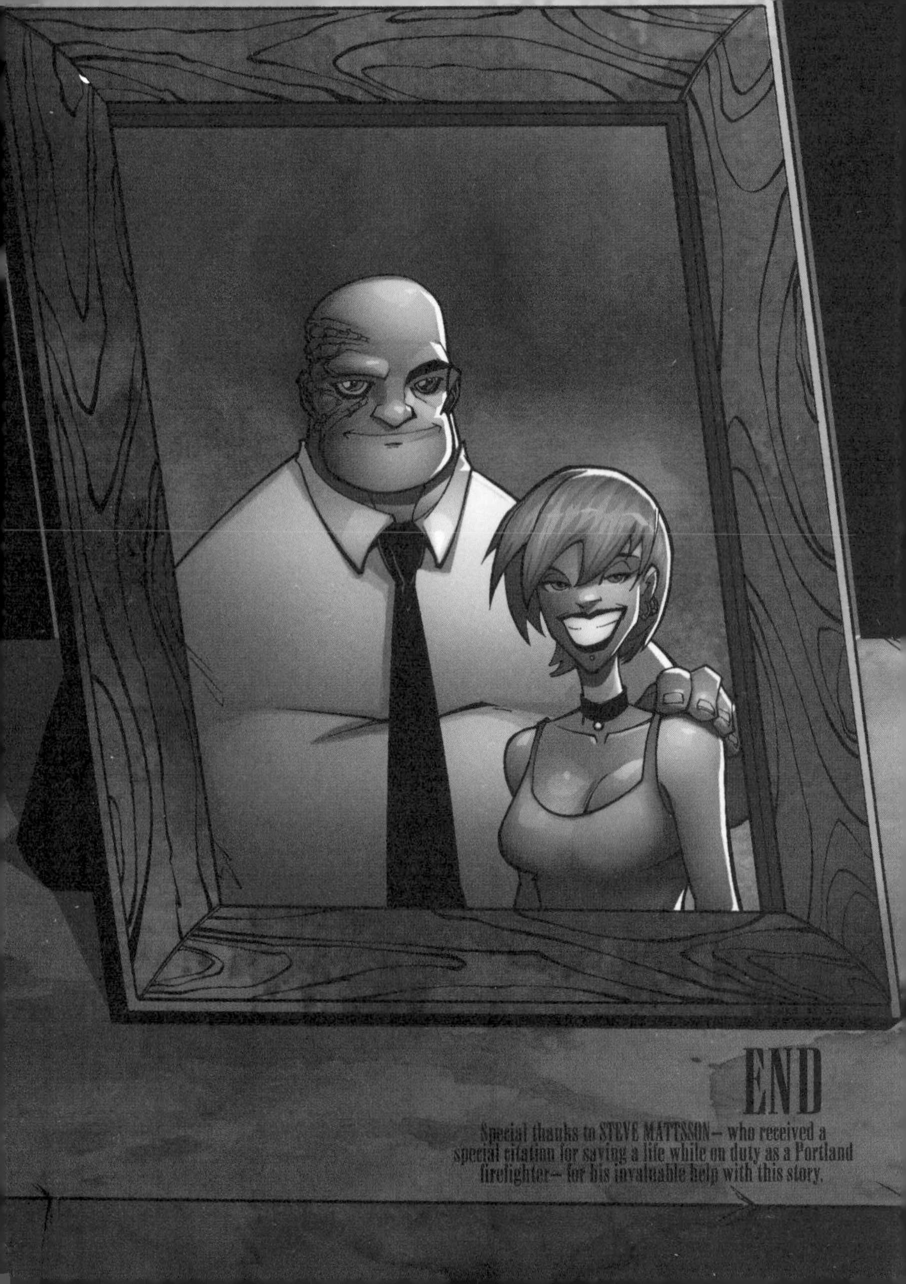
END
Special thanks to STEVE MATTSSON— who received a special citation for saving a life while on duty as a Portland firefighter— for his invaluable help with this story.